THE
CALIFORNIA
LANDSCAPE
GARDEN

THE CALIFORNIA
LANDSCAPE GARDEN

ECOLOGY,
CULTURE,
AND DESIGN

MARK FRANCIS ❧ ANDREAS REIMANN

WITH ORIGINAL ILLUSTRATIONS BY YAN NASCIMBENE

UNIVERSITY OF CALIFORNIA PRESS / BERKELEY LOS ANGELES LONDON

University of California Press
Berkeley and Los Angeles, California

University of California Press, Ltd.
London, England

All photographs by the authors unless otherwise indicated. "California Spring, 1875" by Albert Bierstadt
(p. 2) reproduced by permission of the Fine Arts Museums of San Francisco, presented to the City and
County of San Franciso by Gordon Blanding, 1941.6. Topographic image of the United States (p. 6)
with detail of California (p. 8) reproduced by permission of Raven Maps. Borders for bioregions for
California detail by Bill Nelson.

Library of Congress Cataloging-in-Publication Data

Francis, Mark, 1950–
    The California landscape garden : ecology, culture, and design / Mark Francis, Andreas Reimann ;
illustrations by Yan Nascimbene.
        p.   cm.
    Includes bibliographical references and index.
    ISBN 0-520-21450-1 (alk. paper): cloth
    ISBN 0-520-21764-0 (alk. paper): pbk.
        1. Natural landscaping—California.   2. Natural gardens—California.   3. Gardening to attract
wildlife—California.   I. Reimann, Andreas.   II. Title.
    SB439.24.C2F735   1999
    635.9'51794—dc21
                                                                                    98-35421

PRODUCED BY BOOKMATTERS
Project manager: David Peattie
Cover/text designer: David Peattie
Editor: Anne Canright
Proofreader: Karen Stough
Indexer: Janet Vail

Printed and bound in Hong Kong

9   8   7   6   5   4   3   2   1

Printed on acid-free paper.

For Kirsten and Christine

CONTENTS

ACKNOWLEDGMENTS

We began work on this book in the early 1990s with the goal of helping people create gardens that better reflect their own contemporary environmental values. As landscape architects we were finding that although our clients and students were increasingly interested in "ecological" gardens, they were often unsure how to create one. Few books addressed the idea, especially within the unique context and culture of California.

In 1992 we received a two-year grant from the University of California's Elvenia J. Slosson Endowment for Ornamental Horticulture that allowed us to pursue the initial research and writing of this book, a process that has involved several stages. The first year was spent collecting data and building a network of experts to expand our vision of ecological gardens. During the second phase of our research we conducted three "Ecological Garden Design" workshops: the first in Davis (April 1993), covering the Central

Valley and adjacent foothills bioregions; the second at the Strybing Arboretum in San Francisco (May 1993) for the central and north coastal regions; and the third in Irvine Ranch Water District (June 1993) for the southern coastal region. These conferences, each attended by garden experts and home gardeners, produced ecological garden design examples of differing scale and character, responsive to the various regions of the state.

We would like to thank all the workshop participants: at UC Davis, Margot Anderson, John Brode, Mark Brown, Robert Bugg, Ron Cole, Dennis Dahlin, David Gibson, Patricia Gouveia, Reed Hamilton, Dave Kelley, Robert Kourik, John Mills, Warren Roberts, Ted Swiecki, Robert Thayer Jr., Craig Thomsen, Brent Thrams, Ed Whisler, and Steven Zien; at San Francisco, Larry Burkam, Jeff Caldwell, Paul Cowley, Rosalind Creasy, Janet Green, Ginny Hunt, Robert Kourik, Gary Lazar, Dan Mahoney, Jane Miller, Patrick Miller, Baile Oakes, Beverly Beaver Rudolph, Rick Storre, and Joanne Typpett; and at Irvine, Ilene Adelman, Tom Ash, Jeff Bohn, Rick Fisher, Lisa Iwata, Michael Moquin, Michael O'Brien, Robert Perry, William Roley, Tom Scott, Mark Skinner, Robert Smaus, Gary Stewart, and Susan Van Atta.

We are indebted to the University of California Slosson Endowment for Ornamental Horticulture and its directors, Michael Reid and Robert Webster, for providing crucial financial support. The Landscape Architecture Program at UC Davis provided valuable administrative support. We also called upon several experts to assist us with conceptual and technical aspects of this book. In-depth interviews were conducted with Jeff Caldwell, Barbara Deutsch, Phyllis M. Farber, and Ron Lutsko.

Several people had useful comments on various chapters of the book, including George Waters, Michael Moquin, and Reed Hamilton. Jane Miller contributed expert advice about California native plants, and her review of the plants chapter was most useful. Kathryn Devereaux gave invaluable conceptual advice as well as important editorial and writing assistance. Joan Wright's Davis garden was made available to us to us to develop and test our ideas. Also helpful throughout the editing process were Joan Wright and Marilu Carter. Patrice Diaz-Migoyo and Mary Bedard served as research assistants. Robin Souza provided administrative support for the book. Yan Nascimbene immediately understood our ideas and translated them into expressive drawings that tie our diverse thoughts into a coherent whole. Sarah Washburn prepared the site plans for our prototype designs. Jim Clark, director of the University of California Press, took an early interest in this project and was supportive and encouraging throughout. First Valeurie Freidman and later Katherine Bell of UC Press helped us take our scattered thoughts and shape them into a publishable form. David Peattie of BookMatters did a masterful job of designing and producing the final book. Reviewers Jane Miller, Bob Perry, and Michael Barbour provided invaluable comments and suggestions.

INTRODUCTION

Gardening, as a cultural activity, matters deeply, not only to the look of our landscape, but also to the wisdom of our thinking about the environment.
Michael Pollan, "Beyond Wilderness and Lawn"

The garden has always been about people and plants. Recently, a variety of scholars and practitioners, including psychologists, horticulturists, philosophers, and landscape architects, have expanded the subject of gardening to include larger ideas of culture and nature. Today we know that a garden expresses personal and cultural values, manifests political and economic power, provides a setting for individual healing, conveys personal meanings and memories, and reflects environmental concerns. This book is about how expressions of nature and culture can be best brought together in the garden.

There is an emerging social and ecological conviction among landscape architects and gardeners that the designed landscapes around our homes and community spaces can become the crucible of an environmentally sound and culturally expressive world. While lawns remain a stylistic and utilitarian element in the human landscape, growing popular opinion holds that expansive lawns are too artificial and tend to exclude more interesting garden elements. A change of values is also evident in concerns about chemical overuse and the associated risk in the garden: this chemical warfare is viewed as an untimely, even irresponsible, approach to gardening. The plight of our environment leads us to question the traditional approach to gardening in terms of design style, horticultural practice, and history, and to view traditional gardens as overly static and fabricated, lacking in the mysterious animation of a more wild, natural world sustained by a vast and highly efficient life-support system.

These concerns have spurred a back-to-nature movement in American backyards. Some gardeners use native plants to create wildlife habitat. Others replace front lawns with displays of ecological cycles and processes. Through their experiments, these gardeners are redefining the very notion of the garden as nature under control. A Chicago man, for example, realizing that he never set foot in his front yard except to mow it, transformed the space into a prairie habitat for local rabbits and foxes, saying, "We've taken over all this habitat that used to belong to other species. . . . This is my way of sharing the living space."[1]

This interest in the natural garden is not unique to California or even to the United States. In Britain gardeners are also transforming their gardens into more natural places. Chris Baines, a landscape architect and the creator of a BBC-TV program on gardens, proposed in one of his shows that gardeners should dig a small pond for wildlife in their gardens.[2] He showed examples, including his own front yard in Wolverhampton, and suggested plants that would be supportive of wildlife in the garden. The morning after the program, the BBC received more than ten thousand phone calls from people asking for a transcript of the program and for more information on how to create wildlife gardens. Within a few years British nurseries had adapted their stocks to respond to the surge of interest in plants for wildlife and habitat. Today hundreds of garden clubs, publications, and support groups provide information on natural gardening in Great Britain.

In stark contrast to this back-to-nature ethos, commonly advertised garden products seem oddly contrived and synthetic—hybrids that emulate other species; seedless flowers lacking fragrance; a wide array of products specifically designed for the care of excessively crossbred plants, such as hybrid tea roses; and such ornaments as prefabricated waterfalls, requiring great inputs of energy. These may be important ingredients for picture-book gardens, but they do not reflect deeper environmental concerns and personal meanings.

With increasing frequency, however, new garden products are appearing that promote a more environmentally responsible stance, allowing the creation of gardens in harmony with the natural cycles of the surrounding landscape. Native and drought-tolerant plants have become more popular and more widely available. An "eco-green" industry is emerging, steered by businesses such as the Nature Company, Gardeners Supply, and Smith and Hawken that offer "meadows-in-a-can," native plant seeds by mail, and a wide range of prefabricated compost bins and efficient watering systems. All these resources encourage individuals in their search for their own small Eden, or what Michael Pollan calls a "second Nature."

Interest in environmentally sound gardening has also affected the billion-dollar nursery and landscape industry in major ways, especially in California. Concern for pesticide use has led the turfgrass industry to provide organic or safe chemical products, which have enjoyed brisk sales. Brochures on lawn products feature "environmentally responsible, organic products for a healthy garden" and caption pictures of children and pets playing on a lawn "guilt-free gardening."

Landscape professionals and gardeners are changing their design and management practices to follow ecological principles, experimenting, for example, with nontoxic, renewable materials, such as adobe and rammed earth, for garden construction. Greater consciousness of the need for water conservation is reflected in a growing reliance on well-adapted native plants. Local nurseries, building supply centers, and catalogs are catering increasingly to the demand by the gardening public for these drought-tolerant natives, and water-saving demonstration gardens are on view at botanical gardens and many water district offices in California, illustrating the techniques of "xeriscaping."

The idea of the environmentally responsible landscape has been advanced by many writers and designers, including Sarah Stein, Rosalind Creasy, Jeff Cox, and Robert Kourik. They have produced useful guidebooks demonstrating the important role of habitat, native plants, and recycled materials in the garden. Woven into their writing is the philosophy that by improving the quality of our human environment we can create a more sustainable world, one in harmony with nature. In this view the everyday environment of parks and gardens serves as a metaphor for the greater natural world and reconnects us with nature and natural processes.

Environmentally responsive gardening is supported as well by a growing body of literature describing a different sort of garden, one that reconnects people with the cycles of the earth. In *Natural Habitat Gardens,* the photographer and writer Kenneth Druse presents an inspiring pictorial record of the beauty of native environments in the United States and discusses the potential of restoring some of these qualities in developed landscapes such as gardens. His lectures and other writings also promote the use of native plants. In *The New American Garden,* Carole Ottesen discusses the art of massing plants to produce aesthetically pleasing gardens with regional character and individuality. She suggests that the imported style of the picturesque English lawn is giving way to a new American landscape—one based more on natural process than on predetermined design aesthetics. The perceptive gardening observer and writer Michael Pollan, in *Second Nature: A Gardener's Education,* argues that the wilderness ethic in America has traditionally fostered a strong duality in our thinking about nature: either preserve the land in pristine condition or accept its demise. The historical notion that nature and culture are diametrically opposed is not, however, valid for the American garden. When we understand that nature and culture in fact inform each other in the making of a sustainable and regenerative garden, we forge a new environmental ethic, a garden ethic, that allows us to create ecologically vibrant and culturally rich environments.

The rethinking of the American garden is greatly informed by current explorations of the idea of watersheds and bioregionalism by such individuals as the poet Gary Snyder and landscape architects Robert Thayer Jr. and the late John Lyle. Bioregionalism is a useful concept that can help nurture deep connections to natural processes and provide the context for developing regenerative gardens. For our purposes, a bioregion is defined by the biotic and geographic features of an existing landscape and its natural resources, such as water, soil, and climate. It is a landscape delimited not by arbitrary political boundaries of city, county, and state but by natural systems that work on and shape local conditions. The bioregional ethic ushers in a mounting admiration and concern for the natural landscape, for it demands that we understand the region in which we live and protect its resources. In turn it gives us a way to experience these things as part of our own lives and cultural heritage. Every landscape has a history, a life cycle, an equilibrium of resources, and seasonal rhythms. All of these qualities can find expression in the ecological garden.

It is our belief that the California landscape should serve as a source of inspiration and knowledge for home gardens. To prepare the way for bringing the beauty and processes of the native California landscape into the garden, we pose several questions: Why are home gardens so disconnected from the larger landscape in which they exist? How can gardens be designed or modified to reflect the natural systems of the surrounding bioregion? How can home gardeners participate in transforming the California garden into a place that is at once ecologically responsible and culturally responsive to our times?

This book is intended to inspire new actions in the California home garden. It is grounded in an understanding of the superiority of an interdisciplinary design process over single-issue, specialized approaches, such as creating butterfly gardens, conserving water, or using methods of organic maintenance. We hope to excite our readers, taking them on a journey of the heart and the mind and making new proposals for what this new California garden can be.

We are landscape architects with strong interest and experience in creating meaningful and sustainable landscapes. Both of us have helped clients design and build ecological gardens. This book, which is informed by our combined professional and academic experience, including extensive research conducted over the past five years on ecological gardens, is the result of our keen desire to make garden design more accessible to home gardeners.

Andreas Reimann brings to the project a broad international background that begins with his birth and childhood in Baja California; includes his training in landscape architecture in both southern California, at Cal Poly San Luis Obispo, and northern California, at the University of California, Davis; and today finds him teaching at an institute for urban open space and recreation at the University of Dresden in Germany. Mark Francis was raised in California, trained in landscape architecture and urban design at the University of California, Berkeley, and Harvard University, and has taught and practiced in New York City and Boston. In 1980 he returned to California, settling in Davis to teach and practice. The natural California environment has been a source of inspiration for both authors in their work as landscape architects.

Our intent is not to be rigid or deterministic in our approach to garden design or gardening practices. For example, we do not profess that gardens must contain only native plants; they do not work in every situation, and gardeners may want to (and should) include plants that speak to their personal histories and interests. Although we criticize the sacred lawn, we do see a place for irrigated turf in the home garden, especially in areas of human use and activity. Our view is that many approaches and techniques can transform the garden into a more hospitable and environmentally responsible place.

This book is intended for Californians searching for ways to express personal environmental values and concerns in their home garden. It offers, in equal measure, an environmental vision, practical information, and principles of design. This book is also intended for professionals interested in the garden as a reflection of cultural and environmental values, including landscape architects, ecologists, and horticulturists, and for students of landscape architecture, environmental studies, and ornamental horticulture.

It is our intent to update the history of the California garden with the environmental and cultural concerns of our time. California has long been a leader in garden design; the modern garden has its roots in the design innovations of California landscape architects such as Thomas Church, Garrett Eckbo, and Lawrence Halprin. Almost every California garden to some degree expresses their ideas, notably the idea of a space for outdoor living. A number of contemporary landscape architects, including Ron Lutsko Jr., Robert Perry, Owen Dell, Patrick and Jane Miller, Jana Ruzicka, Ann Christoph, Isabelle Greene, Joni Janecki, Rick Fisher, Steve Chainey, and Achva Stein, are working on a new California garden expressive of the beautiful landscape and multifaceted culture that have evolved here. We highlight the work of some of these innovative designers as well as prototype designs we developed as part of the research for this book.

The book is divided into six chapters and an epilogue. The first chapter explores California's nature, beginning with the way the state was dynamically assembled from island arcs and drifting continental plates over millions of years. With the rise of the Sierra Nevada in the east and the Coast Ranges in the west, for ages California was isolated biologically and ecologically, like an island. Isolation, varied topography, and a Mediterranean climate produced a diversity of fauna and flora unprecedented in North America. First settled more than twelve thousand years ago by native peoples who shaped much of California's landscape through fire, California was isolated no longer after the arrival of Spanish explorers and missionary priests in the 1700s and a flood of gold miners in the mid-1800s. California has since become home to over thirty million people from all continents and cultures. Garden traditions imported from many countries, the rampant spread of introduced plant species, the population explosion following World War II, and a culture dependent on private automobiles have all taken their toll on California's nature. In this chapter we introduce the new garden paradigm and critique the old, which was driven by a desire to dominate rather than cooperate with nature. In the modern view, nature itself becomes teacher and mentor; the gardener's task, then, is to understand the "eco-logic" of

California's landscape and the ways in which fitness and purpose are expressed in its details.

Chapter 2 explores the concepts and possible meanings of the California landscape garden, a place that reflects the habitats, native plants, wildlife, and local resources of the surrounding landscape, either contemporary, if the landscape is ecologically intact, or historically, if it is not. The California landscape garden conserves natural resources, sustains biodiversity, and relies as much as possible on locally produced or harvested building materials. Aesthetically, functionally, and ecologically, it is dedicated to seasonal processes of growth, rest, and decay; in it one may experience nature in a more intimate way while living lightly on the land. Just as important, it is also a personally meaningful place that reflects the gardener's needs, desires, and heritage. By taking an active interest in California's nature, the gardener is able to create a highly personal sense of place in the California landscape and a feeling of community with all the life in the region.

Chapter 3 takes readers on a tour around their own gardens and vicinity, where, with the eye of a naturalist, nature's designs are studied. We observe regional habitats and make an inventory of habitat features such as landforms, creeks, meadows, woodlands, grasslands, and plant communities. We then discuss how to model these nearby natural habitats in the garden and how to attract local wildlife. Patterns useful for the home gardener are included throughout this and remaining chapters.

Chapter 4 explains, in a step-by-step approach with many design examples, how to go about designing an ecologically sustainable garden that is functional and beautiful, serves multiple purposes, and is personally satisfying. Chapter 5 narrows the gap between the possible garden and the real garden with an examination of California's native plants: their cultural and ecological significance; selection, propagation, and horticultural requirements; and principles for using them in landscape design. Perennial dry borders, annual beds, and other traditional garden features are described. Lists of native plants with proven garden and wildlife value are provided, with attention given also to the functional requirements of a garden designed for relaxation and play.

Chapter 6, an overview of sustainable garden resources, demonstrates how to apply ecological principles, processes, and materials in the home garden. We discuss water conservation, including the use of such design and management tools as drought-tolerant plants, graywater and rainwater harvesting, and drip irrigation systems, and explain how to use planting patterns to manage solar energy that reaches the garden site in order to reduce home energy use for heating and cooling. Local resources also include accessible and appropriate garden building materials, such as locally harvested, collected, recycled, and salvaged wood, plastic, cement, and metal, to name but a few. We examine ways in which these materials can be used creatively and imaginatively in the garden to achieve both functional and aesthetic effects. The chapter concludes with a sobering look at California's vanishing wildlife and discusses how a garden may provide assistance to some endangered species.

The epilogue draws together the main themes of the book, summing them up with two words: *healing landscapes.* These words have a dual meaning. The goal of the landscape garden is to heal the larger garden of California through a gardener's knowledge, experience, and appreciation for the nature expressed here. In the process of putting nature's things back where they belong, the gardener is also restored spiritually. The garden thus becomes a living, active place where people may reconnect with nature and see it for what it is rather than what it has been contrived to be.

Throughout the book we present stories about gardens and wildlife and illustrations of design patterns that illuminate the discussions in each chapter. This book is a journey through and discovery of California's awe-inspiring natural landscape. At the end of the book, an appendix provides practical information for creating an ecological garden.

Despite the large number of recent books on environmental gardening, this book is unique in several ways. First, it sets forth a viable, contemporary vision of garden design based not on principles of design geometry or modernism, but on sound environmental concepts and gardening practice. Second, it focuses on California's natural landscape, both as it once was and as it exists today, as a source of inspiration for home gardeners. Third, it takes a strong bioregional approach, arguing that gardens need to be connected physically, naturally, and culturally to the regions in which they exist. Finally, it emphasizes the central role of the design process, with its ability to accommodate complex and multiple goals, in the creation of ecologically sound gardens.

We hope this book will inspire you to think, look, and act differently when you step into the garden. If you begin to see the connections between the landscape that is California and your own backyard, our effort will have been successful.

CHAPTER ONE

THE NATURE OF CALIFORNIA

Ultimately the Universe throughout its vast extent in space and its transformations in time was seen as a single multiform celebratory expression. No other explanation is possible for the world that we see around us. The birds fly and sing and perform their mating rituals. The flowers blossom. The rains nourish every living being. Each of the events in the natural world is a poem, a painting, a drama, a celebration.

Thomas Berry, *The Bush*

Nature is a word we endow with diverse layers of meaning. Depending on our intent, the word might refer to the intrinsic character of a person or thing; the physical world, including living things and natural phenomena; or temperament. The native peoples who were the first inhabitants of California may have used a word like *spirit,* another deeply resonant term, to embrace all of these meanings at once, recognizing as they did that physical reality was but the surface aspect of something deeper. They struggled to understand this unseen power through myths, and in many ways mythology remains the

The California landscape served as inspiration for settlers and artists alike, as evidenced by this painting, California Spring, *by Albert Bierstadt, 1879. (The Fine Arts Museums of San Francisco)*

cultural vehicle for much of our collective understanding about humankind's place in and relationship to nature.

Throughout this book we use the word *nature* in the more encompassing sense captured in the word *spirit*. We see the California landscape garden as a microcosm of nature, a special place where humans can witness the awe-inspiring creativity of the natural world and experience its life-giving energy. In form, we view the garden as intrinsically tied to its biological and geophysical setting, as an important part of the larger landscape or bioregion. In meaning, we understand the garden to represent a link between the past and future, in that it is a crucible for habitat. Habitat provides shelter for indigenous species of plants and animals, natives that, having evolved in specific settings over time, are the surface details of deeper ecological forces at work.

By reflecting on the form and meaning of natural landscapes, we can begin to comprehend the overarching, interwoven processes of nature. By restoring our garden environments to a uniquely Californian matrix of life, we may again establish within the California landscape a creative balance

between each bioregion's essential nature and the attentive gardener's respect for the remarkable processes of life. This shift from domination of the landscape to thoughtful collaboration with it places nature itself in the role of mentor. A renewed relationship between mentor and student will help us to understand and accommodate the ancient processes that gave rise to life and sustain it in the long term.

In contrast to the rampant, shortsighted hubris that too often accompanies human presence, this new model for relating to the landscape relies on the recognition of a sovereign system that has produced fitness in its details. The intricate workings of this system have long been pondered, first inspiring a complex mythology and eventually leading to the scientific study of natural phenomena. Mythology explains this sovereign system in terms of a supernatural being or beings, who test the mettle of unwary mortals and exact severe punishment for poor judgment. Perhaps science has arrived at a similar conclusion: human activities that contribute to global climate change and the depletion of natural resources are also likely to have painful consequences.

The oak with its thirty distinct varieties is an important symbol of the nature of California.

The new model also embodies another familiar Western tradition, the ethics of the Hippocratic oath (the most familiar tenet of which is the exhortation to physicians to refrain from doing harm), and combines this ethical stance with modern principles of ecology and evolution. Whether understood through myth or science alone, or through a synthesis of the two, the elements of place, form, meaning, and biological fitness are central to the concept of the gardener and garden evolving together as a manifestation of California's unique, dynamic nature.

Looking from hundreds of miles out in space, we see California's nature revealed: from a magnificent coastline in the west to rugged mountains in the east, framing verdant valleys and arid deserts. Everywhere a mosaic of urban development and agriculture is framed by remnants of ancient beauty and wild vigor that once characterized the natural landscape.

To grasp the contemporary spirit of California, we must appreciate how its geologic past made possible what exists today; how this place came to be home to a multitude of particular plants and animals; how these resources

were shaped by indigenous peoples over thousands of years; and, more recently, how a collective character has been assembled from a flood of immigrants meeting on this fertile land. Finally, we must understand the role technology plays in how we think and live today. To see California as it is now and to remember what it once was—to gain a new sense of familiarity and belonging—will inspire our own garden designs. Regional characteristics of landscape, indigenous plants and animals, and history can all be echoed in a California landscape garden and experienced as embodying an authentic spirit of place.

Above: *A heritage rose bramble in a historic garden along the Mendocino coast*

Opposite (top): *Seasonal wildflowers in the hills near Lancaster*

Opposite (bottom): *The diversity of the California landscape is evidenced by the mixture of old-growth forest, working agricultural landscape, and coastal fog at Philo in Mendocino County. (Patrick Miller)*

CALIFORNIA'S GEOPHYSICAL PAST AND PRESENT

The California we know today is on the leading edge of the North American continental plate, under which an oceanic plate slides. Physically a place of diversity and restless change, California is one of the newest additions to North America, dynamically assembled from island arcs and submarine

California is part of the richness and diversity of the larger landform of North America. (Raven Maps)

bedrock that have crashed into the continent over eons, like ships ramming into a dock. We now understand this process through the science of plate tectonics, which explains the characteristic physiography of California as having been formed by the subduction of the thinner, heavier Pacific plate under the thicker, lighter North American plate.[1] In a cross-section from west to east, we see the rolling Coast Ranges leveling off into the flat Great Central Valley and then rising again majestically as the Sierra Nevada (see map above).

Somewhere between 150 and 140 million years ago, in the middle of the Mesozoic era, a cataclysmic event occurred: the oceanic and continental plates became stuck in the zone of underthrusting. Volcanic deposits and marine sediments caught in the crunch between the plates folded upward and were sheared into a series of eastward-tilting slabs. From this upheaval, the mountains we call the Sierra Nevada emerged.

When things became unstuck, the Pacific plate once again was forced under the North American plate, and an undersea trough, which later would become the Great Central Valley, was formed. This trough was slowly filled by eroding sediments from the still-rising Sierra Nevada, creating a shallow sea on the continent's edge. Here, dinosaurs roamed for millions of years: the huge, aquatic Mosasaur hunted fish, and the giant Pteranodon hunted in the skies.

As the centuries passed, marine sediments from the top of the eastward-moving oceanic plate piled up on the continent, marking the beginning of the Coast Ranges. With a barrier now rising in the west and the Sierra

Nevada continuing its upward thrust in the east, the shallow sea was filled in and its marine animals died. The decay of these animals' remains created the natural gas deposits that later became an important resource in California.

The Mesozoic period ended along with the dinosaurs about 70 million years ago, and the Cenozoic era, the age of mammals, dawned. The climate warmed and the ancestors of magnolias and redwoods thrived. Mastodons, camels, horses, pollinating insects, and flowering plants flourished in the now lushly fertile Central Valley. The Sierra Nevada rose in a second thrust, and as its igneous rock weathered and streams intersected the gold-bearing veins that had formed during the Mesozoic era, gold cascaded downhill to river channels in the valley. The stage was set for the gold rush that would take place millions of years later.

From the middle of the Cenozoic to just prior to the Ice Age, a series of violent volcanic eruptions interspersed with quiet periods continued to build the Sierra Nevada. Volcanic mudflows reached down into the valley, trapping animals in the mire. Today, their bones help geologists date the last mountain-building events that formed the Sierra Nevada we see today.

The coastal forests of California provide a rich ecology for diverse animal and plant life.

The bioregions of California (adapted from The Jepson Manual, 1993*). (Raven Maps)*

1. Northwest
2. Cascade Ranges
3. Modoc Plateau
4. Central Coast Ranges
5. Great Valley
6. Sierra Nevada
7. Eastern Sierra Nevada
8. Southwest
9. Mojave Desert
10. Sonoran Desert

As the Sierra Nevada reached skyward, the climate gradually grew cooler and drier. About three million years ago, an abrupt cooling period set in and glaciers formed on the rising mountain crest. The glaciers carved and polished the rocks of the high Sierra and sent huge amounts of debris down into the valley, forming the rolling foothills that eventually became covered in chaparral and woodlands. Gardeners today may still turn over the soil and find a polished quartz pebble from these alluvial fans of debris.

The continent-forming, mountain-building, resource-producing power of nature is still at work today, as California remains one of the most tectonically active places on earth. The Pacific plate continues to rotate in a counterclockwise direction, causing friction and movement from south to north, and from west to east. This intense tectonic activity not only shakes the state from time to time but also gives California its diverse topography, highly disparate climatic regions, and equally distinct ecological habitats. Contrast Mt. Whitney, for example, the highest point in the contiguous United States, with Death Valley, the lowest and hottest—two California landmarks that are a mere eighty miles apart. In the diverse habitats that characterize these two places, fauna and flora have emerged that are as different as night and day. The immediate geophysical setting, then, offers important clues about the form a bioregionally sensitive garden may take, and its native beauty serves as a source of inspiration for the home gardener.

CALIFORNIA'S NATURAL DIVERSITY

Climate and the availability of water have had a major influence in shaping California's terrain. Climate patterns, local weather (temperature, precipitation, fog, evaporation, and wind), and soils determine to a great extent the ecological characteristics of indigenous plant and animal life. Thus, each of California's eleven bioregions (see map on this page) has its specific climate pattern, as well as a mosaic of habitats, plant communities, and wildlife.

West of the Sierra Nevada, patterns of rainfall are influenced by latitude and altitude; average yearly rainfall ranges from over one hundred inches in parts of the Klamath Mountains in the north to less than ten inches in many low-lying areas of coastal southern California. However, rainfall totals tend to differ capriciously from year to year in most parts of the state. West of the Sierra Nevada, too, temperatures are generally mild, which accounts for the successful introduction of many exotic plants that have displaced entire native plant communities.

A benevolent climate, coupled with regionally varied topography, has bestowed on California a remarkable diversity of natural resources to garden with. One of the most significant bioregions, in terms not only of natural resources but also of economics, is the Great Central Valley, comprising the Sacramento Valley to the north and the San Joaquin Valley to the south. More than 430 miles long and an average of 50 miles wide, this vast trench, which drains two major river systems, is California's modern heartland.[2] Nurtured by the prevailing Mediterranean climate and fed by a network of streams that transport spring runoff and silt from the mountains, this emerald-in-spring and gold-in-summer place is the richest agricultural region in the world. Besides yielding a cornucopia of fruits, grains, and vegetables, the fertility associated with this area has had such by-products as the oil fields of the lower San Joaquin Valley, formed from decaying organic matter trapped in folded layers of sedimentary rock. In other bioregions, California's natural riches support fishing, lumber, natural gas, and mineral industries. These diverse resources have placed California's economy on a scale larger than that of most nations.

Resources that have economic value are perhaps the best known of California's riches, but one also finds an abundance of resources with no recognized direct economic value, including a remarkable variety of indigenous plant and animal species that reflect the climatic and topographic diversity of this state. It is in this heritage of fauna and flora—wealth that is being lost at an alarming rate through habitat destruction[3]—that we find California's most exceptional treasures. As the abundance of native plant species adapted to various habitats declines in the wild, home gardeners have benefited from the increasing number of native plants available to them at local and specialty nurseries. Many gardeners who use local native species experience a special payoff as they witness the ingenious strategies these plants have developed to survive and reproduce. Admiring nature's ingenuity is in itself a kind of beauty, a new garden aesthetic.

CALIFORNIA THEN AND NOW

Descriptions by early explorers of California are filled with breathtaking imagery. Ample water drainage from the mountains once produced vast expanses of wetlands, dominated by tules, and wide bands of beautiful riparian (occurring near a river, stream, or creek) oak woodlands. Magnificent flocks of swans, geese, sandhill cranes, white pelicans, and ducks reportedly

The picturesque Sacramento River and the Marysville Buttes, as rendered by R. Swain Gifford in 1872

darkened the sky during migrations or when disturbed out of estuaries and inland marshes. Grasslands in the Central Valley resembled an American Serengeti and supported populations of tule elk, deer, pronghorn antelope, grizzly and black bear, mountain lion, fox, and coyote.

Just after the gold rush of 1849, the Scottish immigrant John Muir (who would go on to found the Sierra Club some forty years later) looked out onto a still-pristine Central Valley and captured in words the teeming abundance, which he likened to that of "bee pastures":

> At my feet lay the Great Central Valley of California, level and flowery, like a lake of pure sunshine. . . . Magnificent Oaks, from three to eight feet in diameter, cast grateful masses of shade over the open prairie-like levels. And close along the water's edge there was a fine jungle of tropical luxuriance, composed of wild rose and bramble bushes and a great variety of climbing vines, wreathing and interlacing the branches and trunks of Willows and Alders.[4]

Only vestiges of these grand and inspiring landscapes are left in California. Organizations such as the Nature Conservancy and the Trust for Public Land struggle to protect and sustain the last remnants of California's pristine natural heritage, and the Wildlands Project seeks to reconnect living landscapes, fragmented ecosystems, and ancient animal migration routes.

Nonetheless, enough remains of California's biological richness that, though vastly reduced in scale in most places, it still produces a sense of wonder in the careful observer. Seasonal rhythms finely tuned by evolution continue to orchestrate a symphony of activity in even the smallest biological

The form and geometry of the valley oak bring interest to the garden.

kingdoms, surrounded though they may be by urban development. No single snapshot can capture the diversity of life one might encounter during any one seasonal cycle in California. Indeed, it would take many albums to show the interplay between habitat and occupant, the unique ways in which the adaptive process for each species whittles down to a manageable size a large and complex world. Every plant and animal here has its own story.

California's remaining native oaks are among the grandest illustrations of how plants are shaped by place, developing qualities that in turn shape major biotic communities. At present California has eighteen species of oak, with nearly thirty distinct varieties, and the life cycle of each has been finely tuned to regional water availability, soil, and climate. Some drop their leaves in the fall, while others keep a thick canopy year round, strategies designed to cope with resource scarcity in different regions.[5] When moisture is limited, tiny gas-exchanging pores in the leaves close to conserve water. Evergreen oaks do lose their leaves, but only gradually over two-year cycles, so that some leaves remain on the tree at all times. Deciduous oaks, in contrast, drop their leaves all at once and go dormant during the winter. In this way they save energy during the cold months, putting out leaves only when conditions improve.

Trees exist at the top of most terrestrial ecosystems, with life pulsating in and around them. In the branches, among the roots, and on the leaf-littered soil surrounding native oak trees are sheltered hundreds of species of insects, lichens, fungi, and vertebrate animals that depend on the oak and each other. Hundreds of companion plants are associated with an oak-dominated native plant community. Acorns make up between 25 and 50 percent of the yearly diet of at least thirty species of birds. In turn, scrub jays, Steller's jays, and magpies help the oak extend its range by burying caches of acorns as a future food supply. One bird can bury five thousand acorns in a season, small hordes of food that half the time remain unclaimed.

Native oak trees also tell us another story about California. They serve as living reminders of the incredible loss of habitat California's plants and wildlife have suffered over the past two hundred years. Once part of thick woodlands that covered much of the Coast Ranges and the Central Valley's riparian corridors, countless acres of oaks—one of the most prized resources of native peoples—were destroyed by settlers and grazing animals. Riparian belts were among the areas hardest hit. Whereas formerly more than 775,000 acres of oak woodlands lined rivers in the Sacramento Valley, forming protective bands of habitat hundreds of yards wide on each bank, today fewer than 12,000 acres of riparian habitat remain.[6] From southern to northern California, towns named for their oak woodlands—Thousand Oaks, Live Oak, Oakland— now have only token trees to remind residents of their native heritage.

Hundreds of native species could tell a similar story of being over-whelmed by rapid change during the past few decades. One species that reveals to us the fragile beauty of California's spring and the special relationships that exist between plants and insects is the endangered mission blue butterfly, now found only in cool coastal scrub and grasslands near San Francisco.[7] Females lay their eggs on just three species of perennial lupines: silver *(Lupinus albifrons)*, Lindley varied *(L. varicolor)*, and summer *(L. formosus)*. Seven to ten days later the larvae hatch, and for three weeks they munch on the lupine leaves. During this feeding period, caretaker ants stroke the larval caterpillars with their antennae, and the larvae secrete a sugary fluid called honeydew, which the ants feed upon. In return, the ants protect the vulnerable larvae from predators and other parasites. The caterpillars then crawl into the leaves scattered on the ground beneath their lupine hosts and become dormant until the following spring. Sometime between early March and early July, following pupation, the caterpillars emerge briefly (for six to ten days) as violet-blue beauties, the timing synchronized with the appearance of the lupine blossoms on which they depend for nectar. Recently, loss of habitat to housing and industrial development has propelled the small butterfly toward extinction, while its only remaining lifeline, the lupine, is being overtaken by grazing animals and invasive exotic plants, particularly European gorse.

While surviving oaks and butterflies tell the story of the overwhelmed, lichens tell the story of the overlooked. During the transition months from cold to hot weather, clouds of fungal spores find footholds on gravestones, rocks, and the bark of trees and shrubs—anywhere there is a stable surface. Those spores then colonize with algae, cyanobacteria, or both to yield the colorful symbiotic organisms known as lichens. Neither plant nor animal—nor entirely fungus, alga, or bacterium—lichens form tiny ecosystems that can thrive for centuries, perhaps even millennia, and support entire communities of microorganisms, insects, birds, and animals. Scientists, for example, speculate that a wind-transported lichen supplied the biblical manna from heaven, and it is known that several Native American tribes turned to this foodstuff during times of famine.

Long ignored, approximately 3,600 species of lichen grow in the United States and Canada, each with a representative color and form, ranging from a soft green filigree draped on trees to a bright orange crust on rocks. Dormant when dry and metabolically active only when damp, lichens serve as sponges for environmental pollutants; because of this extreme sensitivity, they can, like toad skin, be used to measure air quality. Even as the number and diversity of lichens decrease owing to pollution and loss of habitat, appreciation for their medicinal and decorative properties is growing. Substances derived from lichens—nearly six hundred pigments, toxins, and antibiotics that these organisms have developed to survive—historically have been used by many indigenous peoples as dyes and medicines.[8]

In a garden, portions of the larger landscape, with its natural diversity of spaces and species, can be emulated, reflected, and recreated on a small scale to provide refuge for increasingly embattled insect, bird, and plant populations. For instance, the beauty and richness of the lush canyon habitats of southern California may inspire richly contrasting arrangements of vegetation: A decaying tree trunk on the garden border might mirror the legacy of life that on a larger scale sustains entire forest ecosystems. Nearby might be an area dense with the golden-colored fronds of native buckwheat, next to which rests a large clay dish filled with water to symbolize the vital role water plays in all ecosystems. These elements contrast richly with the dark green leaves of adjacent shrubs and the rock border of a patio. Taken as a whole, the garden forms a scene reminiscent of so many rugged California canyons.

Through recreation of an entire ecosystem in miniature, many of the overlooked and overwhelmed among California's native species can find a place in the California landscape garden. This reflection of the surrounding physical and biological environment inspires in both the gardener and the garden visitor an awareness of many unique natural processes and a sense of communion with the larger home in which we all live.

THE FIRST CALIFORNIANS

In addition to climate and topography, human hands played an important role in shaping the nature of California. Archeological and ethnographic evidence argues convincingly that native peoples arrived here over the Bering Strait land bridge between twelve and forty thousand years ago—well before the first Spanish missionaries arrived in 1769 or gold was discovered near Sacramento in 1848. Through their wide-scale land management practices, California's native peoples left us a legacy of ecological diversity and respect for nature that we have yet to honor.

Traditionally, native Californians lived in a close relationship with the land, their way of life integrated with the natural environment through judicious harvesting of animals and botanical resources for food, clothing, medicine, and construction materials. In addition, native Californians believed that all of material nature was endowed with spirit; in their biocratic, or "life-governed," metaphysics, humans were neither superior nor subordinate but simply part of the whole. Human benevolence was seen as the key to sustaining harmony within this biocracy so as to reap nature's bounty and live well. This deeply intuitive and highly practical sense of ecology was taught to each succeeding generation through stories and traditions that sanctified life and through the maintenance of sacred places. Such reverence is an important part of our heritage and can lead us to rediscovering ways of living lightly on the landscape in a sustainable manner.

The first Californians lived among large game animals such as mastodons, camels, great sloths, and saber-toothed cats. Around 6000 B.C., perhaps because of climate changes, many of the larger game animals disappeared. During this same period, newly arrived tribes, though still hunting game, acquired tremendous knowledge of plants and their uses. California, thanks in large part to its moderate climate and plentiful food resources, now became the most densely populated section of the Americas north of modern-day central Mexico.

Although California, with its abundant tangle of resources, may have looked wild to early explorers and settlers, it was not the untended, uncharted wilderness these newcomers imagined they saw. In fact, native Californians are known to have managed and cultivated the natural landscape for richer

Native Californians tended a mosaic of different plant communities to harvest fuel, food, and building materials. (Sacramento Valley Indians, 1877; artist unknown)

productivity, both to satisfy their own needs and to nurture the rich array of wildlife around them, over thousands of years.

> The extremely rich, diverse and apparently "wild" landscape that so impressed Europeans at the time of contact—and which traditionally has been viewed as a "natural, untrammeled wilderness" ever since—was to some extent actually a product of (and more importantly dependent on) deliberate human intervention. In other words, particular habitats, in a number of important respects, had been domesticated.[9]

Indigenous peoples managed their environment in various ways. One of the most important techniques they used was fire. Fires were set regularly throughout California to renew and encourage grassland vegetation, such as bulbs and a wide variety of grass seeds, for human consumption and animal forage. Care was taken that fires did not grow too hot and burn the important oak trees or crowns of other trees.

Native Californians' management skills also extended to maintaining healthy stands of basket-weaving materials, which they both collected from the wild and cultivated. Highly valued species included deergrass, California redbud, and sedges. Deergrass was set on fire annually to rejuvenate it; redbud was pruned; and the sedges, of which great quantities of long, straight roots were necessary for baskets, were root-pruned and weeded.

Management techniques also included taboos. For example, native

Californians often curtailed the amount of a resource they harvested, such as salmon from a river where they had built a dam. They did so to ensure that there would be enough fish left to reach the spawning grounds, thus guaranteeing a subsequent harvest, and to reduce conflict with neighboring tribes who relied on the salmon as well. Although we may interpret these measures as sound practices for ensuring a sustainable yield, native peoples were conscious primarily of the sacred cycle of nature: greed and hubris were denied so that the spirit, made manifest in salmon, would be pleased with the people and return to honor them again as life-giving food.

From generation to generation the native peoples of California taught their children to respect the environment and its natural laws—the ways in which nature operated as a result of spiritual forces working beneath the surface. Discovery of these laws was based on perceptive observation of seasonal events, climatic changes, and other aspects of the physical world over generations. The cumulative store of shared knowledge that resulted helped native peoples make full use of seasonal resources and formed the basis for a rich spiritual and community life.

Native American cultures offered a broader framework for life experience than the ego- and ethnocentrism of the Europeans, which drove westward expansion and led to the cultural collision between indigenous peoples and immigrants. For the native peoples, every aspect of the landscape was sacred; everything in nature—including humankind—was understood to be interrelated. The taking of something from nature, whether for food, shelter, or some other purpose, was often attended by ceremonial displays of gratitude to the Creator and always by prayer. The anthropologist Dorothy Lee was especially struck by the Native American traits of courtesy and mindfulness with respect to the natural world. Native Americans, she said, acted in the name of

> a wider democracy which includes Nature and the divine. . . . The courteous speech to the bear about to be killed, the offering to the deer world before the hunter sets out, . . . the refraining from intercourse, or from the eating of meat (in particular times) or from touching food with the hand, are expressive of such an attitude. . . . The great care with which so many of the Indian groups utilized every portion of the carcass of a hunted animal was an expression, not of economic thrift, but of courtesy and respect.[10]

The care with which native Californians related to the land and its resources reflected their cultural and, hence, personal values. Echoing their worldview, John Muir—who quietly observed that when we try to pick out anything by itself, we find it hitched up to everything else in the universe—understood that every detail in nature is part of an all-encompassing tapestry. It was this awareness that drove him to become one of the foremost champions of California's natural landscape, at a time when most people considered nature ours for the plucking.

It is estimated that less than 10 percent of California's native human population survived the hundred-year period following the arrival of the Spanish in 1769. During the next hundred years, California's native plant and animal species would likewise vanish in large numbers. Only during the last few decades, with the growth of the environmental movement, has a contrary trend begun to emerge, one based in part on the ideals and symbols of a way of life that was vanquished and is now often portrayed as lost. Stereotyped images of Chief Seattle and Black Hawk and symbols such as the circle of life are now familiar icons of mainstream America. Though commandeered to some degree for corporate advertising, these images are still used by environmental groups to help regenerate a vision of biocratic universality and to reshape attitudes on resource use and environmental protection.

The idea that the torch of Native American culture has been passed to all people is reflected in the words of the artist and poet E. Roger Apodaca:

> The way of thought is what is important to preserve, not particular, individual bodies. . . . It is silly to talk about a flower dying, because its essence is preserved in the seed. The seed produces a remanifestation of a glorious spring bloom. And people are very much like flowers. Their essence is preserved not in their body, but in their way of being, in the way of thought.[11]

Although precious little remains today of the physical landscape in which native Californian cultures developed and thrived, their beliefs and practices offer a source of meaning not found in contemporary gardening and landscape design. Native peoples' ideals provide us, in particular, with a vocabulary with which to envision a renewed relationship with nature, allowing empathy to be restored to Western culture's worldview, beginning with one's home landscape and extending into shared community and public spaces. A sense of divine mystery about the origins of life motivated prescientific peoples' relations to the earth and its inhabitants. At the dawn of the twenty-first century, scientific rationalists who have popularized theories of evolution and cosmology express a similar notion of the divine. Now, however, the physical mechanism through which the divine operates is

An early California garden in Bakersfield (Carleton Walker, 1888. Reproduced from the collection of the Library of Congress)

understood by deep ecologists in terms of the Gaia hypothesis—the notion that planet Earth is a living, sentient organism.

CALIFORNIA AS MYTH AND REALITY

Despite overwhelming odds, Native American ideals survived to shape the philosophy of the environmental movement, and today they permeate Western ideology generally. The notion of preserving or restoring fragments of wild areas left in modern California has its roots in these ideals. Today's landscape, however, is still being shaped and imprinted, as successive waves of diverse groups of immigrants arrive, leaving physical signs everywhere that serve as a living history.

The name *California* originated in a sixteenth-century Spanish legend describing a mythic island "rich in pearls and gold and very near to the terrestrial paradise."[12] Today, biologists again refer to the "island" of California because, ecologically speaking, it essentially was an island for millions of years. Mountains to the north, east, and south, deserts beyond, and the ocean in the west long functioned as effective barriers to the free movement of most plants and animals. At least until the Spanish colonial period, unique ecological communities were able to evolve in the protective embrace of isolation, typically narrowly restricted in range and developing few defenses against diseases, predators, or competitors. Once the natural barriers were breached, however, the "island" of California changed character for good.

The landscape traditions we live with now derive largely from the immigrants who arrived in California during the past two hundred years. Anywhere one looks today, those things that are considered typical of California, from exotic palms to architectural styles, farming practices to attitudes toward nature, were brought piecemeal by Spanish, then early American and European, and more recently Asian and Latin American immigrants and visitors in an attempt to recreate more familiar surroundings.

California's vast, relatively open land and ample resources, along with its benevolent climate, promised a life of abundance and well-being for a growing population of immigrants. Here, an eclectic, highly progressive society emerged, to which much of the world looks today for leadership. Inventiveness, unconventionality, and an individualistic approach in a multicultural society have become the hallmarks of this land, though accompanied, to be sure, by a plethora of social and environmental problems. We have already examined the physical landscape and the Native American worldview that inform contemporary gardens and gardening. Here, then, the contemporary cultural ingredient gets added to the mix.

In *California Gardens: Creating a New Eden*, the landscape historian David Streatfield traces the cultural history of the California garden. Early mission gardens like that of Santa Barbara (1772) were simple and utilitarian, reflecting a fledgling society on a colonial frontier. On land that thus far had seen no permanent buildings, corpulent architectural structures arose to surround central courtyards, refuges from the arid environment of coastal California and reminders of the walled-in garden of Middle Eastern and Spanish tradition, symbolic of the Garden of Eden.

In early California gardens, a variety of wild native species were domesticated, and flowering plants were imported and tended for church decoration. The imports included the calla and Madonna lily, Castilian and musk rose, jasmine, lavender, tamarind, anise, hollyhock, oleander, nasturtium, sweet pea, and portulaca. European giant reed was grown as a windbreak and for making mats. The date palm was planted for its leaves, which according to the New Testament were used to celebrate Christ's entry into Jerusalem.

The mission became a lasting theme in California, even serving as the architectural style of choice for numerous college campuses and shopping malls. The style can be attributed partly to a literary romanticism that emerged after the missions were secularized in the early nineteenth century. With the introduction of cattle grazing and development of the Spanish rancho, the transformation of the California landscape proceeded rapidly. Helen

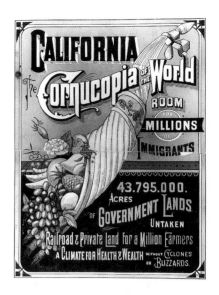

The lure of the California cornucopia, circa 1900. (Landauer Collection, New York Historical Society)

A walled garden at Rancho Santa Anita
(Saxon Holt)

Hunt Jackson, in her 1884 novel *Ramona,* described the "half barbaric, half elegant, wholly generous, and free-handed life" of a typical rancho. Speaking of the alluring classical gardens with grape-covered trellises, decorated with great clay jars containing colorful plants, Jackson observed that gardens were not isolated terrains but intimate parts of the landscape in which they resided. In her words, the "river meadow" over which a rancho garden looked comes vividly to life:

> All was garden, orange grove, and almond orchard; the orange grove always green, never without snowy bloom or golden fruit; the garden never without flowers, summer or winter; and the almond orchard in early spring a fluttering canopy of pink and white petals, which seen from the hills on the opposite side of the river, looked as if rosy sunlight clouds had fallen and become tangled in the trees and the clouds.[13]

By the mid–nineteenth century, the nation was transforming rapidly from an agricultural to an industrial society. California was in the midst of the gold rush, and all Americans were faced with the enormous changes posed by mechanization. As the population expanded on the eastern seaboard, immigration to the western regions of the United States was exuberantly touted as fulfillment of a dream: not only could one buy plenty of land, but the West enjoyed an idyllic climate as well. The transformation of the California landscape into a cultural mosaic of human influence and domination was about to be complete.

California's mild climate, a welcome relief for many easterners, provided ample material for writers such as Charles F. Holder of Pasadena, who, like Jackson, romanticized southern California's leisurely life:

> When the blizzard blows in the East, the warm trade wind sighs through the orange blossoms here. When the ice is forming there, the birds are singing here. There is no lost time from one end of the year to the other. Nature seems always at her best, and the products of nearly everyone meet here. The banana and the pine, the palm and the apple grow in the same dooryard, and when the summer comes, and sunstroke and other ills visit the East, perfect immunity is found here in cooler days and perfect nights.[14]

From the gold rush to the modern day, California's landscape has allowed, even encouraged, the pursuit of dreams and the expression of mythic stereotypes. For many immigrants, the verdant hills dotted with California oaks brought to mind the mythic land of Arcadia—a world, according to Greek mythology, without work, war, or real danger. Many people in fact called the state Arcadia, and the name still belongs to a town in the San Fernando Valley.

The actress Helena Modjeska, fleeing Poland's oppressive Russian rule in the 1870s, settled in a canyon in the Santa Ana Mountains. She had long had "wild dreams" of living in an untamed and free country, and now they were realized: "Oh, but to cook under the sapphire-blue sky in the land of freedom!" she enthused. "What a joy! To bleach linen at the brook like the maidens of Homer's *Iliad!* After the day of toil, to play the guitar and sing by moonlight, to recite poems, or to listen to the mocking-bird! It seemed like being born again." To her delight, the actress discovered her California property had "everything that Shakespeare speaks of . . . on the spot—oak trees, running brooks, palms, snakes, and even lions—of course, California lions—really pumas."[15]

Other mid- and late-nineteenth-century immigrants to California, just as extravagant in their praise of the "idyllic" surroundings, transformed their enthusiasm into eclectic gardens. They created geometric beds in elaborate mosaic-like patterns of annuals and succulents around cast-iron statues and reproduced idealized landscapes in miniature through alpine plantings and the creation of canals. European ideas were taken to new heights, especially in gardens around the San Francisco Bay.

During this time, collections of exotic plants became symbols of wealth and social status. Curiosities such as unusual rocks, shells, and gems were eagerly displayed in home gardens. With a moderate climate and copious amounts of water, an exceptionally broad range of temperate and semitropical plants could be planted. A great diversity of plants imported from all

The wildness of Yosemite inspired early visitors such as John Muir and Frederick Law Olmsted Jr. (Marc Treib)

Fantasy and expressiveness have always been a part of the California garden, as in this shell garden pool at Lotusland, Montecito. (Jerry Pavia)

over the world were found to thrive in California, establishing the state's identity as an exotic place.

The California gardens of this immigrant society were, and continue to be, largely out of step with their environmental setting. According to Streatfield, this tendency is associated with two factors: technology that allows water to be moved over significant distances and the ease of growing just about any plant in California. In addition, Streatfield describes the influence of the landscape designer Andrew Jackson Downing, whom many nineteenth-century immigrants considered the authority for what constituted good taste. Downing, a New Yorker, stressed the importance of a proper, harmonious connection between house and grounds and between grounds and the surrounding scenery, so as to avoid "any violent contrast to the eye." Appalled by gardens full of ornaments that had no connection with the immediate surroundings, he urged his readers to reject such "scenes of rural bedlam" in favor of the "natural and tasteful." The "natural and tasteful" style he advocated, however, was modeled on a distinctly eastern American landscape. "It was Downing," writes Streatfield, "who was responsible for the American public acceptance of a new kind of garden design—the broad lawns, distant vistas, gently rolling terrain, winding paths and artful clumps of trees of the English picturesque style."[16] In short, the California immigrants who so eagerly sought his advice overlooked the fact that the California landscape and the environment of the East Coast suggested very different solutions to problems of "harmonious" garden design.

The 1920s witnessed a new effort to import other cultures and visions into California, this time steered by landscape architects seeking to make more regionally appropriate gardens. This subgroup of the Arts and Crafts movement, reacting to the aesthetic and botanical excesses of Victorian gardening and to the dominance of international tastes in American horticulture, stressed the importance of local materials and plants suited to local conditions, finding inspiration in other Mediterranean-climate regions such as Spain and Italy.

European innovations have continued to shape the California landscape. In Germany in the 1920s, the Bauhaus design school sought new forms to express an increasingly industrialized society, with rapidly growing populations and a need for new housing. In the view of these practitioners, the hope for the future lay in the new technologies of reinforced concrete, steel, and glass walls, which soon informed an internationalist style that was eagerly adopted by California architects. Although the spaces and buildings created in this tradition have been criticized for their dehumanizing properties, the modernist consciousness inspired a popular new approach to gardening, reflected in the austere functionality of designs by landscape architects such as Thomas Church and Garrett Eckbo.[17]

Prior to World War II, too, California landscape architects were exploring other creative ways of achieving aesthetic effects. Led by Church and Eckbo, designers now brought modernism and modern outdoor living together in the garden during the middle period of this century. The unified space defined by Chris Grampp in his 1985 article "The California Living Garden" has become the California standard, with the sliding glass door and outdoor barbecue merging house and garden. These explorations of the multiple uses of gardens set the stage for development of a truly Californian landscape garden.

Particularly since World War II, a huge and increasingly pluralistic middle class has put its own stamp on the vernacular landscape (despite efforts to the contrary by *Sunset* magazine and landscape architects), opting for a plethora of individualized styles in house and garden. Far from displaying the conformity of, say, a Cape Cod community with its distinctive architectural look, today California's developed environment is marked by an often runaway eclecticism. Such a lack of a style has in fact become the style in and of itself. From the Italian villas of Los Angeles to the Victorian homes of northern California, a great variety of imported forms are now both familiar and acceptable. The California vernacular has become so all-inclusive that even more elaborate ethnic constructions, such as the Scandinavian theme-

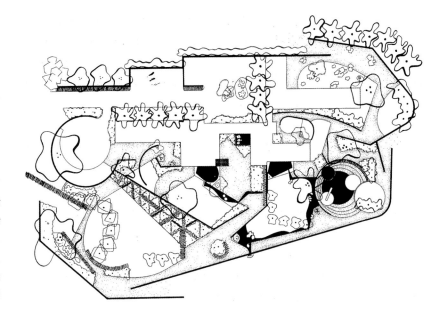

Modern landscape architecture brought form and geometry to spaces such as the Burden Garden by Garrett Eckbo, 1945. (College of Environmental Design, Documents Collection of the University of California, Berkeley)

world of Solvang and a host of smaller Santa Claus and Swiss villages, provide some longtime California residents with a sense of cultural connection. For others, not only do these constructions fail to appear out of place, but they also impart a Disneyesque, matter-of-course feeling that California is and seemingly always has been like a small United Nations.

Much of the California vernacular landscape, of course, looks as it does because of our relatively short history as a rapidly assembled pool of many peoples. Yet while the variety of styles—and particularly, in the context of this book, the associated plants—helps make California what it is today, it is important that we assess the imported flora in terms of what it contributes to the landscape and what, if anything, it is displacing. Eclecticism and regional gardening practices are not necessarily incompatible but can continue side by side. At the same time, however, we must recognize that ecological factors should play the major role in directing the form and function of the California garden.

TECHNOLOGY AND THE CONTRIVED LANDSCAPE

While the mythic California of an earthly paradise lives on in our literature and in our imaginations, inconsistencies with that picture are everywhere evident. The past 150 years have been characterized by massive immigration to the state. In 1848 the population of California comprised approximately 100,000 Europeans and about the same number of Native Americans. By the year 2012, in stark contrast, the state's population is predicted to swell to sixty million. Now, massive changes in the landscape and in people's quality of life are possible within a single lifetime, and often within a few years. Loss of open space, declining air and water quality, and urban sprawl are daily reminders to many Californians of the demands we are putting on resources and of the limits to further growth.

Driven by large population increases—and the quick profits to be made catering to these newcomers' needs—technological quick fixes and short-sighted planning strategies for growth and development are hastening the ongoing process of environmental degradation. Rather than benefiting from much-needed ecological restoration and repair, remnants of wilderness near our homes and communities are often leveled and replaced by biologically impoverished, resource-dependent, "landscaped" open spaces.

Many scientists have characterized the twentieth century as an Age of Extinctions. The cultural distance we maintain relative to our natural environment has allowed an often severe decline in the number, extent, and integrity of once-common ecosystems. The rushes that not too long ago graced large sections of the Santa Clara Valley can scarcely be found today. Gigantic stumps among young, uniform stands of trees remind us of the rich forests that once dominated hills and valleys in northwestern California. Many creeks and streams, habitat corridors through which plants and animals once dispersed, have been replaced by ecologically disastrous concrete or channeled drainage ditches. A generation ago, the horned lizard was still common in southern California; children growing up today know nothing of it. As of this writing, 115 species of threatened and endangered wildlife are protected by state and federal laws, and 25 percent of plant species are threatened with extinction. At the current rates of human population increase and habitat loss, it is estimated that over 60 percent of California's native flora and fauna will become extinct within the next few decades.[18]

Because native species of plants have been crowded out by urban and rural development and displaced by imported competitors, scientists find it increasingly difficult to reconstruct significant habitats, such as prairies and riparian landscapes. The ongoing loss of wild, open spaces is a painful experience for people who remember a more diverse and intriguing environment. What we miss perhaps most of all are the small, wild places close to home, those fascinating (and up to a certain age, even magical) places that we explored and experienced with such intensity. This critical loss of habitat and species diversity has resulted in what one naturalist calls the "extinction of experience": "When we lose the common wildlife in our immediate sur-

The natural qualities of the California landscape have often been lost due to its engineered fields, roads, and canals. Aerial photo of Mendota Canal (William Garnett)

Suburban development ignores the natural environment as it sprawls across the land. (Richard J. Meisinger Jr.)

roundings, we run the risk of becoming inured to nature's absence, blind to delight, and, eventually, alienated from the land."[19]

The term *landscaping* has come to mean a cosmetic furnishing of the landscape, a form of interior decoration done outside. Instead of emulating the natural environment in all its complexity and stimulating a positive experience of nature, many gardens today are purely decorative. In deference to transient lifestyles, tract houses that go up in a month are landscaped in a day with instant sod lawns and mature trees and shrubs. The desire for an instant yard has tended to supersede thoughtful, deliberate plant selection that places value on ecology, fitness, and meaning.

In his book *Out of Place: Restoring Identity to the Regional Landscape,* the landscape architect Michael Hough suggests that the "contrived human environment symbolizes the imbalance between the vision of a utopian Garden of Eden and the ability of the environment to sustain the idea."[20] It is our goal, as California landscape designers, to remedy this imbalance and reestablish close contact with both nature and the native environment.

Reliance on Technology

Why has more of the natural environment not been preserved? The reasons lie first of all in our fascination with engineering, which has resulted in elaborate aqueducts, road systems, and power and communications systems, all having enormous environmental implications. Although technology is a necessary part of our lives, it seems that the more we depend on its products, including power tools, pesticides, and fabricated materials such as fiberglass, the more we use these innovations to create contrived landscapes:

> Technological products allow a more antiseptic, durable, low maintenance landscape; however, the result is less apt to be truly "alive," since the generation, deterioration, recycling, and regeneration of natural materials in the landscape is what enables life to exist. The hard urban landscapes of today, while more durable and maintenance-free than ever before, and often animated by high technology, are also more sterile and lifeless.[21]

Besides controlling more of the environment, technology has allowed us to distance ourselves increasingly from the larger world. Many of the materials we use regularly in daily life are from places we ourselves have never been; indeed, we may have no idea just where they do come from. Nor do we know how they are made, much less who makes them.

Similarly, technology removes us from a sense of accountability for our actions. This is especially true in water and energy use; since we don't pump the water or harvest the wood or coal ourselves, we often take for granted the availability of these resources and sometimes squander them needlessly. Meanwhile, the continuing importation of water from distant sources to the highly populated urban areas of California impoverishes lakes and flood plains in the inland valleys and foothills. And the coal-burning Four Corners power plant, though located in one of the least populous areas of the country, produces more pollution than the entire city of Los Angeles as it provides electricity to an area that extends from southern California to Texas.[22]

While the media, an influential technology, have their positive aspects, they, too, have served to separate us from the world around us. As Robert Thayer Jr. writes in *Gray World, Green Heart,* our love of the outdoors increasingly is satisfied not by direct experiences of nature but by simulation. The media, moreover, promote contrived landscapes—an immaculate lawn and manicured shrubbery in a Sierran yard, for example, or an alpine garden in urban San Fernando Valley—that bear no connection to local ecology. The result is a great potential for harm by the overuse of resources required to maintain them, including water and pesticides, and by the displacement of indigenous plant species needed by local wildlife.

Landscape architects themselves, influenced by the media, often help to blur the line between fantasy and reality. A growing segment of the profession is preoccupied with designing landscapes aimed strictly at entertainment, simulation, and illusion. The result is an everyday "reality" that is not authentic. The cultural historian Thomas Berry discusses the dangers of turning our backs on the real world in *The Dream of the Earth:*

> The natural world is subject as well as object. The natural world is the maternal source of our being as earthlings and the life-giving nourishment of our physical, emotional, aesthetic, moral, and religious existence. The natural world is the larger sacred community to which we belong. To be alienated from this community is to become destitute in all that makes us human. To damage this community is to diminish our own existence.[23]

Lack of a Sense of Place

The Native American activist and author Vine Deloria notes that, unlike Western societies, which tend to identify strongly with historic tradition, Native American cultures have a deep relationship with place.[24] Local geographical features govern daily rituals, religion, an entire way of thinking. Sutter Buttes in northern California, for example, was a sacred place for four tribes and functioned as the center of their universe. It would have been inconceivable for them to alter this landscape or move away and still retain their personal identity.

The Western focus on social history may help to explain why our gardens refer more immediately to the green lawns of England than to California's golden summer landscape. Many Californians seem to feel that place is temporary and not a significant part of one's identity. What rules our daily life is not "intimacy with the larger earth community," as Berry calls it, but a system of schedules, money, laws, and social expectations.

> Indigenous peoples live in a Universe, in a cosmological order, whereas we, the peoples of the industrial world, no longer live in a Universe. We live in a political world, a business world, an economic order, and a cultural tradition. Even more significant in its consequences is the fact that we live in cities, in a world of concrete and steel, of wheels and wires, a world of business, of work. We no longer see the stars at night or the planets or the Moon. In the day we do not experience the Sun in any immediate or meaningful manner. We live in a world of highways, parking lots, shopping centers, and malls. We read books written with a strangely contrived alphabet. We no longer read the book of the Universe.[25]

From the perspective of an industrial society such as our own, a backyard seems strangely irrelevant to what happens in nature. Nature is something found in Alaska or in Yosemite, but not at home or even nearby. Louise Lacey, publisher of *Growing Native,* a newsletter about California native plants, once quite literally lived in two worlds: during the week she worked in Silicon Valley, the heart of industrial technology, but on the weekends she returned to her small house in the wild canyons of the Berkeley hills, where she wrote her newsletter. She described her sense of living in a community dominated by *technosapiens,* a word she coined to describe people whose feet never touch the earth:

> Near my workplace [in Silicon Valley], a creek has been turned into a channel. There used to be rushes and sedges there, as well as elderberry. I used to bring twigs and seedheads home from there and put them in a vase. It was all destroyed. There is no ecology there. When it rains I can't smell the soil. My apartment, where I live during the week, is in a planned community with lawn and bushes. There is only a tiny space of bare soil in front of my apartment, and it is poisoned with herbicides. The pool smells of chlorine. The place is pleasant looking but not real. It can't live on its own.[26]

A garden can create a meaningful connection between people and nature. (Kathryn Devereaux)

Nature and Culture in the Garden

California's contrived landscape also reflects the popular notion that only one of two possible conditions may occur in a place: either a nature preserve or an artificial, high-input, human environment. According to the writer Michael Pollan, the wilderness ethic, fostered by such influential figures as John Muir and Henry David Thoreau, has led us to preserve 8 percent of the nation in nearly pristine condition but has done little to sustain an environmentally sound condition in the rest, including our home gardens. We seem to be stuck in the notion that nature and culture are separate entities: that on the one side there is the wild, on the other the manicured.[27]

In the 92 percent of the country where the wilderness ethic is silent, Pollan suggests instituting a "garden ethic." The garden, he says, is a place where nature and the human influence are thoroughly mixed, where we are forced to make decisions about contents and care. "Gardening tutors us in nature's ways, fostering an ethic of give and take with respect to the land: being solicitous of nature, self-conscious and responsible, mindful of the past and the future."[28] He draws on our obsession with the lawn to suggest a different relationship with our gardens:

The gardens at the Sea Ranch development in Mendocino County blend personal gardens with the larger natural north coast landscape.

The culture of the lawn discourages the very habits of mind needed to make good gardens. . . . As soon as someone decides to rip out a lawn, he or she becomes, perforce, a gardener, someone who must ask the gardener's questions: What is right for this place? What do I want here? How can I go about creating a pleasing outdoor space on this site? How can I use Nature here without abusing it?[29]

Confronted by pressing environmental problems, many people today look to ecologically sound landscape design as part of the solution. This attitude may encourage us to view our own gardens in a very different way, for it allows us to desire something more authentic and fulfilling, akin to what Thomas Berry calls "the real world of insects on up to the stars in the galaxy."[30]

Environmentally conscious landscape design helps us to shift our focus from a world of illusion to the living functions of plants and ecosystems; it also forces us to be clear about our needs and wants. There is no "default" landscape, to be applied interchangeably in the hot, dry summer climate of the Central Valley and the cool marine climate of the coast. Environmentally conscious design allows us to really see a site and appreciate the unique characteristics of its natural setting as part of the larger California landscape.

As in every significant cultural revolution, sophisticated cultural values inform this process. George Waters, the editor of *Pacific Horticulture,* writes that, just as toward the end of the eighteenth century the "tonsured" gardens of France were ridiculed by the new zeitgeist that brought us the English

Left: *The Home Demonstration Garden at the Santa Barbara Botanical Garden shows homeowners how they might create a garden reflecting their environmental concerns.*

Below: *A California landscape garden is one that strives to be part of the larger California landscape, as in this Stoney Hill residence. (Landscape architect: Ron Lutsko Jr.; photograph by Lutsko Associates)*

pastoral landscape, so today "from every quarter we are called upon" to abandon the old artifices and "garden with Nature."[31]

California possesses a young and flexible immigrant culture, fully able to respond to the unique opportunity that is at hand. Our gardening conventions are less deeply ingrained than is the case with older cultures. The tolling of the environmental bell has signaled, to our horror, that we can indeed alter the most fundamental mechanisms supporting life on earth. The challenge for California's gardeners and garden designers will be to attempt to reverse this course, by heeding sound principles of conservation and sustainability. Our task is to develop a new landscape tradition that reminds us of our ethnic backgrounds and addresses our modern needs, but in a way that is respectful of the nature of California and its priceless value in our lives and the lives of all that inhabit it.

CHAPTER TWO

MEANING AND FORM

Things are pretty, graceful, rich, elegant, handsome, but, until they speak to the imagination, not yet beautiful.

Ralph Waldo Emerson, *The Conduct of Life*

The California landscape garden is meaningful in a biological sense because of its ecological relationship with the surrounding environment. The gardener, however, brings another important quality—imagination—and with it creates an entirely new set of meanings arising from personal experience and values.

The meanings associated with a place have many sources—personal, cultural, physical, and political. Simple familiarity, an imaginative association of time and memory, may imbue a place with meaning as we recall or once again

The home garden can be a place of experience and meaning.

enjoy a favorite garden flower. There may be a warm association between a place and family or friends—where grandparents lived or children grew up. Some places incorporate meaningful ideas, such as a wall made with recycled bottles, a drum that stores rainwater, a windmill that captures energy, or a wind sculpture that draws our attention to the moving air. We tend naturally to create meanings for personal places, and it is through this faculty that we develop a *sense of place,* a term that will be used often in this book.[1]

To begin to define the garden elements that might inspire a sense of place and personal engagement, ask yourself first what childhood memories you have of gardens. Then imagine the sounds, colors, or smells that engaged you and that would draw you to the garden. What garden elements, such as rocks, shrubs, or trees—or wildlife associated with them—evoke strong feelings or memories? What would motivate you to observe, learn, and be attentive in the garden? Think of things that do not necessarily require time or effort or planning, but rather can be experienced on the spur of the moment, such as reaching out a finger to see if a butterfly will land on it or eating a ripe tomato warm from the sun. For it is through the fullness and immediacy of the moment that gardens best work their magic on the spirit.

The cultural historian and environmental philosopher Thomas Berry describes a childhood experience at his family's new house:

> It was an early afternoon in May when I first looked down over the scene and saw the meadow. The field was covered with lilies rising above the thick grass. A magic moment, this experience gave to my life, something, I know not what, that seems to explain my life at a more profound level. It was not only the lilies. It was the singing of the crickets and the woodlands in the distance and the clouds in a clear sky. . . . It had none of the majesty of the Appalachians or the western mountains, none of the immensity or the power of the oceans, nor even the harsh magnificence of desert country; yet in this little meadow the deep mystery of existence is manifested in a manner as profound and as impressive as any other place that I have known in these past many years.[2]

The meadow of lilies inspired a sense of place, a connection not only to his new home but to a larger home, the living world with its "deep mystery of existence." In the same way, there is a living California all around us, in nearby places, including gardens, that offer not the grandeur of Yosemite Valley but rather the life processes of wildflowers blooming in the mild days of spring or a heavy crop of acorns fruiting in the autumn.

Gardening, beyond the physical activities it entails, is an aesthetic expe-

Gardens are important places to grow up in as well as to grow old in. Elliot in his Davis, California Garden.

rience that is part sensory—involving sight, smell, hearing, and touch—and part spiritual. Although the kind of encounter that inspired transcendent empathy in Berry cannot be willed or created solely by design, it can be encouraged by allowing a place and the imagination to come together to work their magic.

Jana Ruzicka, a landscape designer in Newport Beach, uses the aesthetic impulse—her intuitive sense of a place—to make authentic gardens that inspire a deep awareness of time, place, and change: "I think about what used to be there and relate to it, the writing on the air one can still read when you are by yourself, quiet, almost like you are not there. Your consciousness becomes part of the whole consciousness. Inspiration and intuition overwhelm, not in a rational way."[3]

A living relationship with the surrounding landscape becomes more meaningful, a place more authentic, when we understand the character of that locale and discover for ourselves a role in its life. The authentic landscape garden has nothing to do with make-believe or illusion; rather, it is a place to be in tune with natural forces, to nurture our fascination with the mysteries of the universe. The sounds of birds filtering through dense fog, the sun projecting patterns of light that change throughout the day, the scent of wet earth after a rain—these are ingredients of the authentic garden.

The impetus to make such a garden comes from what Jim Armstrong calls the poetic self: "The poet knows that, while science may help us to discover general laws, only the sympathetic imagination—the poetic force in all of us—can help us to draw near to things, to stand by them and care for them,

This garden located at Soka University in Malibu was designed to showcase native plants common to the Santa Monica mountains (Envicom Corp. and Toyon Design; photograph by K. Patey)

because only the imagination will let them be."[4] William Carney adopts this sense when he says that the California landscape garden

> foster[s] the identification of people with the earth by creating intensely sensual places in which harmonies of color, texture, line and form awaken perception and invoke a sense of connection with the larger harmonies of the biosphere. In the tradition of the great gardens, we would deploy our plans and plantings to serve not so much as cosmetic screens, but as active enrichment of experience.[5]

Thomas Berry observes that "the driving force of the scientific effort is nonscientific . . . the driving force of the technological endeavor is non-technological." Albert Einstein said it another way: "The cosmic religious experience is the strongest and noblest driving force behind scientific research." According to Berry, science has helped us to "sketch the great story of the universe from its beginning until now. We can recognize the earth as a privileged planet and see the whole as evolving out of some cosmic imaginative process."[6]

Although scientific knowledge may be an important primer for a poetic view of the world, it is not sufficient in and of itself. The world we experience needs to speak to our imaginations if it is to be truly meaningful. In a prosaic, mechanical view, the trees in a forest might be assessed merely in quantitative terms of size and number or in utilitarian terms of board feet of lumber. Once the encompassing, "poetic" view is invoked, however, those trees, now understood as life forms with a singular role in planetary ecology, can never again be viewed simply as lumber.

For the most insightful observers, scientific discovery nearly always arouses a sense of awe—the soft whistle under the breath when the power and ingenuity of nature shine through—which in turn catalyzes the imaginative leap from the singular fact to the profoundly universal. Even as a young child, Thomas Berry could make this leap of understanding; for those of us lacking his gifts, science can inform and foster this deeply harmonic alliance with nature.

FORM AND THE CALIFORNIA LANDSCAPE GARDEN

California landscape gardens recreate natural habitat and involve humans in the biological web of the local region. Neither ecologically dogmatic nor indifferent to environmental issues, they provide a context in which people can rethink their relationship with nature, by emphasizing local resources and by encouraging personal and cultural expression. Because they make a direct impact on regional ecology and allow us to protect what we consider valuable, they are places where our experiences and actions can have meaning.

Here, the perception of value is defined not by the arbitrary rules of politics or economics, but rather by the biocratic processes of the natural world. In this new spirit, the gardener seeks to transform the traditional yard, which too often is divorced from the surrounding environment and isolates its human inhabitants, into a dynamic garden habitat that embraces local conditions and native flora and fauna and encourages creative human engagement.

The California landscape garden differs from traditional gardens in significant ways. The following list (intended not as a slate of rules but to provide a sense of direction) summarizes the major goals of the California landscape garden:

BIODIVERSITY

- ❧ allows interaction between people and native plants and wildlife

- ❧ creates an environment attuned to local conditions and features

- ❧ restores a seasonal procession reflecting California's nature

Right and opposite: *Before-and-after illustrations of the Wright Garden in Davis, showing how even a traditional front yard can be transformed into a landscape garden. (Landscape designer: Andreas Reimann)*

↜ is not fully planned but rather allows for spontaneous, evolutionary developments

RESOURCE USE

↜ promotes awareness of the value of water and energy through frugal use

↜ employs locally derived natural building materials creatively

↜ ensures that the materials used have a benign impact on the environment

↜ applies passive design principles

↜ depends minimally on pesticides, artificial fertilizers, and energy sources

CULTURAL EXPRESSION

↜ initiates observation of and participation with natural processes, including interrelationships between organisms and seasonal patterns

↜ allows expression of personal heritage and recreational and aesthetic needs

↜ provides flexibility for changing aesthetic and cultural values over time

↜ has a deep meaning for its makers

BIODIVERSITY

More and more Californians today realize that to ignore the biological web of life poses a great risk for present and future generations. Groundwater contamination and overdrafts and loss of habitat are a few of the many signs indicating the need for a course correction. Unless the problem is in our own backyard, however, we sometimes have trouble taking environmental issues seriously. It is one thing to say that a sunflower or a salamander has lost its habitat; but when we realize that by driving these creatures out we humans lose a crucial dimension of our own habitat, the situation becomes perhaps more meaningful.

Only a half century ago the bulk of the California population still lived on or close to a farm; even the cities were patchworked with agricultural lands and wild areas. Family farmers worked their fields to the sun's rhythm. Children turned the stones of a field or creek, certain that sooner or later something would skitter out. People could daily delight in the dew on golden grass stems, the fragrance of sage, the magical unfolding of a swallowtail from its chrysalis, the footprints of quail, or the midnight sounds of crickets. The rural habitat offered people a mentally engaging sensory buffet.

The landscape garden seeks to restore this sensory feast, first by creating a habitat that is able to nurture a living web of plants, insects, birds, and other creatures, and then by allowing complex biological systems to operate. To achieve the latter, essential component, we do not plan every last detail of the garden; instead we give things that can be shaped by nature's processes the space and time to change, just as they would in wild places. Allowed to operate on its own with a minimum of human intervention, a landscape garden becomes a transition zone between nature and culture, providing the opportunity to see nature for what it is rather than as we think it should be.

When nature's own processes are brought up close and made familiar in this way, the human habitat regains the potential for meaningful, formative experiences. By yielding some control over the details and form of the garden, we are enriched by the fact that evolving complexity naturally tends toward novelty and surprise. As the garden changes with the seasons we have the chance to observe the biological rhythms of plants and wildlife intimately. Just as in any functioning ecosystem, where a process of give-and-take enables each species to achieve a working balance with all the rest, by restoring a natural habitat to plants and wildlife we restore it to humans as well. To the extent that we can encourage native plants, birds, and insects to reside in our garden, we benefit by helping other species survive in a world increasingly hostile to their existence—and to our own.

RESOURCE USE

The California landscape garden is marked by the intelligent use of resources, which can be seen in part as an effort to mitigate environmental degradation. These resources include the materials used to build the garden, the water needed to maintain the plantings, and the various amendments incorporated into the soil. Especially to be avoided are imported building supplies; overreliance on water; and chemicals that are toxic or upset ecological balance, such as fertilizers and pesticides, which contaminate food and water for humans and wildlife alike.

Why rely on lumber from Southeast Asia, bricks from the East Coast, or stone from Italy when in many areas of California we have high-quality native resources that are ideal for hard surfaces or walls? The resource in question might be clay, which can be easily made into adobe, stone, or even tree trimmings. Where local materials do not suffice, other environmentally friendly alternatives with landscape potential exist, such as recycled plastic, which can be compressed into durable boards, benches, and poles. Then too, if we use plants that are adapted to the local climate, we reduce the need for artificial support systems like the application of chemicals, excessive maintenance, and irrigation.

By hand-crafting our garden or using local folk art such as chairs made out of branches, we intensify our knowledge of our own surroundings and its resources. Building the garden ourselves, including such components as walls, benches, and basins, elevates its construction to a craft. By weaving a wattle fence, for instance, the worker acquires knowledge of material limitations and possibilities as well as a personal stake in the longevity of the creation. Such projects can also provide an opportunity to find new uses for and recycle materials that otherwise would end up as landfill.

Reliance on local resources means making full use of what is available in or near the garden site, including rainfall or sunshine, soil or rock outcroppings, a wood supply—even a wide, sweeping view. It takes advantage of local character and builds on that: the very opposite of scraping a site clean and imposing a whole new order on it. To echo Emerson, the results of a wholly transformed garden space might be pretty, but they cannot be beautiful, for they are unable to engender a sense of place.

In addition to local materials, the ecological vision challenges the gardener to employ environmentally sound principles of design. These include use of passive energy features, such as plant screens or glass to deflect or enhance the sun's heat; use of built or natural barriers to control prevailing winds; and installation of graywater systems to reclaim water that has already been used once in the home or garden. In gardens designed with "eco-logic," ingredients have multiple uses or functions: a shade tree may also yield a harvest of fruit or nuts, or a wide roof overhang may cool the house, support a beautiful vine, or create a porch that increases the usable living space.

AN EXPRESSION OF HUMAN VALUES

Gardens serve basic human needs, providing a safe place for children to play, a cool refuge in summer, shelter from the wind. Culinary herb plantings, decorative touches, and design features such as sculptures and entry gates can all reflect a family's heritage and attitude toward garden spaces. The California landscape garden is therefore defined in part by the way not just other living things but also people are included in the habitat design.

One way people can achieve an intimate relationship with the garden is to put in plants that carry some sort of meaning. A garden with a tree that has been planted for a new baby in the family is like no other garden, and the tree is like no other tree because it has meaning: it symbolizes new life, growth, and strength. Certain plants are treasured for their foliage, fragrance, or fruit,

such as lemon and pomegranate trees, beloved and ecologically benign imports with year-round beauty. The lemonade or pomegranate jelly made from the harvested fruit is special; its origin is known. Plants used in producing crafts, such as twigs for weaving baskets or flowers for making decorations or arranging in bouquets, bring nature very close and can engage children and parents in shared activities. Many gardeners find satisfaction in pursuing organic gardening methods, which do not harm the environment and are healthier for the family.

Another way in which gardens and plants become especially meaningful to people is by serving as a connection to culture, heritage, and philosophy—one's personal needs and values—and rejecting mass consumerism.

Some naturalized plants—ones that help give the local region its character and are known to grow especially well—may go back to a family's immigrant roots. These are often old races of plants, like the roses that were planted over a hundred years ago in coastal northern California. Other plants are associated particularly with the southern California bungalow style, such as palm trees and bougainvillea, or with the Spanish revival period, including the century plant. Materials such as terra-cotta likewise make us think of the Spanish colonial style.

Some plants have religious associations. The olive tree and incense cedar, for example, are mentioned in the Bible, and the lotus is an important flower in the Buddhist tradition. Some of these plants were brought here by Spanish missionaries and early settlers as a means of expressing their faith.

In the more worldly realm, early immigrants brought favorite foods with them, which remain in home gardens as heirloom species. The special traits of the various kinds of maize, which evolved both in response to the specific

Left: *A small backyard can include rocky places, low wet spots, and diverse plants. (Landscape designer: Andreas Reimann)*

Below: *The garden can inspire multicultural exchange; in this case, Eureka residents have opened up their backyard for a Hmong family to garden in. (Deborah D. Giraud)*

ecological characteristics of the surrounding bioregion and under the influence of human cultivation, well illustrate the principle of genetic diversity—a crucial principle for us to grasp if we are to restore balance to the earth.

It is a joy to be the caretaker of a grapevine or rose many generations old. Such plants often have a long life—a longevity that partly defines their character—and are relatively easy to cultivate, unlike many hybridized varieties that have been bred to narrow specifications. Today, however, infertile, hybridized cultivars of fruits, flowers, and vegetables that have been developed from heirloom varieties predominate in nurseries and seed catalogs. As these engineered plants have gained in popularity, sadly, many heirloom varieties that evolved with humanity have become increasingly unavailable, and some are even endangered.

In thinking about imported plants, it is important to remember that a plant's cultural value cannot outweigh its ecological significance. Consider, for example, French and Spanish broom (*Spartium junceum* and *Cytisus monspessulanus,* respectively), which were imported as ornamentals by immigrants from Europe. Spanish broom, for one, is an attractive green shrub that grows four to ten feet high and bears fragrant yellow flowers in the spring. In the past, its branches were bound together to make household brooms. Today, children still take pleasure in finding the "trigger" at the base of the mature blossoms and surprising an opponent with a puff of golden pollen dust. Both species of broom, however, escaped cultivation early on and have since become serious, invasive pests in many parts of the state, displacing much native vegetation.

THE IDEAL VS. THE REAL GARDEN

In a California landscape garden, environmental concerns are not ignored; instead, they are deliberately expressed—in the types of plants featured, in wildlife amenities such as a bird box or pond, and in a reliance on local building materials. Of course, gardeners will always be confronted by real-world dilemmas—such as whether to use herbicides in certain situations, what to do when wildlife becomes a nuisance, or how much of the garden to dedicate to habitat—and the need to make compromises will frequently arise. It is in this tension between the ideal and the real that true environmental learning takes place.

The transition from a traditional garden to an ecological one requires knowledge, feeling, insight, and creative flexibility. By keeping the central issues of the new garden paradigm in mind—namely, sense of place, diversity of form, meaning, and fitness—the designer or gardener will more easily be able to make crucial decisions. It is equally important to remember that a successful California landscape garden is a complex biological community arranged to serve multiple purposes. Such complexity does not allow for rigidly dogmatic rules. Conflicts naturally arise among diverse goals, and here, too, compromises are frequently necessary.

Perhaps it is useful to reiterate what a California landscape garden is *not:* it is not a place of conspicuous mass consumption, a space bereft of meaning and values, maintained with copious amounts of water and pesticides. A lawn bordered by a few shrubs and rosebushes is a resource-intensive, biologically impoverished still-life, not an ecosystem. It takes, but it gives nothing back in terms of ecological values. Our goal in expressing the ideals of the California landscape garden is to restore balance, a sense of positive give-and-take, to our environment and to ourselves.

Fitness

The California landscape garden ideal does not, for instance, insist on the abolishment of lawns. When it comes to a living ground cover that can withstand frequent, heavy use, few plants hold up as well as healthy turfgrass. Lawns per se do not deny a sense of place (awareness of and ability to fit into the bioregional ecosystem as a whole), diversity of form (the existence of

Lawn is appropriate in the garden as a surface for human activity.

various regional habitats), or fitness (adaptiveness of garden plants to local conditions), and they certainly can have meaning. Since lawns are wonderfully inviting sites for human activity, and since they effectively increase the living and recreation space of a home, it may be perfectly logical to include a small lawn in the garden. Besides functionality, lawns have aesthetic value as well, helping to set off surrounding planting beds or paved surfaces. Nonetheless, lawns are traditionally much larger than they need to be to satisfy most such functional or aesthetic demands. Depending on how a family intends to use lawn areas, other materials can often be found, such as drought-tolerant ground covers and simple mulches, that will satisfy most, if not all, typical needs.

The California landscape garden also does not require that only natives be planted. Within a local setting—one, that is, that includes both native plant communities and readily adaptable plants brought to California, generally from regions with a similar climate—there is room for naturalized plants that are culturally meaningful or possess proven wildlife value. What matters is that natural processes are supported, and the evidence shows that in this regard certain nonnative plants may serve just as well as natives. Their inclusion, moreover, does not make a garden "nonecological" or "nonbioregional." Again, the point is to use knowledge about plants, wildlife, and habitats intelligently and effectively, not inflexibly.

Many naturalized Mediterranean plants, for example, do well here and require no more water than a native plant. Some of these imports are so well established in parts of California that they now contribute substantially to regional character. Think of a vibrant bougainvillea blooming on a southern California porch or a patch of violets adorning a Central Valley front lawn. Historic use has made these imports authentic parts of the California landscape.

The use of nonnative plants, particularly in situations where no native species are available to accomplish a particular task, is a matter of judgment. One must start by asking certain questions: Does the plant alter the composition of the soil or cause loss of moisture? Is its growth pattern appropriate to the site and the surrounding vegetation? Can it succeed under local, natural conditions? Does it support regional wildlife? The answers to these questions—which will be easier to arrive at the more one knows about the region—will determine the ecological, bioregional appropriateness of the plant under consideration.

The same questions can be useful in the rehabilitation of an older garden, when decisions have to be made about which plants should stay. Here, the best course is to follow nature's rule of thumb: if a mature plant needs excessive help to survive, it is probably in the wrong garden.

Diversity of Form

The California landscape garden does not have to be a backyard museum of plant species once common in the native landscape, nor does it have to lack aesthetic appeal. Numerous styles, geometries, and visual qualities are eminently possible. A landscape garden may well juxtapose wild-looking spaces, such as are found in untouched natural areas, with more formal or structured spaces, where order and clean lines predominate. The native plant garden, the ethnic garden, and the formal garden—or some combination of these aesthetics—are all possible manifestations of the California landscape garden.

With this new approach we are countering the traditional model of the yard—especially the front yard—that conforms to an accepted norm, one usually involving a mown lawn and clipped shrubbery. This conformity may simply signal a lack of awareness of alternatives. Tellingly, a recent study of atti-

tudes about highly personalized front yards found that people generally appreciate unconventional-looking yards and respect the gardeners who built them.[7]

Seasons—California Style

The California landscape garden is diverse in form and visual character. Gardens that allow seasonal processes to prevail are not always tidy places, but neither do they need to be overgrown tangles. To be sure, experimenting with unfamiliar native plants and relying exclusively on low-maintenance strategies will probably not produce desired effects. A seasonally disheveled appearance can, however, be controlled to a certain degree with good design. In time, and with experience, a conscientious gardener will learn how to make the dry spots, bare spots, and weedy-looking spots blend in with the whole.

Seasonal processes, untidy or not, are signs that a garden is an ecosystem. It is these natural processes—not form—that link a garden to the surrounding bioregion. Nature can accommodate many styles, aesthetics, and personal meanings, as long as these in turn support ecologically meaningful change, succession, and diversity.

The mechanics of nature can be designed into a landscape garden in myriad ways. A garden pond that, like a vernal pool, fills up and dries out according to the season is one example. Likewise, assigning plants to spots that provide congenial soil conditions, light, and moisture will help different plants thrive. Sage, for example, prefers dry places; wild parsley, damp; columbine, mottled shade; and sunflower and Indian paintbrush, bright sunlight.

California seasons are reflected in the state's native plants, which may

The norm for most California gardens is the manicured front lawn (below), although more naturalistic front yards, as pictured at right, are becoming increasingly common and accepted.

exhibit summer dormancy or winter deciduousness. Many people scoff at the notion that California has seasons, but that is partly because California's native plants are rarely used to beautify our homes. Rich colors and forms abound in all the seasons, everywhere in the state. Hillsides resplendent with masses of grays and greens, brilliant orange fields of pollen-laden flowers, velvety deep green foliage, bold purple spires, and clusters of copper and brown seed heads all offer seasonal inspiration—California style.

Being in tune with the seasonal spirit of a place is not an abstract idea; indeed, it offers the gardener a healthy dose of reality. Knowing about the water cycle, and about frugal plants that live on small reserves of moisture; being aware of species living intensely on the edge of survival, like hummingbirds that require large daily doses of nectar; appreciating the diversity that adapts to seasonal patterns in endlessly imaginative forms—these are some of the goals of cultivating a California landscape garden. These temporal dimensions tell us where we really are: not in the illusory pretense of an English garden or a tropical bungalow compound, but in a California garden that is as real as the ancient seashore that now rests atop local mountain peaks.

Timing has to do with change—with rejuvenation, maturity, and death. It has to do with the real forces that make California what it is. When the natural progression of time is overridden in the garden, we lose the significance of those shifting moments, and of the living fabric of which they are a part. The truth is, people who act without regard for the world around them, who

California nature provides abundant patterns to inform and inspire home gardeners, including grasses, stones, flowers, and water.

attempt to control all elements regardless of the environmental costs, are not the best garden designers. It takes an interplay of natural forces and human savvy, curiosity (probably), and empathy (certainly) to design an effective landscape garden.

For native peoples and farmers back to the dawn of agriculture, the seasons have been a matter of life-giving importance. Today, environmental timing is not a consideration in most gardens and therefore, in much of California at least, is outside the view of most people; that timing is, however, one of the triumphs and pleasures of a true California landscape garden. In nature, all the ebbs and flows—the rising sap, the first profusion of green, flowers and seeds, drying soil, woody stems, falling leaves—are critical natural processes signified by form. In exchange for nurturing this life, the alert gardener gains an understanding of the meaning of form—artfully expressed in fragrances and sounds, in the dancing light on iridescent butterfly wings—and of the wisdom it signifies.

CHAPTER THREE

THE
GARDEN AS
LANDSCAPE

> Once a garden comes alive ecologically, it displays a humor and richness of
> meaning that have been missed by narrow views of horticulture. Signifi-
> cance expands. Meanings multiply. Each plant or planting becomes much
> more than what nurseries believe they sell, or gardeners suppose they grow,
> or visitors would notice.
>
> Sarah Stein, *Noah's Garden*

Private gardens account for a sizable portion of the best land that has been
removed from the earth's custody. The California landscape garden, however,
attempts to reverse this process. In a sense, the landscape garden is analogous
to a protected national park or seashore, where children are admonished to
"put it back where you found it." Even very young children can understand
that "it"—whether a plant, a sea star, or a butterfly—has a place where it
belongs and needs to be in order to live. In the same protective spirit the
California landscape garden, by restoring native elements of regional ecosys-

Gardens can be designed as small-scale models of larger natural systems.

tems, gives them back their place in the land. The gardener, then, is as much a keeper of wildlife as a keeper of garden plants. The challenge is to find a balance between human activities—entertaining, pursuing hobbies, playing, working, or simply enjoying the outdoors—and the biological needs of the garden, including those of both introduced plants and the wildlife that will come naturally: the more so with the right incentives.

As a small-scale model of a larger natural system, be it a forest, a prairie, a rocky hillside, or a creek, the landscape garden supplies the basic elements of water, soil, and climate, as well as appropriate host plant communities. This provides habitat for a variety of insects and microscopic organisms, and it also sets the stage to draw birds, butterflies, amphibians, reptiles, and small mammals, all of which interact to create a stable food chain and a thriving ecosystem. To achieve this outcome, we do not need to abandon traditional garden design principles or functional requirements. Being a keeper of wildlife in the garden does, however, mean that we invite nature to participate in the design of the home landscape, allowing it to take care of food, housing, and other basic amenities of life for members of the extended biological community. This translates into relinquishing some control and allowing natural phenomena to occur in the garden, such as leaving a downed tree branch to serve as a wildlife condominium or letting mature seed heads disperse to unplanned garden locations. As we will see in this chapter and throughout the book, wildlife and natural process can be included within a pleasing home landscape very effectively.

BIOLOGICAL DIVERSITY IN THE GARDEN

Because all species are opportunistic, they will make use of any place that meets their needs. The key to attracting diversity in the garden is therefore to provide a diversity of habitat types, and in this respect wild areas yield many valuable clues. Although a natural landscape comprising many square miles of continuous forest or grassland might at first glance not seem very diversified, in fact a variety of niches are to be found there—spots that are wetter or drier than the immediate surroundings, open or sheltered locations, uneven vegetation heights, layers of vegetation and decaying matter—allowing a greater concentration of wildlife. Many animals depend on diverse amenities in a small area in order to live, finding food, cover, water, lookout sites for defense, or nesting cavities in the varied terrain. Logs, rotting wood, and leaf litter, harboring food and providing shelter; burrows for hiding in; rocks for basking in the sun; and loose soil or gravel for digging in—these are all ingredients of a diversified environment, enabling more species to live side by side. Such amenities, not surprisingly, are largely lacking in planned environments around most homes.

Nature also supplies the gardener with important clues about interdependence. One familiar example is the interaction between fruit trees and pollinators, which then benefits us humans: the insects find a nutritious food source in the trees' pollen, and as they travel about they carry the pollen to receptive flowers, thus enabling the many varieties of fruits and nuts we enjoy to grow.

Over the millennia species have evolved to rely on other species in ways that are benign, advantageous, or detrimental. The result is an array of strategies that allow the greatest number of species, and a critical mass of each species, to advance over time. In short, Nature does not put all her eggs in one basket; she has devised a fierce elasticity in planetary life through the woof-and-warp of diversity. Butterflies, for example, have evolved with specific host plants that nourish the newly hatched larvae. Birds need insects to feed

The use of natural materials to build unique objects also creates habitat for native insects such as solitary bees.

The Adler Garden, Walnut Creek.
(Landscape architect: Ron Lutsko Jr.)

JANE ADLER'S
LANDSCAPE GARDEN

Gardeners throughout California are striving to implement more ecologically and culturally sound principles in the design of their yards. Jane Adler is one such innovator. In 1978 she built her garden in Walnut Creek, California, from bare ground. In the early 1990s she hired landscape architect Ron Lutsko, one of the leading proponents of the emerging California landscape garden approach, to redesign the garden in a way that would express her strong environmental values.[1] Her garden is now recognized as a backyard wildlife habitat by the National Wildlife Federation.

Ms. Adler, a specialist in environmental education at Mt. Diablo State Park, east of Oakland, wanted to incorporate into her garden plants found in that beautiful mountain habitat, and she also wanted a garden that would invite birds, butterflies, and other wildlife. In the early stages of planning she sat down and imagined how the new garden would look and what she most wanted from it. She wrote out this list for Ron Lutsko, expressing what the garden's design should do:

1. Include many Mediterranean-climate plants while emphasizing California natives

2. Include as many drought-tolerant elements as possible

3. Make sense in terms of the open spaces around the site

4. Incorporate many sensual elements—plants with interesting textures (e.g., lamb's ears) and fragrances (various herbs, perovsika, lilacs, roses, daphne)

5. Supply cut flowers

6. Offer something of interest in each season

7. Provide enough maintenance tasks so that the garden will be interesting but not burdensome

8. Have a naturalistic look

9. Have a style reminiscent of the English cottage garden but with plants appropriate to arid California

10. Have space for entertaining large groups

on, and many insects need plant litter to complete their life cycle. Numerous flies, aphids, mites, moths, and tiny wasps have evolved to take advantage of the life cycles of oaks, poplars, and cottonwoods. By injecting a chemical, the insects force a leaf or a twig to put out an exuberance of growth, called a gall, programmed for size, shape, and color, which then provides food and shelter for insect families without hurting the tree. Humans did not invent genetic engineering; nature did, and this is a familiar example of it.

These types of biological activity often go unnoticed or are trivialized, but they are crucial parts of a working whole. The ability to bring these processes up close where they can be observed over time is one of the most enriching aspects of the California landscape garden. By turns through the seasons, performers take center stage and then depart. It is not always immediately apparent how all the seemingly isolated events fit together, but finding out is one of the best ways for us to deepen our relationship with nature (see "Jane Adler's Landscape Garden," p. 54).

Nature invites such understanding by pulling out of her tool kit all the things that can amuse, disconcert, and awe an observer. Bats, for example, dart through the twilight sky to capture insects by a sensitive process known as echolocation—bouncing sound off of prey to determine its whereabouts. Their very flight is a marvel in the world of mammals; their sonar abilities are an ingenious adaptation for nocturnal hunting. If that scene were observed and unpacked piece by piece, we would find dozens of convergences that allow that bat to have that meal at that moment. The season, the time of day, the insects present, and the way the bat is engineered are just a few of them. What do the insects eat? What predators do bats have? By asking questions such as these and piecing together observable events in a particular place over time, we can begin to discern a larger sense of purpose and direction; with patient attention, we may be able to identify the missing links, the unseen web that, unintentionally, can be broken. No species lives in isolation from other species.

RECREATING REGIONAL HABITAT IN THE GARDEN

Landscape ecology, first developed as a way to understand and manage very large ecologically disturbed areas that include cities and agricultural zones, has focused more recently on restoring to health smaller disturbed areas that are close to or even within human communities. A major focus of effort has been untended strips of land alongside roads, railways, and creeks and other

A small birdhouse attracts life to the garden.

A habitat for amphibians can be easily constructed in the garden. (Peter Latz)

waterways. Through ecological restoration, habitat and travel routes for wildlife through and around communities can be created, naturalized corridors that give animals greater access to food and cover and greater reproduction opportunities. The result is greater diversity at an intermediate scale.[2]

This new emphasis on urban ecology aims at integrating *people* with nature as well. Using the same kinds of problem-solving strategies developed by ecologists in cooperation with city planners, garden designers can create habitats that, like local wildlife corridors, actively invite nature into an urban space. Although the natural systems approach to design and management employed by professionals is based firmly in the environmental and natural sciences, a home gardener need not have an advanced degree in ecology or urban planning to learn about habitat restoration. Much of the pertinent information has been prepared in nontechnical language for public use and is available from libraries, state and local resource agencies, National Audubon Society chapters, and California Native Plant Society chapters, most of which have sites on the World Wide Web. In addition, there is a wide selection of specialty books about the natural history of California's various bioregions.

Deciding how best to recreate regional habitat within a landscape garden requires careful, thoughtful deliberation combined with footwork and investigation. First and foremost, the unique features of the garden site must be considered—such things as soil conditions, drainage, prevailing winds, need for noise abatement, views to capture or screen, and water availability. Second, the immediate context surrounding the site must be considered, including the proximity of neighbors, the character of nearby natural places, and the larger residential context, be it a subdivision or a rural site. Regional factors such as rainfall and climate and plant communities will all influence the garden's design as well (see Chapters 4 and 5).

An ecological approach to home gardening involves incorporating desirable elements of nearby native and naturalized environments into the private yard. For example, if birds use certain shrubs for food or shelter, very likely these shrubs will serve the same purpose in the garden and attract the same species. The obvious caveats apply, of course: the plant must be able to survive in the garden, and birds must be able to find it. Handbooks that identify local plants and wildlife are available to make this task easier.

Urban habitat intermediate between city and country in terms of wildlife value includes vacant lots and abandoned property. These ruderal sites (that is, sites where the natural vegetation cover has been disturbed by humans) can provide a great deal of information about local plants and wildlife. Now usually overgrown, these places may have been scraped in the past, used as parking lots, or been changed in contour by the addition of fill material, such as gravel or sand. However, if there has been no extensive maintenance or disturbance for some time, such a site is likely to have attracted diverse species—including native ones—that have come to depend on it. Observe a ruderal site for a while to determine the types of wildlife that nearby gardens might soon attract: Are there any lizards or wildflowers? Do butterflies frequent the site? Are there temporary puddles or drainage lines that might serve as breeding grounds for toads? Have ground squirrel holes been claimed by burrowing owls? By creating gardens that encourage these and other creatures to expand their distribution beyond the ruderal site, we take advantage of the accessible, ready-made bounty available in what might once have been simply an eyesore.[3]

Also not to be overlooked in the inventory of places, plants, and wildlife are certain naturalized weedy plants that have considerable wildlife value. Several butterflies, for instance, use introduced species as hosts for their eggs: nettle for the red admiral, an introduced variety of mallow for the western lady, and European anise for the anise swallowtail. If a nonnative plant supplies good cover, fruit, or nectar, by all means consider retaining it as part of the garden habitat, provided it doesn't dominate the site and limit diversity. An example of a dominant weedy European import that does prove troublesome, especially in sites with persistently wet areas or seasonal creeks, is Himalayan blackberry. Even though this import affords birds, snakes, rodents, and other mammals a protective cover of brambles that is inaccessible to cats and dogs, not to mention people, it has no problem blanketing entire native plant communities. Originally planted in rural areas to provide cover for quail, it has spread rampantly through ravines and creeksides and would do the same in a garden.

Top: *Even in the smallest areas it is easy to create a wet habitat; this pool in a Sacramento garden is made from a recycled barrel. (Landscape designer: Joe Balesteri)*

Bottom: *Foxgloves and a wooden fence make up a north coast theme in a landscape garden.*

Study of nearby hillsides and other naturalized areas may also net information about native plants and wildlife that are still in the area and the types of habitat they require. In particular, look for natural habitats that have been isolated by development and could benefit from expansion of a particular amenity, such as food plants, cover plants, water, or nesting sites.

Once we have considered what local plants and wildlife are suitable for our garden, we must tie them together using one or more well-chosen themes. Such themes, preferably inspired by the large-scale natural features of the region, are central to forming a stable foundation on which nature can build its circle of life.

Ecosystems are often formed from mixed habitats of great complexity, yet careful observation will bring important forms and functions to the foreground. A typical California ecosystem of mixed chaparral, oak woodland, and grassland, for example, has rock outcroppings, here and there splashed with the colorful hues of lichens. Lizards sun themselves on the rocks and on downed trees. Plants characteristic of each habitat burst into new growth and bloom in late winter and early spring, providing shelter for migrating songbirds that feast on the abundant insects. A small pool of water has collected in a shallow depression in the grassland, and a trail of trampled grass leads to a copse of oak. Dragonfly nymphs emerge from the pond to molt on reedy stems at the water's edge and, after a few days, fly away, becoming one of the most feared predators of other insects. These agile fliers create further links between aquatic and grassland habitats when they themselves become food for frogs, toads, birds, and small mammals.

One thing to notice about the above ecosystem is that diversity and interdependence are encouraged by numerous edges, the places where habitats meet and overlap to create the greatest variety of amenities for wildlife of all sorts. By modeling the garden on these edges, especially ones within the immediate bioregion, we can create a similarly multifaceted habitat congenial to local species. It will also mirror the most common California landscapes, such as the grassland/chaparral or woodland/chaparral transition zones. Other landscape patterns can provide an organizing element within such gardens: a small stream corridor may reflect nearby riparian conditions; a small urban forest, inspired by local forests or historic groves, may serve to recapture a sense of the past; a low, wet area in the garden may suggest formerly large wetlands in the area.

Habitats, or biotic communities—interdependent associations of plants and animals—are named according to their dominant vegetation cover. Since the details vary from source to source, we use the system outlined in Benyus's *Field Guide to Wildlife Habitats of the Western United States,* an easy-to-find book written for a lay audience that offers a good overview of California habitats and their characteristic wildlife. Out of the eighteen biotic communities described in that guide, California has seventeen, including the oak woodland, an increasingly rare habitat found only here. The others are the rocky coast, coastal salt marsh, lake and pond, mountain stream, inland marsh, mountain meadow, Sonoran cactus desert, sagebrush desert, pinyon-juniper woodland, aspen forest, lowland river forest, redwood forest, ponderosa pine forest, old-growth Douglas fir forest, lodgepole pine forest, and subalpine forest.

The garden can be connected ecologically and visually to the larger neighborhood landscape.

HABITAT VALUES IN NATURAL ECOSYSTEMS

A major barrier to habitat restoration and repair is our lack of understanding about the natural history of a majority of species. If individual gardeners were to carefully observe a single species of native bird, insect, or plant in the garden and report what was seen, the critical needs of many more species could be better identified and addressed. Meanwhile, the litany of losses among California's native ecosystems is escalating. According to Michael Barbour in *California's Changing Landscapes,*

> About one-fourth of our plant species are threatened with extinction, as are twenty-seven percent of our freshwater fishes, ten percent of our mammals, and six percent of our birds. Less than ten percent of such old-growth forests as riparian and coast redwood remain. Less than a fragmented ten percent of our coastal wetlands and a meager two percent of interior wetlands are still with us. The quality of most remaining cover types has been compromised by adjacent development. Oak woodlands are not reproducing, beaches are eroding because distant dams reduce sand movement into the ocean, desert scrub is damaged by off-road vehicles, grasslands are dom-

Community open space can provide valuable habitat as in this neighborhood greenbelt in Davis. (Landscape architects: CoDesign, Inc.)

inated by exotic species, forests have dense, flammable understories because of fire suppression policies, wetlands are no longer large and continuous enough to be valuable for waterfowl, and montane forests are weakened by ozone that has traveled hundreds of miles.[4]

Home landscapes alone cannot restore ecological health to urbanized areas, yet they can make significant contributions. For every species that has been placed on state or federal endangered lists, there are dozens more plants, insects, and birds in decline to which gardeners could extend a helping hand. Ecological gardens that are part of a larger, communitywide effort to create habitat and wildlife corridors are especially important in this regard. The link provided by corridors between restored habitats near human settlements and nonurban areas is crucial to maintaining healthy wildlife diversity.

Species that do adapt to life in urban areas still need protective cover, to permit escape from speeding automobiles and from unrestrained cats and dogs. The existence nearby of cats, especially, must be factored into any plan to attract wildlife to a garden. Cats have been human companions for thousands of years not only because they are wonderful animals but also because they are supremely efficient at keeping rodents under control. Unfortunately, cats' hunting instincts do not stop with unwanted pests like house mice. Even well-fed pet cats hunt birds, small reptiles, and many small mammals other than mice, and they are of course extremely agile: it takes more than just a fence to keep them out of a garden. Since neighborhood populations of cats can be quite high, this all adds up to a tremendous impact on wildlife in gar-

A hillside in north San Diego County has become part of the coastal sage plant community. (Landscape designer: David Buchanan)

dens and nearby natural areas. One Wisconsin study estimated that cats kill nineteen million songbirds each year in that state alone; studies done in Texas and England arrived at similar results.[5] Managers of wildlife preserves throughout California report that domestic and feral cats hunt and capture endangered species that are protected by law. It is difficult to come to terms with the trade-off represented by a desire for garden wildlife and the wish for feline companionship. Attempts to disarm cats by declawing them or having them wear bells have poor records of success. The only really effective solution may be to keep them indoors, letting them outside only under close supervision. Neutering and spaying are also essential to keeping burgeoning cat populations, domestic and feral alike, from overwhelming already severely disadvantaged wildlife populations.

The ultimate survival of countless species may in the end depend on how well we succeed in integrating them into human communities and surrounding areas. Because sound information on how to do this remains scarce, attempts at habitat reconstruction must be considered "experimental," for now at least, as we continue to study the deeper ecological relationships in nature and assimilate the lessons learned. Using gardens to mend fragmented habitats and broken food chains involves a large element of faith that if water and appropriate plants and spaces are provided, the wildlife will come back. Although allowing seasonal processes to operate ensures a greater number of bird and animal sightings, we must look to wildlife itself to teach us just what it will take to secure these species' long-term residency and reproduction.

An adventure garden for children might include space to grow flowers and vegetables, as in this garden in Village Homes, Davis. (Kathryn Devereaux)

Simple observation of these creatures in our yards, however, is a step in the right direction. By bringing living things into our day-to-day existence, the garden serves as a showcase for nature that is real and at hand. This feature is of special importance for children. Just as many adults can easily recall favorite places they had in their yard when they were young, today's children, who enjoy far less freedom to roam on their own, will find in their own garden the same special hiding places and memorable experiences (see "An Adventure Garden for Children," opposite).

Over time, the California landscape garden illustrates the intricacies of seasonal patterns, the many needs of plants and wildlife, and the strategies they have evolved to succeed at life. John Hay, writing about barn swallows, captures the way in which a well-designed garden can lift our spirits and evoke a sense of the faraway nearby:

> Every morning, I open the barn door to hear the rapid twittering with which they keep in rhythmic communication. I find it cheerful, and reassuring. Sharing space with swallows is a comfort in an age that is all too likely to be indifferent to their fate. As long-distance migrants, they are also a link between this barn and the oceanic space beyond it. And the intensity with

AN ADVENTURE GARDEN
FOR CHILDREN

Participatory habitats invite kids in to look, touch—by all means touch—smell, hear, and even taste. There are sounds to hear on still nights—a mockingbird, say, or crickets—and on windy days—leaves scattering, branches bending. There are ants to study as they busily tend a nest, birds to observe as they swoop in to catch a moth. An adventure garden for children allows physical experiences as well as sensory ones, by providing organic litter, a sand pile, thick bunches of grass, shrubs and trees, and perhaps a wet area where water accumulates, all of which can be interacted with up close and examined for the mysteries of life.

An adventure garden may provide the perfect design solution for yard spaces that are too small, narrow, inaccessible, out-of-the-way, or shady to be useful for recreation or socializing. Children love such unkempt, hidden corners. Imagine, for example, a thickly planted grove of willow in an out-of-the-way garden area, or a twenty-by-twenty-foot "jungle" featuring downed wood, a big cavity-riddled old root, or rough-barked trees to climb. Every element is chosen so that it can be played with, on, or under. With a proper screen of plants, this type of play area might serve as a green backdrop for the rest of the garden, looking very tame from the vantage point of, say, a patio.

Native trees, shrubs, and grasses are well suited to adventure areas because they are tough and resilient; in addition, they are very attractive to wildlife. If native shrubs are interspersed with tall bunchgrasses, a child will have what looks like an African savanna, though ecologically it is closer to what California grasslands used to look like. Hardy native plants that can achieve this look include willow and perennial *Muhlenbergia* grasses. In arid areas the willow of choice would be the native desert willow, which can be grown from seeds or hardwood cuttings. In moister areas the Fremont cottonwood would be appropriate. Children can cut basketry materials from stout tufts of grass and willow or climb on the shrubs without causing permanent damage to the plants.

which they follow through the season, win or lose, wakes me up to major changes in minor phenomena that I might otherwise ignore. They make this garden wilder than I realized.[6]

A number of natural habitat patterns can easily be scaled to a California landscape garden, including creeks and riparian areas, wetlands, chaparral and coastal scrub, oak woodlands, grasslands and meadows, and coastal and mountain forests. Many gardeners will find that they live within a transition zone that has characteristics of more than one biotic community—such as the mix of grassland, light chaparral, and woodland that one finds in much of the Sacramento Valley region. Such variety is likewise readily adaptable to a garden setting.

Creeks and Drainage Ways

Creeklines are important corridors that link urbanized areas with surrounding hills and mountains and provide habitat for wildlife. Plant ecologist Michael Barbour, commenting on one particular creekside habitat type, puts it this way: "The cottonwood zone of the riparian forest has the most complex architecture of any California vegetation, and the richest collection of animal species. More species of birds nest in this forest, for example, than in any other California plant community. Also, twenty-five percent of California's 502 kinds of native land animals depend on riparian habitat."[7]

The value of such drainage ways has been increasingly recognized in the past few decades, leading to more frequent and more concerted restoration efforts. For instance, the Santa Fe, Whittier Narrows, and Tujunga floodways in southern California are now part of the regional park system, and in 1996 California voters approved a $320 million bond measure to restore natural vegetation along portions of the Los Angeles River, currently a sixty-mile concrete-lined flood control channel, and turn it into a continuous greenway.

Naturalized stream corridors, whether continuously flowing or seasonal, supply lush habitat congenial to plants and wildlife of all sorts. Native deciduous vegetation that today is more typical of the humid eastern part of the country—willow, cottonwood, oak, sycamore, walnut, alder, and various shrubs—is still common in these drainage ways, and creek habitat is invaluable for many animals, particularly amphibians and aquatic insects that spend all or part of their life cycle in water. In addition to affording a ready source of water, naturalized creeks offer multilayered vegetation (from trees to shrubs to grasses) and diverse conditions for nesting, feeding, and hiding. Old tree stumps serve cavity nesters, and a moist layer of organic ground litter provides food and shelter for a variety of insects and their prey. Also, the flowing water produces multiple conditions—sandy surfaces, gravel bars, silted areas, boulders, and steep embankments—to which many creatures have adapted for laying eggs, feeding, or hibernating. For songbirds, creek-side habitats serve as refueling spots during migration, without which many birds would perish en route.

In many urban and suburban areas in California, houses back up to drainage ways and creeks. Because urban creeks often lack such original natural elements as vegetation and banks, even just a few backyards can give local wildlife a needed boost by extending these habitat features. For example, people who live in a developed area that once featured summer water or shrubby riparian hiding places can, by creating a small seasonal creek with a few plants typical of California drainage ways, embark on a fun project that adds both ecological and aesthetic dimensions to a garden.

Where riparian areas still exist, imports such as pampas grass, fig trees, salt cedars, and giant reeds have replaced much native vegetation and discouraged nesting by imperiled birds such as the yellow-billed cuckoo and least Bell's vireo, which prefer thickets of wild rose, poplar, willow, and cottonwood. In such areas, a larger-scale effort may be needed to eradicate the exotics. However, the work of restoring the native plants is worth it, for it will help to feed—by encouraging a greater diversity of insects and providing nectar and fruit—and shelter many native animals, including endangered species.

Wetlands

Low spots in the terrain that either collect water in temporary, isolated pools or seasonally expand into larger bodies of water are another notable landscape pattern found throughout California. Wetlands support a teeming diversity of migrating waterfowl and other types of wildlife. Only in the past few decades, however, has there been any serious effort to protect these small- and large-scale natural systems critical to the ecological health and water quality of California. Now strict regulations and permit processes govern their preservation, and mitigation is required if they are to be altered or destroyed. More recently, attention has been directed to actually restoring disturbed wetlands and constructing new ones. It is not unusual now in new suburban developments to have water detention ponds designed as wildlife habitats, or for public agencies like CalTrans to construct small ponds on parcels of public land bounded by highway interchanges.

The small-scale wetlands known as vernal pools are both unique and rare: approximately 99 percent of vernal pool habitat has been lost to agricultural and urban uses. Near the few remaining pools on the valley plains of California, which arrive with the spring rain and evaporate with summer drought, one can still see tiny, specialized bees that emerge from underground homes near the water's edge just in time to pollinate the new blooms of their specific plant host. It is one of the wonderful mysteries of nature that the bees somehow know exactly when their host will bloom. Now in danger of extinction, these bees and their host plants are found only at the vernal pools, where, during the ensuing weeks, dozens of invertebrates and amphibians will spend all or part of their life cycle as well. By turns, small communities of flowering plants bloom in concentric rings, thriving for a time at the edge of the receding water: sky blue *Downingia,* marked with frothy splashes of yellow and white; a frothy circle of meadowfoam; yellow goldfields, a tiny relative of the sunflower; owl's clover (ask the kids if they can find the tiny owls' faces); quilworts; pillworts; and liverworts, relative to the mosses and shaped like the human liver. Their presence indicates the former botanical complexity of these valleys and the enduring marvel of symbiotic relationships. Here, insect pollinators, special plants, and an ephemeral place evolved together over eons and today share the same fate.

Wetlands, especially vernal pools, are among the most difficult habitats to recreate in a garden because their biotic communities are unique and highly interdependent, with very narrow seasonal requirements of water level and water quality (often in terms of mineral content). Nevertheless, these wet environments offer inspiration for building backyard ponds that will support wetland plants and wildlife (see "Providing a Wet Spot: Garden Ponds," pp. 68–69). And while the wet area in a garden will have a different quality than its wild counterpart, its habitat values are considerable, adding a small bit of moisture back to a landscape that has largely dried up thanks to human activities.

When it comes to water, our influence on the land has been considerable, even without considering the myriad dams we've built. Groundwater overdrafts and ground leveling have eliminated seasonal pools, small springs, seeps, and wet meadows—all the hollows that once held water into the summer months. Other drying factors include the many introduced trees such as eucalyptus and Lombardy poplar—the "water-pumping" species, so called because they absorb great quantities of soil moisture and extrude it into the air through transpiration. Even the Monterey cypress, a California native

A low depression in the garden collects rainwater to create a small seasonal pool.

whose range has greatly increased owing to human influence, removes a large quantity of soil moisture in this way.

Topsoil denuded by overgrazing also loses moisture quickly, a condition that favors the survival of the many annual grasses introduced into the state. The rapid cool-season development of weedy exotics like slender oat, brome-grasses, Italian ryegrass (often used for erosion control), and rabbitfootgrass tend to speed the drying of the soil in late spring. Unlike the once-abundant native perennial grasses, which in dormancy remain green near the base, forming spots of dense shade that keep the soil from drying out too rapidly, exotic annuals survive the scorching California summer by dropping dried, dormant seeds onto the parched ground to await the next wet cycle.[8] Not surprisingly, therefore, native perennial grasses play a useful role in the California landscape garden, especially where small, moist areas are provided as well; together, they help other life forms survive the harsh California summer.

Chaparral and Coastal Sage Scrub

Chaparral and coastal scrub are the dominant habitats of southern California coastal areas. Buckwheat, prickly pear, and California sagebrush are just three of the characteristic plant species that can be found in these distinctive, diverse communities. Wrens and many other birds adapted to dry conditions depend on this habitat, taking advantage of the dense shrubs and the layer of litter, where they find moisture-rich insects. Mixed flocks of chickadees, titmice, kinglets, and other small birds band together outside of the breeding season

PROVIDING A WET SPOT: GARDEN PONDS

Water is an inimitable substance. Without water, life never would have begun. Earth is a water planet, unique in the universe for all we know so far. Humans—indeed, all animals—have a deeply instinctual response to water: one must stay within reach of it or perish.

Perhaps places with water are so familiar, so inviting, because of the many ways we can experience water—as a vital resource, as a matter of convenience, as an element that brings pure sensory pleasure. It can make a hot day seem cool. Its very fluidity in a world that is so solidly material is something of a daily miracle. Too, its aesthetics are undeniable. Water is nature's mirror, reflecting colors, shapes, and birds that fly by. It makes wind visible with surface ripples and waves. The look, the feel, the sound of it—poetry has hundreds of references to the way water sounds, all as metaphors for human emotion. A multimillion-dollar sound recording industry produces ocean waves, gurgling streams, and the pitter-patter of rain in lieu of the real thing. Maybe, when all is said and done, sound is what is so captivating about water.

For all its pleasures of sight, feel, and sound, a naturalized water feature is also the one element that will attract the most wildlife into a garden. In California's arid environments (remember, even coastal areas suffer from a lack of fresh water), water availability is a matter of survival for many creatures. As soon as a small pool of water is in place, the spinners, whirligigs, damselflies, and dragonflies appear as if by magic. If the water moves—sprays, trickles, splashes—singly and in flocks the birds arrive. Native plant seeds blown in by the wind or carried by birds form a band of crowded green around the water's edge. California monkey flower *(Mimulus guttatus)*, Hooker's evening primrose *(Oenothera hookeri)*, and wet-soil grasses like *Juncus* and *Carex* spp. take hold and provide food and cover for butterflies.

Water features offer many possibilities for the gar-den, including a range of forms and scales—anything from a large buried kettle or free-standing clay container (at least twelve to eighteen inches deep if it is to support aquatic plants and fish) to a pond that serves as the centerpiece to an aquatic garden—and a diversity of surrounding vegetation. Something as simple as a moss-covered stone placed where a spray of water reaches it may evoke memories of a favorite shaded picnic spot by a river. A garden pond may stand alone or be incorporated as a pool into a stream; it may be allowed to dry in the summer to reflect seasonal wet-dry cycles. The use of rocks and sedges can create a convincing dryland waterway that spills into the pond.

Larger systems—holding from fifty to six hundred gallons of water—can easily be designed not to require mechanical aids for aeration or filtration; the water surface functions as a highly efficient aerator. Smaller water features, especially in warm climates, need a pump for water movement. Evaporation is also more of a problem for small water features, though a trickle or spray that periodically refills the pool is generally sufficient to maintain a sufficient water level.

In designing a garden pond, an understanding of the role standing water plays in the natural biological cycle—a process that involves bacteria, plants, oxygen, and sunlight—is useful. Bacteria decompose fallen leaves and other organic debris; to accomplish this they require, and therefore deplete, dissolved oxygen. This is perfectly natural, and not usually a problem. The problems, however, arise when the amount of dissolved *nitrogen* in the water becomes elevated—usually because of excess fertilizers, plant material, or fish food and excrement, all of which contain nitrogen. The nitrogen encourages algae to bloom, which in turn cause huge increases in bacterial populations. An overabundance of bacteria inevitably means a precipitous decline in dissolved oxygen. Fish die at this point, as do the aerobic ("with oxygen") bacteria; anaerobic ("without oxygen") bacteria quickly move in, and thrive, producing the foul smell of putrified water.

Generally, the larger the volume of water, the more stable the system will be, the greater margin of error it will allow, and the less maintenance it will require. Think of a fishbowl on a windowsill, which requires more management and diligent observation than a hundred-gallon tank—or a garden pond. Small-scale systems, like fishbowls, require periodic cleaning. As organic debris decomposes, it increases the acidity of the water and adds methane and sulfides, which over time make the water toxic.

The oxygen level of water can be increased in various ways. Cooler water raises oxygen saturation, so limiting a pond's exposure to full sunlight—by means of buildings or shade-producing plants or by a layer of aquatic plants—helps keep algae in check and ensures that aerobic bacteria serve as the main decomposers of organic debris. Water can be oxygenated as well by channeling it in a thin layer over rocks, trickling it, or spraying it. Certain aquatic plants, such as water lilies, are very efficient at removing nitrogen from the water and can head off a bloom of algae. In addition, rushes, cattails, and tules offer a natural means of pond biofiltration, acting much like a filter in a home aquarium. Simple measures such as maintaining a fertilizer-free buffer zone around the pond are also helpful.

Wherever there is a standing pool of water, mosquitoes will be a problem during warm weather. Two biological measures exist to control mosquitoes. Mosquitofish, available free from mosquito abatement agencies, eat mosquito larvae and are often introduced into ponds for this purpose. Alternatively, the microbial pesticide *Bacillus thuringiensis* (sold under various brand names) parasitizes mosquito larvae; unfortunately, it also kills lepidopteran larvae, though otherwise it is harmless to wildlife.

Since pond installation can be laborious, time-consuming, and expensive, the pond's design needs to be carefully assessed. Child safety is perhaps the number-one consideration. Any water feature more than a few inches deep may need a barrier, especially if small children will have unsupervised access to garden areas. Shallow banks and rustic limbs that are lying partly in the water and partly on the bank will allow small mammals, including children, to climb out of the pond should they fall in; they will also allow small birds to drink.

Location is also a critical consideration. A garden's natural features—a natural depression in the landscape or a wet area, for example—may determine where a pond should be located. Avoiding impediments such as tree roots, old masonry, underground utilities, and sewer lines will in turn rule out many potential pond sites.

It may be an option to site the pond in the front yard rather than the back. Generally, backyard pools are more practical because people's lifestyles are geared toward privacy and family recreation, which the backyard better provides. The front yard also tends to be more difficult to control. Fences may be required for safety, and plant screens for privacy. If a pond is deeper than eighteen inches, most municipalities require a permit.

A pond offers a whole realm of possibilities in terms of garden plants. Some aquatic plants will root in deep water and rise above the surface in tall fronds; others will float on the surface or anchor themselves in the mud at the pond's edge. A naturalized pool should also be colonized with small aquatic organisms such as small, native fish, freshwater crustaceans, aquatic worms, and algae. The first place to look for plants and pond amenities is at a local nursery. Friends or neighbors with an established pond, or a sympathetic landowner with marshland, may be able to help as well. To get a pond off to a faster start, collect a few aquatic plants from a local marshy area, along with a bucket of mud from around their roots. This mud contains a culture of established microorganisms that will help the new pond on its way.

for insect-hunting forays, a survival strategy of safety in numbers by which they avoid predators. Gardens with a link to nearby chaparral or scrub might expect visits from the brush mouse, California mouse, cottontail rabbit, gray fox, and spotted skunk, which are well adapted to live in the dense vegetation and may even prefer a garden on the urban edge in which to forage and breed.

Oak Woodland

There is no better choice for a garden than one of the local species of native oak. Though ranging considerably in size, shape, and specific needs, all of the twenty or so oak species have one thing in common: they have been crafted in every detail to thrive in the California landscape. Contrary to popular opinion, oaks grow quickly and are easy to raise: an oak seedling may grow up to three feet every year and, once established, will thrive in well-drained garden soil that is not overwatered in summer. An oak tree ties the garden to an ecological cycle wholly characteristic of the wild California that early settlers witnessed.

The California oak woodland is a heritage landscape of the valleys and foothills, a mosaic of habitats crowned by majestic oak trees. Whether found scattered like solitary sentinels in a parklike sea of grass or with a dense understory of gray pine or manzanita, native oaks are a central feature of the life cycles of hundreds of vertebrate animals, thousands of specialized insects, and uncounted forms of microscopic life.

Acorn season is feast time for many birds and mammals, including mule deer, wood ducks, quail, and pocket gophers; meanwhile Steller's and scrub jays, gray squirrels, and chipmunks busy themselves burying the calorie-rich nuts underground, thus inadvertently planting many oak seedlings. The influx of small mammals from the surrounding grasslands also brings predators, such as owls and weasels.

Not just acorns, but every part of deciduous and evergreen oak trees is a source of food. Leaves, stems, woody tissues, buds, and roots are eaten in diverse stages of growth and decomposition. The tree also serves as a home for a huge assortment of insects, such as beetles, leaf hoppers, aphids, wood borers, and leaf miners, whose tiny larvae extract the green juices of the leaves.

Through all this nibbling and gnawing, an oak flourishes to provide a centuries-long foothold in the ecosystem, a stable anchor for the shorter life cycles of myriad other species. A tree may live for two hundred years and then take another two hundred years to die. Old, dying, and dead oak trees provide thick, insulating bark to protect birds and mammals from very hot or cold weather. Snags, or standing dead trees, are used for nearly all basic activities: foraging and food storage; a perch for hunting, roosting, or courtship displays; a snug overwintering spot. Acorn woodpeckers, for example, use snags as "granary trees" for stockpiling acorns that will feed a group of birds throughout the winter. Trees that have passed their prime supply nest cavities for at least thirty-nine avian species and fourteen mammalian species, including bluebirds, swallows, owls, squirrels, and bats.

During the active afterlife of a tree, decomposition takes many years. Nothing goes to waste. Once a snag falls to the ground, it invites use by diverse species, such as insect larvae, lichens, fungi, and microorganisms. As nitrogen-fixing bacteria enrich the decaying wood and mushrooms sprout and die (sometimes producing a bizarre array of spore outgrowths on a single log), nutrients are carried to the surrounding soil; these in turn foster soil-dwelling microbes and symbiotic fungi, which contribute to the water and nutrient intake of many plants. In addition, as many as three hundred species of insects may colonize a downed tree, constituting a banquet for spiders, salamanders, lizards, and woodpeckers. Thus, downed wood is a very rich habitat, offering a multitude of wildlife amenities—as well as some interesting possibilities for the home garden (see "Garden Art: Downed Wood and Leaf Litter," p. 73).

Grassland

The mixed prairie that once was so abundant in the Central Valley and the grasslands that still blanket the foothills offer many ideas for natural elements of interest and great beauty in a California garden. Grasses are without doubt the most abundant (162 species, both native and imported), widespread, and useful plants in California. Imagine a showy expanse of poppies, goldfields, and lupines surrounding the spare architecture of tall, perennial deergrass with its slender spikes and you have the beginnings of a grassland garden. Place an oak in the corner of this picture and you'll have a savanna, which combines the amenities of both grassland and woodland. Small mammals and birds depend on native bunchgrasses like deergrass for shelter in which to raise their young. Small voles and native mice (not to be confused with pesky house mice) rummage through grassy thickets in search of seeds, vegetative matter, berries, fungi, and insects and escape as best they can from the searching gaze of predators such as owls and weasels.

Burrows, made by rodents like gophers and gray squirrels, are welcome

A fallen tree left to decompose in the garden creates habitat and is aesthetically pleasing.

niches that provide prairie wildlife with a sporting chance to escape danger or the hot sun. Burrowing owls, so fascinating to observe as they stand quietly outside their shelters looking for food and watching for predators, use ground squirrel burrows in the vicinity of houses, though unfortunately their food supply—large insects and lizards—and the open ground they require for security have become scarce.

Coastal or Mountain Forest

Forests, found along the coast and in the mountains, in both dense stretches and small, isolated patches, are another significant component of the California mosaic. As is true of other biotic communities, a life-giving characteristic of forests is their structural diversity. A robust forest includes shady areas broken up by golden patches of sunlight; small creeks, seeps, and boggy areas; and vegetation in various stages of growth and decay. As many as fifteen hundred invertebrate species make their home in aerial lichen gardens growing in the canopy of old trees. A tree snag may stand for a century, providing shelter for bats under the loose bark or food for woodpeckers in the form of carpenter ants and termites; it may then take another century to decompose into a heap of organic matter topped by a rich assortment of fungi, mosses, lichens, and plants. Downed logs, scattered around or piled together like a child's game of pick-up-sticks, offer indispensable forage, nesting, perching, and hiding spots. In the case of forest creeks, downed wood also slows the water flow and so helps to preserve the forest soil.

GARDEN ART
DOWNED WOOD AND LEAF LITTER

One of the things that first catches our eye in a natural landscape, whether at the beach, in the mountains, or in a beautiful meadow, is a downed log. It is where the action is: perhaps a pelican is sitting on it, a lizard has just skittered across it, or a lush vine is draped around it like a shawl. The kids clamber on and around it, and it becomes an imaginary boat. Such logs, in various stages of deterioration, sometimes massive or with an irregular beauty, aren't seen in cultivated environments and for that reason draw our attention.

The angular, twisted shapes and contrasting textures provide an artful sculpture for the garden such as only nature could create. A twisted pine snag combined with ferns and columbines conjures up a living moment in a forest glade. A limb from an old oak in a bed of flowering annuals and bunchgrasses creates a garden meadow. Slender branches of silvery cottonwood piled among a deep, golden cushion of leaf litter near a pond or stream evoke a river's edge.

A diverse environment of organic debris, gravelly and sandy spots, and wet and shady or dry and sunny areas supports a variety of living organisms—in the home garden as much as in the larger forest landscape. In designing a forest-based garden, you might consider focusing on an edge habitat, where the trees are sparser. If you decide on a denser forest planting, a strategic plan that ensures sunny garden spots is critical. In either case, you will be able to supply wildlife amenities characteristic of forest habitats—cavity nests, for example, or a hedge that offers hiding places—that may be in short supply in your local area.

CREATING A GARDEN HABITAT FOR BIRDS

Any garden space is large enough to support some form of bird habitat.[9] Birdhouses, water, and well-chosen plants all can entice visiting birds to the garden; with a full range of amenities, you will even attract residents (see "Providing Nest Sites and Materials for Birds," pp. 76–77; for a discussion of the special requirements of songbirds, see Chapter 5).

Water works especially well to lure birds to the garden. Many birds find

The shady diversity of plant life found on the forest floor can become a garden element.

the sight and sound of dripping or spraying water irresistible, especially in warm weather when water is in limited supply and they seek it for bathing and drinking. If you are creating a permanent wet spot, a shallow basin with a rough surface will prove most effective, since many small birds are afraid of water that is more than an inch deep; alternatively, you can place a grate just under the surface of deeper pools. By situating the water feature—whether a birdbath, a trough, a fountain, or a pool—near vegetation that is dense, prickly, or high enough to allow birds to perch or escape easily, you can help protect them from heavy, relatively slow predators such as cats.

Birds use plants for cover, food, and nesting. In natural areas, a mixed landscape with shrubs, trees, and open fields or meadows has particular appeal, since the various levels of vegetation satisfy an assortment of needs. For instance, some birds may nest in trees, eat berries from shrubs or vines, and search for insects or worms in open ground. If a similar mixture of vegetation types is included in a garden (recall the idea of habitat edges, where elements from two or more habitats overlap), chances are greatly increased that birds will visit or settle there. Not all shrubs and trees provide food or the right type of shelter for birds; by focusing on the native vegetation of the region, you will be more likely both to attract resident birds and reestablish former seasonal visitors.

Making a garden safer and more hospitable for wildlife may require a passive area, where recreational activities and roaming pets do not disturb visitors. The front yard may be ideal for this less trafficked garden component.

The Public Garden in Davis' Central Park uses plants that maximize habitat value for birds and butterflies. (Landscape architects: Mark Francis and CoDesign, Inc.)

Common Garden Visitors

A variety of bird species can be found widely throughout California; they visit gardens frequently, are a joy to watch, and may be enticed to nest. (But don't try to catch one—all wild birds are protected by law; only sick or injured individuals may be held in captivity, and then only temporarily.) Because relatively abundant species such as wrens, finches, cedar waxwings, and hummingbirds represent a broad range of food preferences, by providing for them you will likely draw others in their wake.

Wrens   Wrens are small birds with a distinctively cocked tail that flips up and down (house wren) or from side to side (Bewick's wren). Wrens forage for insects on the ground or in low branches, and their slender, downward-curving bill makes them particularly adept at catching spiders and wasps. The house wren, so called because it readily nests in birdhouses and under the eaves of residences, is largely a migrant species and visits most of the state (excluding deserts) in the spring and summer. The Bewick's wren is generally a year-round resident, undertaking only local migrations.

Male wrens arrive in the breeding area before the females and build rough "dummy nests" to attract a mate. A house wren will cram a nest full of sticks and embellish it with other materials it finds in the area. Once the nest is established and brooded, the home site is vigorously defended; the house wren may even destroy the eggs of other nearby house wrens as a protective measure.

PROVIDING NEST SITES AND MATERIALS FOR BIRDS

Besides water and an old log, nothing stimulates interest in a garden as much as a bird's nesting site. Every day, all day, during the late spring and summer period of nest building, egg brooding, and rearing of the young, avian parents toil ceaselessly. It is garden drama like no other, as the parents search endlessly for food, drive off intruders, and call nervously when the fledglings take their first flight.

Providing garden nesting sites, besides allowing intimate observation of a bird's life, is one of the most important contributions we can make to habitat restoration. The loss of old orchards, natural woodlots with tree snags, and barns with rafters and open windows has created a critical housing shortage for cavity-nesting birds. More than fifty species of American birds accept fabricated nesting boxes; by working with them in this way, we help to reduce at least one of the many ecological pressures these birds face.

Nest boxes should be placed within the natural habitat of the species we hope to attract, with appropriate cover. The entrance hole should point to the southeast, away from prevailing wind and weather, and it should be low enough that it can be checked and cleaned out routinely, especially of ants, wasps, dead birds, rotten eggs, and, if the conservation of threatened native species is a goal, the eggs of unwanted cowbirds, house sparrows, and starlings.[10] Place the nest box out in the fall so that it weathers and becomes more attractive to the birds; in the meantime, it will also provide winter birds with a sheltered place to roost during inclement weather—birds that may stay to build their nests when the weather warms. A thirty-inch metal sleeve around the pole on which the box is mounted may keep cats, squirrels, and raccoons from climbing into the nest.

It is best to use rough, approximately one-inch-thick wood to build the birdhouse. Some birds—chickadees, titmice, downy woodpeckers, and nuthatches—seem to prefer rustic nesting boxes made of slabs of rough-hewn wood with attached bark. Do not stain or paint the birdhouse: that may well discourage birds from using it. And don't provide an outside perch, which would just give starlings and house sparrows a place to sit while they destroy eggs and harass and injure nestlings.

Birds of the same species will generally not nest close together, so there is usually no point in putting up more than one birdhouse for each species you hope to attract. Most bird boxes should also be attached securely to a solid object, such as a strong, stable pole inserted firmly into the ground or a shelf mounted on a building or tree. Wrens are an exception to both these rules: they nest in birdhouses that are suspended from tree branches or any other support, and they will nest where multiple birdhouses are grouped in close proximity.

Birds can be encouraged to nest in an area if you gather and leave nesting materials in a place for them to find. Short pieces of yarn or string, for example, no longer than six inches, can be draped on the limbs of trees and shrubs or offered to birds in a suspended wire basket. The wide-mesh bags in which citrus fruit is sometimes sold can be filled with a variety of nest-building materials, such as short strips of soft cotton or wool cut from old clothes, horsehair from old upholstery, bristles from worn-out paintbrushes, cotton batting from old pillows or furniture, chicken feathers, bits of fur collected from pet brushes or hair from a hairbrush, and straw or other dried grasses.[11]

NEST-BOX DIMENSIONS FOR VARIOUS SPECIES

	Floor (inches)	Height of Bird Box (inches)	Entrance		Height above Ground (feet)
			Height (inches)	Diameter (inches)	
Bluebird	5 x 5	8	6	1½	5–10
Chickadee	4 x 4	8–10	6–8	1⅛	6–15
Titmouse	4 x 4	8–10	6–8	1¼	6–15
Nuthatch	4 x 4	8–10	6–8	1¼	12–20
House and Bewick's wren	4 x 4	6–8	4–6	1¼	6–10
Cavity-nesting swallows	5 x 5	6	1–5	1½	10–15
House finch	6 x 6	6	4	1½	8–12
Flicker	7 x 7	16–18	14–16	2½	6–20
Red-headed woodpecker	6 x 6	12–15	9–12	2	12–20
Downy woodpecker	4 x 4	8–10	6–8	1¼	6–20
Screech owl	8 x 8	12–15	9–12	3	10–30
Barn owl	10 x 18	15–18	4	6	12–18
American kestrel	8 x 8	12–15	9–12	3	10–30

(SOURCE: Terres 1994)

Because wrens are not very choosy about nesting sites, many gardens will attract them. Wrens will accept nest boxes; in fact, they've been known to nest in gourds, cans, and even mailboxes. They especially favor shrubby native vegetation or brush piles that provide them with cover.

Finches   Outside of breeding season, finches travel in large mixed flocks that include goldfinches, house finches, and purple finches. As the time for mating approaches, males begin to don their bright breeding plumage, a progressive change that is very noticeable and interesting to watch, as is the serenade-accompanied dance the male offers the female in courtship ritual. The house finch nests readily near human habitations, primarily in dense shrubs or trees, under eaves, or in building cavities.

Finches are easily attracted with birdseed, and they especially love thistle seed. A thistle feeder designed for finch beaks will also discourage jays, crows, and magpies from staying around for a free meal of seeds—or baby birds. The disadvantage of feeders is that they create conflict as more and more finches arrive, although once the birds pair off the number arriving at the feeder at any one time is reduced.

Cedar Waxwings   Cedar waxwings are gentle birds with a melancholy song that suits the mists of early spring. Soft brown in color, they are named for a bright red waxy substance (perhaps a status symbol) that older birds exude as small spots on the tips of their secondary feathers, and for the fact that they eat cedar berries. Slightly larger than sparrows, cedar waxwings are also recognized by their distinctive black face mask, a pointed crest, and a band of yellow across the end of their tail. After nesting, they stay around until mid- to late summer, feeding on a great variety of insects, fruits, and berries (mistletoe, pyracantha, privet); they then leave to winter as far south as Panama, where they raise a second brood. Unlike the competitive finches and wrens, cedar waxwings display a gentle group dynamic, feeding each other berries, rubbing beaks, and even dancing together during courtship.

Because of their love for berries, a good bet for attracting these small birds is to plant blackberry, dogwood, wild grape, cedar or juniper, elderberry, holly, mountain ash, or hawthorn. Like other birds, they are also attracted to water for drinking and bathing. In nesting season, cedar waxwings can be so tame as to take string or yarn out of your hand for nesting material. Look for their loosely woven nest of grass, twigs, moss, and yarn on horizontal branches in thick plantings of shrubs or trees.

Hummingbirds   Hummingbirds are indigenous to the New World, where the greatest variety is found in South America. Sixteen species are found regularly in the United States and Canada; of these, seven breed in California (the only hummingbird to breed in eastern North America is the ruby-throat), and most then migrate to Mexico in the winter. The hummingbird's dependence on a constant nectar supply not only ties it to the succession of regional flower seasons but also determines the route and timing of migration.

The species most commonly seen in California gardens are the Anna's (a year-round resident), black-chinned, Allen's, and Costa's hummingbirds. The summer breeding range of the forest-loving rufous hummingbird barely crosses into the northernmost part of the state, while the calliope (the smallest North American bird) and broad-tailed hummingbirds remain entirely east of the Sierra Nevada in summer.

Their size, aerial feats, glittering color, buzzing wings, and feisty temper make hummingbirds instantly recognizable and beloved. The architecture of their wings allows them to hover virtually motionless in front of a flower as they obtain nectar and insects, or to move forward, backward, sideways, or up and down. The rate at which hummingbirds beat their wings varies according to their size—the bigger the bird, the slower the beat rate—but can be anywhere from twenty to eighty beats a second. Their eye-catching aerial displays are performed by male birds defending a territory in hopes of attracting a mate.

Hummingbirds, among the smallest of warm-blooded vertebrates, have very high energy needs for flight and for body temperature regulation; as a result, they must refuel on nectar and insects nearly all day long. This poses a real problem during cold or hot spells in the spring, when nectar-producing flowers and insects may suddenly disappear. To compensate, hummingbirds have evolved a survival mechanism by which they may become torpid at night, dropping their body temperature to near-ambient levels and depressing their metabolism by as much as two-thirds.

To attract hummingbirds to the garden in the spring and summer, choose flowering plants that provide a succession of flowers throughout the spring and summer or, for the Anna, throughout the year. Even a small garden full of nectar-producing plants—or a strip of native monkey flowers growing next to a driveway—can help to support a hungry neighborhood hummingbird. Los Altos hummingbird authority Louise Blakey recommends the following plants: fuchsia (especially the very small-flowered varieties), grevillea, sage, California fuchsia or hummingbird flower (upright growth varieties), woolly

Concave stone allowed to fill with water increases the potential for wildlife sightings.

blue curls, tree mallow, tree tobacco, flowering maple, penstemon, eucalyptus, bottlebrush, heath (*Erica speciosa* or *E. mammosa* especially), and honeysuckle.[12]

Because of their agility and speed, hummingbirds have few predators, although hawks and even frogs have been known to catch them. In fact, one of the greatest threats in the home landscape to hummingbirds—and to many other fast-flying birds as well—is from plate-glass windows, which can be made more visible with tape or stickers to help warn the birds off. Stunned hummingbirds that have hit a window and survive the first few hours can be maintained for a recovery period with the following food formula: Dissolve in four ounces of water one level teaspoon of condensed milk, one and a half teaspoons of honey, one to two drops of liquid vitamins (Vipenti), and one drop of beef extract (to replace dietary insects).[13]

Swallows   These swift birds are recognized by their soaring, gliderlike flight, often just inches above the ground or water, as they search for insects. Familiar to most gardeners are the barn and cliff swallows, the latter making a sometimes dramatic homecoming from South America in the spring, often within a few days of the same date each year. Less familiar are tree and violet-green swallows, though some individuals make their year-round home in California, and the purple martin.

In spite of their names, both the cliff and barn swallows build mud-pellet nests and plaster them to houses, cliffs, or bridges, while tree and violet-green swallows and the purple martin nest in cliff crevices or the trunk cavities of old or dead trees. A paucity of cavities suitable for nests limits the population of these swallows relative to the mud nesters.

The two species of mud-nesting swallows are easily distinguished: the barn swallow has a deeply forked "swallowtail" and orange throat, while the cliff swallow has a square tail and orange rump. Both species have adapted to a wide variety of habitats throughout the state, being found virtually everywhere except deserts. They particularly favor grasslands, shrublands, croplands, open forests, and open bodies of water. Their only requirement is a source of mud and a place where they can attach a nest, such as a vertical, sheltered wall.

The tree swallow is blue-green above and white below, and its tail is intermediate in form, with just a medium notch. It is common in wooded habitat near water, particularly in areas with dead trees that offer nest holes, though it will also nest in barn eaves or in a nest box. The purple martin, distinguished by its dark, violet-blue mantle, searches out old woodpecker holes for nesting; however, it is rapidly losing the battle for these valuable homes to the aggressive European starling.

Mixed-Species Flocking

They swoop in suddenly, dozens of chattering, skittish little birds, hopping from branch to branch in a frenzied search for insects, never pausing for more than a few seconds. The chestnut-backed chickadee, plain titmouse, bushtit, white-breasted nuthatch, brown creeper, ruby-crowned kinglet, and other passerines (perching, or "sparrowlike," birds) commonly join together outside of breeding season in insect-hunting forays, a cooperative strategy that has several potential advantages.[14] A group effort may enable more effective detection of predators; it may also confuse a predator as the entire flock flees at once in a flurry of beating wings. In addition, mixed flocks seem to increase the efficiency of feeding; not only is it more likely that a rich feeding patch will be located, with more birds on the lookout, but any insect that escapes one bird is also quite apt to be caught by a second bird. Finally, an individual will encounter less competition in a flock with diverse food preferences and foraging techniques than in a similar-sized flock of its own species.

The flocks of passerines, moving downslope from the mountains in fall and winter or into more southerly regions of the state, eat some seeds, but primarily they consume insects gleaned from leaves or bark. They live in shrubby or open-forest habitats and nest in old woodpecker holes or cavities

A SONOMA BUTTERFLY GARDEN

Louise Hallberg has created a diverse habitat for butterflies in her Hallberg Ranch garden in Sebastopol. Louise's mother planted a Dutchman's pipe vine in the 1920s, and Louise observed that there have been pipe-vine swallowtails on the plant ever since. With encouragement from butterfly garden experts, Louise started developing the garden in 1990 to attract more butterflies. Since then she has cataloged thousands of individual butterflies, from more than forty species, in her garden. She now leads tours of the garden for nearby Oak Lane Elementary School students.

SOME COMMON BUTTERFLIES AND THEIR HABITATS

Butterfly Species	Location (County)	Habitat	Host Plant
San Bruno elfin	San Mateo	hilltop rocky outcrops	stonecrop *(Sedum spathulifolium)*
El Segundo blue	Los Angeles	coastal dune	dune buckwheat *(Eriogonum parvifolium)*
Smith's blue	Monterey	coastal dune	dune buckwheat *(Eriogonum parvifolium)* and coast buckwheat *(E. latifolium)*
Palos Verdes blue	Los Angeles	coastal scrub	southern California locoweed *(Astragalus trichopodus* var. *lonchus)*
Lotis blue	Mendocino	wet meadow	coast hosackia *(Lotus formosissimus)*
mission blue	Marin, San Mateo	coastal scrub and grassland	silver lupine *(Lupinus albifrons)*, Lindley varied lupine *(L. variicolor)*, and summer lupine *(L. formosus)*
Lange's metalmark	Contra Costa	riverine sandy dune	naked stemmed buckwheat *(Eriogonum nudum)*
Oregon silverspot	Del Norte	coastal meadow	western dog violet *(Viola adunca)*
Myrtle's silverspot	Marin, Sonoma	coastal dune, terrace prairie, bluff scrub, and grassland	western dog violet *(Viola adunca)*
bay checkerspot	Santa Clara, San Mateo	canyon	native plantain *(Plantago erecta)* for larvae; then owl's clover *(Castilleja densiflorus* and *C. exserta)*

(SOURCE: Thelander 1994)

that they construct in decomposing snags, except for the bushtit and kinglet, which construct suspended nests. Small passerines are most likely to visit gardens with patches of native shrubs or trees, though cats may well keep these excitable birds away. Making nest boxes available may attract them to the garden as well.

Leaf-Litter Foragers

The hermit thrush, rufous-sided towhee, and California towhee all forage on the ground, preferring areas with accumulated leaf litter. They have catholic tastes, consuming insects, spiders, and other invertebrates but also seeds and fruit. These birds generally seek cover in brushy native vegetation (toyon, coffeeberry, native honeysuckle, native grapevine). Since their cup-shaped nests are placed on or near the ground in dense vegetation, you might consider planting gooseberries and wild rose thickets to help protect the birds from cats and other predators. Thorny plants in combination with irregular elements such as rocks and wood debris offer good habitat value generally.

CREATING A GARDEN HABITAT FOR BUTTERFLIES

The order Lepidoptera (meaning "scale-winged," from the fact that their wings are formed from a multitude of overlapping scales) includes butterflies, moths, and skippers and, with 125,000 species, is second in size only to the beetle order, Coleoptera, with some 300,000 species.[15] Butterflies in particular have captured the imaginations of people for thousands of years because of their fragile, ephemeral beauty, but they have considerable ecological value as well, in that they transform immeasurable amounts of plant matter into animal protein. The majority of butterflies are adapted to narrow ecological niches in terms of reproduction and plant food sources, sometimes relying on a single species of plant; this makes them highly vulnerable to ecological disruptions, and many are now on threatened or endangered species lists.

Butterflies begin life as eggs laid on a host plant. Once hatched, a larval caterpillar eats plant parts, grows, and stores energy until it is ready to pupate. It then seeks out a sheltered spot and forms a chrysalis; the cocoon stage lasts several weeks while the animal metamorphoses into its reproductive form, an adult butterfly.

Encouraging butterflies to lay eggs in a garden requires some knowledge of their larval plant host(s), information that is available in butterfly field guides and in butterfly gardening books.[16] Common plant hosts are thistles, milkweed, carrots, anise, Queen Anne's lace, and parsley, as well as many woody shrubs and trees, such as willows and cottonwoods. Tall native bunchgrasses serve as larval food plants for many butterflies too and, as an added amenity, offer places for butterflies to hide at night or during windy or wet weather.

While the larvae of many species of butterfly eat only specific plants, adults feed on a variety of flowering plants. Common species that supply nectar and on which butterflies are able to perch include lantana, heliotrope,

Top: *Butterfly caterpillars often have specific host plants on which they develop and metamorphose.*

Bottom: *Louise Hallberg has observed more than forty varieties of butterflies in her Sonoma garden.*

verbena, and various members of the mint family. Native plants that are especially attractive to butterflies include yerba santa, wallflower, mock orange, coyote mint, California buckeye, wild buckwheat, and many members of the sunflower and dandelion families.

To create a garden habitat for butterflies, group nectar-producing and larval-host plants together in sunny locations (see "A Sonoma Butterfly Garden," p. 82). From the time they emerge, butterflies thrive in sunlight, spreading their wings to dry, basking, and performing their mating dances. Since the food sources for many species, in both larval and adult forms, remain something of a mystery, butterflies provide an excellent opportunity for amateur naturalists to contribute in significant ways to field lore.

Birds and butterflies are just some of the creatures that enliven a garden and make it a more natural place. A diversity of conditions, such as wet or sheltered spots, and a well-chosen assortment of plants from the surrounding region encourage natural processes and attract living things to the garden. Such visitors reassure us that the mystery of life is in the everyday landscape we inhabit.

CHAPTER FOUR

DESIGNING
THE
CALIFORNIA
LANDSCAPE
GARDEN

Design starts with a sense of the spirit and opportunities that a site presents. It involves the careful observation of the unique qualities and problems of the site such as drainage, soil, wind, sun and relationship to neighbors. It demands an understanding of the unique needs of the garden users. It requires a concern for basic design such as composition, scale, color, line, texture and three-dimensional form. These are all important to the overall look, feeling and function of a garden.

Thomas Church, *Gardens Are for People*

Thus far we have seen how a gardener, by looking closely at local habitats with the eye of a naturalist, can become inspired to recreate those habitats on a garden scale, using primarily native plant species but also carefully chosen imports (see "A Valley Heritage Garden," pp. 140–141). Now comes the time to put a systematic landscape design together, just as a landscape architect would. Though it may be a challenge for the untrained, the overall design process is not difficult; in fact, it should prove stimulating, for it enables ideas to be transformed into a real garden that expresses the gardener's own per-

Right: *Structures such as arbors and low retaining walls organize this Walnut Creek garden. (Landscape architect and photographer: Ron Lutsko Jr.)*

Below: *The Stewart Garden in Burbank combines history and ecology. (Landscape architect: Rick Fisher)*

sonality and values. In essence, the design process provides an opportunity to consider several garden plans before settling on a final one—for it is much more efficient to work problems through on paper, rather than in the garden itself, where they're much more difficult to correct. Through application of a systematic approach, whether starting with a bare site or an already developed garden, it is possible to achieve a garden with both design character and ecological integrity.

An ecologically sustainable garden reflects the climatic, cultural, and ecological conditions of the garden's setting within a bioregion, and it is created as much as possible out of local resources. The natural resources used in the garden are much like an artist's media, such as watercolors or clay, and they must be handled similarly: with knowledge, creativity, and judicious care. Selecting plants that are adapted to local conditions, preparing the soil to meet their needs, aesthetically grouping plants that have similar needs—this design process requires an understanding of local climate and native plant species that is infused with an imaginative vision for the prospects of a new garden experience featuring California's nature.

DESIGN CONCEPTS

Since 1980, an increasing number of landscape architects have been working to create water-conserving gardens that are sensitive to regional conditions.

Their designs are distinguished by a commitment to environmental processes and the preservation of natural form. Top California designers include Ron Lutsko Jr., Robert Perry, Owen Dell, Isabelle Greene, Patrick and Jane Miller, Steve Chainey, Rick Fisher, Ann Christoph, and Achva Stein. Each of these designers has demonstrated an inspiring ability to create unified and innovative landscape designs through a synthesis of natural and cultural factors.[1]

There is nothing mysterious about creating an inviting garden that is visually engaging, indeed, that offers something for all the senses. This is as true of an ecological garden as of a more traditional garden. Landscape design professionals focus on several key concepts to achieve these compelling effects: a recognizable form, a sense of organization, sensory contrast, and elements of surprise and discovery. These design principles are critical in planning any garden, whether from the ground up or as a remodeling project. The following discussion focuses on simple ways to think about garden aesthetics in a way that demystifies landscape design.

Landscape gardens may have multiple forms and styles. The small pool in this formal Berkeley garden attracts urban wildlife, including raccoons and possums. (Landscape architects: Patrick and Jane Miller, 2M Associates; photograph by Jane Miller)

Create a Recognizable Form

A garden gains form and character when its different segments are part of a recognizable composition, that is, when individual elements have a clear relationship with one another. Generally, at least one unifying concept will be readily apparent. For instance, in a front yard designed around a main axis, garden features such as flower beds, hedges, and an entryway will all relate to this axis.

A garden concept may center on a geometrical composition or on a particular theme. Diagonal lines and triangular spaces, for instance, may offer a refreshing alternative to the typical square yard. Undulating lines, used for planting beds or screens, provide continually changing views as one walks through the garden. While concentric or square lines can produce spaces of simple beauty and elegance, more organic, naturalistic forms allow for a more complex composition that refers to nature directly. Sometimes a single, dominating element, such as a large pond or a winding stream, will shape the identity of a garden.

The themes on which a garden can be built are limitless. They may reflect a philosophy—about our relationship to the earth, say, or the place of wildlife in our lives—or a passion—for butterflies or songbirds, perhaps, or for specific plants, such as roses, herbs, or bulbs or luxuriant bunchgrasses and plants native to the region. They may center on an aesthetic idea—imagine a moonlight garden, with white-blooming or grayish-colored plants and

The entrance to this Santa Barbara garden evokes a sense of unfolding drama. (Landscape architect: Owen Dell)

a still pool—or on a meaningful narrative—a favorite children's story, local event, or work of literature. A special appreciation for music or poetry may be expressed in a garden through form, texture, or color or through symbolic gestures. A love of the ocean might be represented by appropriate colors and materials and by the sound of gurgling water. In addition, composition can be oriented around a strong functional purpose, such as an orchard, a vegetable garden, a shaded patio for orchids, a play area, or a sculpture garden.

Organize the Garden into Garden Rooms

Once a unifying concept has been decided on, the overall layout and organization of the garden need to be planned, with an eye to functional, aesthetically pleasing, and ecologically oriented results. Do not discount intuitive understanding and experience of the site during this initial phase.

One key to organization is to think in terms of garden "rooms"—enclosed spaces, either cozy or more spacious, to heighten interest and comfort. Without a sense of delimited areas, small details make little difference and in fact may be nearly invisible. It is also important to provide appropriate pathways for people and to accommodate such basic needs as room for the dog to exercise or for children to play.

Thinking of the garden as a set of rooms is a simple yet useful way to give pleasing character to the garden. Though garden rooms may be open on one or more sides, they *feel* enclosed or protected and exert a strong sense of place. They may be defined by "walls"—anything that impedes a view, such as vegetation, constructed screens, a set of tree trunks, or buildings—but the

VINES FOR GREEN
GARDEN ROOMS

The garden may be thought of as a series of outdoor rooms, which serve different purposes and have diverse qualities. Traditionally, trees and shrubs have been used in many ways to help define these green rooms and give them character. In today's suburban homes, however, small gardens are the rule rather than the exception, and there is little room for shrubs and trees.

One alternative for creating a garden room in any size yard—even a roof terrace, where container gardening is most practical—is to use vines that are supported with wooden or metal frames. Metal bars connected with stout wire make simple structures to display attractive vines, which in turn impart a variety of qualities to the framed space: an open or dense vegetative "wall," diverse patterns and colors, or fruit or fragrant flowers.

An overhead screen or arch, also easily constructed, might further serve to shade the garden area below. Such a device makes a garden room feel intimate and comfortable and is often very effective in combination with house entrances, patios, or green rooms along the outside edges of the garden or on the narrow side of the house. Especially appealing vegetation for overhead covers are luxuriously blooming rose vines or fragrant vines such as California honeysuckle *(Lonicera hispidula)*, but there are many to choose from. You might consider, for example, Dutchman's pipe *(Aristolochia californica)*, a deciduous native of northern California Coast Ranges and Sierra Nevada foothills; pipestem clematis *(Clematis lasiantha)*, a deciduous native of the chaparral, Coast Ranges, and Sierra Nevada foothills; greenbriar *(Smilax californica)*; wild cucumber *(Marah* spp.); California grape *(Vitis californica)*; or desert grape *(Vitis girdiana)*.[2]

sheltering space under a tree in an otherwise open landscape may also be considered an outdoor room. Rooms may be small, private, and hidden from view, perhaps with an overhead structure (see "Vines for Green Garden Rooms," above), or they may be more open and sunny. They may be somewhat architectural in character, or defined only by plants. Fragrances, sounds, details in the building materials used, and small accentuating objects will further define the character of a garden room.

Because garden rooms have different functions, it makes sense that they

CONCRETE PILLARS FOR RUSTIC TRELLISES

A hand-crafted pillar is a simple, elegant solution for holding up a garden trellis. It can be made with rammed earth, an ancient fabrication method still common in many Mediterranean countries, but it also can be constructed of concrete. Concrete is especially useful where a high degree of resiliency and longevity is required.

Crafting a trellis using concrete pillars is very simple. Concrete is poured into a Sonotube (thick cardboard tube) in which a length of rebar has been centered; after the concrete has hardened and set, the paper tube is peeled off. Slender logs or poles are then secured to the column, or a series of columns, by means of horizontally placed brackets. With the passing of years, the transitory wood cross-beams can easily be replaced.

The most important structural element of this trellis, however, is permanent—and personal. Unlike a manufactured column made with a slick faux-marble surface, the homemade concrete pillar can be imprinted with the hands and names of children or a significant date. With a mold, concrete can be shaped into multiple forms to fit many purposes in a garden, including benches, a table for children's play, retaining walls, and posts.

will have different characters. At the front of the house, for example, a garden room may be intended specifically to complement the building or to form a small, multipurpose courtyard. A narrow side yard may serve as a pleasing thoroughfare. A backyard might consist of a single room or several rooms, each with its own function, whether it be play, entertainment, or quiet retreat. Vegetables and fruit trees may define a productive, functional space, while an informal hedge can be used to create a room with a protected feel, perhaps with a small pond in its center.

A set of diverse rooms around the exterior of the house not only produces a practical organization but also makes for a stimulating sequence of experiences. The typical home landscape, a narrow ring that surrounds the house, is not particularly satisfying as a garden form; by shaping individual rooms along the ring, all different but somehow interconnected, the designer gives a garden a unique look and functionality.

Let's take an imaginary walk around a property to see how garden rooms can create a compelling environment. Picture walking out into a narrow side

Each garden "room" has its own form, function, and detail. (Landscape architect: Rick Fisher)

garden with a simple, accessible surface of adobe block and decomposed granite. The space is shaped by a property-line fence and a fruit tree or two tall enough to walk under. As you head toward the backyard you can see in the distance a pretty wall with colorful mosaic inlays. Next to the mosaic wall, you soon discover, is a small, sunny patio with adobe-block surface and some wrought-iron furniture. Nearby is a small bed of perennials in the dappled shade of a twisted mature madrone or manzanita. Nudging into the patio from the perennial planting is a small pond with aquatic plants and a trickle of running water. Walking on, around the next corner of the house you encounter a sunny lawn surrounded by small trees, shrubs, and perennials, connecting to the wide double doors of the living room. Not all of the open area is visible at once because of the undulating nature of the plantings. Some large embedded rocks help define the edge between the planting beds and the lawn.

The view from the house toward this larger garden room is framed by a pergola with thick, woody grapevines adorning its columns. Under the pergola you find a table surrounded by chairs, and hanging baskets; on the far end a short path leads to a garden gate covered with rose brambles. On the other side of the gate is a small cut-flower and vegetable garden, fenced off to protect it from dog intrusions. The rectangular shapes of the planting beds and walkway make it formally clear that this garden space leads somewhere—in this case, to the garage. On the south side of the house kiwi vines clamber up wooden frames to the roof and spill over the garage entry.

Part of the pleasure of such a sequence is the variation between covered

Plants can be used to create an outdoor room that accommodates a variety of activities, as in the Thomas Garden. (Landscape architect: Topher Delaney, of Delaney, Cochran & Castillo; photograph by Topher Delaney)

and open garden rooms. Whether a room is open to the sky or not makes a big difference and may clearly define diverse spaces around a house. Other variables in this example include the differing character of walkable surfaces; the shape and style of planting beds; the size and shape of the garden rooms; and individual features such as the gurgling pool, a space-defining wall, and furniture announcing that an area is used for playing games and dining.

Besides helping to define garden rooms, shrubs and other screens also help to guide the eye, even making small spaces seem bigger, more complex. The garden is not seen all at once, and that is part of its great charm. By encouraging exploration of all the corners and details in a space—or by leaving some aspects to the imagination—you, as designer, intensify the garden experience.

Not just screens, but any object or area in the garden can mold the space, serving as a foreground, midground, or background landscape element. Columns, tree trunks, and rectilinear or sinuous flower beds, for example, by framing the scene, may constitute a foreground; larger-scale perennial plant-

Left: *The front garden need not be just lawn and trees, as this Burbank garden shows. (Landscape architect: Rick Fisher)*

Below: *The Oliver Garden shows how contrasting textures and colors help to define form. (Landscape architect: Topher Delaney, of Delaney, Cochran & Castillo; photograph by Topher Delaney)*

ings, a lawn, pieces of furniture, and other medium-sized garden elements may form a midground view; and fences, trees, shrubs, and buildings can all function as backdrops. The interplay and layering of foreground, midground, and background give depth and interest to a garden.

Create Sensory Contrast

Creating patterns of harmony and contrast, especially of textures and colors, is another important consideration in planning a garden. A monochromatic garden, with continuous plantings of green foliage that cover even the surrounding walls, will lack a definable form and offer no clues for orientation. In contrast, by using a variety of surfaces, such as brick walkways, embedded stones, and small lawns or ground covers, and architectural structures, such as pergolas, screens, or fences, a designer can give a garden dominated by plants a recognizable structure (see "Concrete Pillars for Rustic Trellises," p. 90). Besides manufactured materials, plants with sculptural interest, such as irises, perennial bunchgrasses, and artemisias, may be used to add contrast.

Obviously, a garden may become busy if too many colors or textures are included. However, a strong underlying concept usually prevents such overload. The trick is to include just enough contrasting elements to accentuate the main theme. For example, if the primary goal is to emphasize the beauty of bunchgrasses, a strongly contrasting shape or form, such as a group of large, harmoniously curving vases, can effectively set off the long, grassy wands. Similarly, textured structural objects and surfaces—bricks, blocks, stones,

ADOBE: A GARDEN OF EARTH

Adobe lends itself to nearly any style, but it seems especially fitting surrounded by Latin American cultural elements in a warm, sunny place like Ventura. Formal patios with potted plants, whitewashed walls, a *barbacoa* (hot rock) pit, and architectural accents like a fountain and a wall shrine for the Virgin of Guadalupe characterize this earthy garden design, which draws together a love for outdoor living and the spiritual values of a Latino family. The adobe also has an aura of permanence, which is appropriate for a family with six young children.

The family wanted an edible landscape—vegetable gardens, a small orchard, and a flock of chickens—and a special place to cook and entertain outdoors. The kids wanted a "jungle" to play in, and they got it: their play space has reverted to the wild, which suits them just fine. A mixed vegetation of shrubs, weeds, and grasses is diversified by open ground and a wet zone, which means jungle wildlife is likely to include lizards, butterflies, and perhaps a field mouse or two.

Double French doors connect the living room to the formal courtyard, and the kitchen and carport adjoin the vegetable garden, patio, and orchard/chicken run. Here, the transition from indoor to outdoor living spaces is deliberately immediate, a reflection of the fact that this family uses outdoor rooms as intensively as any room of their home.

Paving in the courtyard is a combination of adobe and pebble stone crafted from local materials. Rainwater from the roof either flows into a water sink in the backyard or into a rainwater and graywater tank that is used to irrigate the vegetable garden. Solar panels and native plantings are further amenities that conserve energy and water.

---

gravel, and wood—can emphasize the aesthetic effect of leafy or shrubby areas, and brightly colored furniture may enhance an earth-colored pavement.

Even small accents help define the garden space. A blue glass ball lends refined character to a small pond, though the pond may be filled with duckweed and algae. A sculptural birdbath placed on a lawn gives the lawn a focal point, transforming its visual effect. A small birdhouse hanging from an oak tree lends an added point of interest to the tree.

Inject Elements of Humor and Surprise

Elements of discovery are abundant in natural environments—mushrooms growing in a ring, a rugged rock outcropping, brightly colored lichens, a burrow under a tree root. Cultural landscapes supply their own unexpected

Adobe Garden

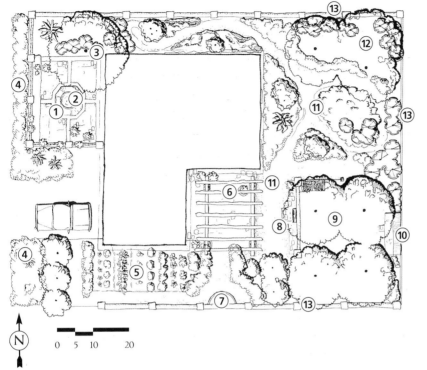

Above: *A small wall shrine is a form of personal expression in the adobe garden (see item 7).*

1. Formal display garden with flowers and potted plants
2. Spanish tile fountain
3. Flowering tree
4. Native succulents
5. Vegetable garden
6. Patio with large timber wood structure
7. Shrine (see drawing)
8. Barbecue
9. Orchard
10. Chicken house
11. Decomposed granite path
12. Willows and poplars
13. Twig fence

details: an unusual fountain, a small chapel, celebratory banners, and music broadcast through outdoor speakers all help create a sense of novelty in the larger human environment. Such elements of surprise and wonder can easily be incorporated into the home garden, for instance through plants of contrasting form or color, colorful Tibetan streamers and chimes, the playful use of water, aromatic flowers or herbs, or a wall shrine (see "Adobe: A Garden of Earth," above). Seasonal changes and processes of decay, apparent, for example, on moss-covered wood, may provide something to study over time. And of course, wildlife is always a delight to see.

Surprise is further created by half-hidden or unexpected elements. Perhaps water can be heard, but its source is not immediately apparent; or a ceramic ball or a bust in a perennial bed causes a visitor to do a double-take.

In the Donahue Garden in Berkeley, found objects create a sense of surprise and discovery. (Designer: Marcia Donahue)

Interrupting otherwise clear forms is another way of providing an element of surprise. A circular patio that is interrupted by a small stream meandering across one side, for example, is unexpected and has flair.

A rich experience is possible with a relatively small backyard, as artist and landscape designer Marcia Donahue's garden in Oakland illustrates. The space combines vegetation, winding paths, small open areas coupled with archways, and, in one location, a small pond. Little details such as glass balls and sculptures appear here and there. At the edge of one path, tiny oval ceramic shapes are strewn. At first they look like pebbles; only on closer observation does it become apparent that each one has a face carved into it.

THE DESIGN PROCESS

Brainstorming

Even with thorough preparation—after looking around the local region for ideas, reading up on native plants, and learning how landscape designers achieve professional results—many people still find it difficult to design a garden from scratch. Where to start? The best way to get some momentum going is to brainstorm: gather together all the possible ideas for main features, important functions, and basic layout of the garden.

How does a garden express a unique "personality"? It does so in part by mirroring personal interests and values and by presenting spaces that are varied in form and function. Consider what you want from your garden in these regards, and write down words or phrases or draw pictures that express those desires. Write whatever comes to mind, uncritically and without evaluation, even though it may sound ridiculous or inappropriate. "Ridiculous," after all, is relative: writing down "a place to pick my toes," for instance, might later be interpreted as "a place for total privacy," thus becoming an important aspect of the final design. Involve the whole family in this process, including children. Children might spontaneously say something or draw something that will lead to a great idea. You might also want to brainstorm with friends; the more people involved, the more likely it is that innovative ideas will arise that you might not otherwise have considered.

If you're just beginning to think about designing a landscape garden, start a wish list: jot down key ideas and begin assembling a file of images clipped from garden books and magazines of eye-catching garden features, efficient recreation spaces, or planting areas that are particularly attractive. These can help you imagine how design options might look in your own garden. In this idea-gathering stage, don't be too concerned with what is realistic in terms of cost or space. The goal at this point is simply to let the creative juices flow. Space and budget constraints will be addressed later in the design process.

Often people think that what they see in a published photograph will only fit in a larger garden. In fact, however, most garden themes can be effective even in very small gardens. For instance, if oak trees or good-sized chaparral shrubs, grasses, and ground covers set the tone in a spacious garden, a similar effect can be achieved on a smaller scale with relatively compact native shrubs and ground covers placed around a patio, say. Keep in mind that although the specific planting composition depicted in an article or a book may not fit your garden site and climate, without doubt an equally attractive and effective alternative exists.

Site visits to gardens both private and public may be useful for generating ideas. Many communities have demonstration gardens as parts of arboretums, botanical gardens, or water district offices (some are listed in the Appendix). Local garden clubs and nurseries can also be very helpful, especially in identifying the most appropriate plants for various situations. Even just ranging out into the community can spark thoughts. For instance, if you know you want a hedge that screens an area where laundry will hang to dry, keep an eye out while walking in nearby neighborhoods; you may well spot a local native shrub that can be clipped into formal shapes—the perfect thing.

Also, don't neglect the natural environment—the bioregion within which your garden will exist. If part of your goal is to make an ecologically sound California landscape garden, it's crucial to attend to habitat interactions, native plant communities, and historic or cultural features of the surrounding area that may be integrated into the garden layout. This might be brainstormed on its own, as a sort of checklist for locally available resources and themes.

Once you've written down as many garden wants, needs, and whimsies as you can think of, and noted aspects of the surrounding bioregion that may play a role in the layout, it's time to sort and prioritize. It is not time to make any firm decisions yet, but specific ideas may start to come together, and these should be jotted down. A "wish list" from a brainstorming session might, for example, include a row of fruit trees with a path, a trellis with native California vines over a patio, a wild area with willows for the kids to climb on, native shrubs with contrasting forms and colors that reflect seasonal change, raised vegetable beds made with adobe brick, and a spring that can be turned on to attract birds. As you continue the planning, the viability of these various options will be tested and the list shortened. The point at this juncture is simply to get away from the clichés of what a garden "should be" and discover what is most useful and meaningful for you.

Making a Diagram of Functional Areas

A rough diagram of functional areas—called a "bubble diagram" because these areas are most easily represented with roughly circular shapes—provides an overview of how the garden will be used and of site limits to those uses. Keep in mind that it is still too early to decide on specific shapes and materials for the various projects involved, or even on the overall form of the garden. The general siting of functions is what counts at this stage.

In making a bubble diagram, of course, the aim is to site compatible garden functions in close proximity. Often, however, incompatible areas will need to be located next to each other, usually because of space or access considerations. In these cases—as when a children's play area adjoins a flower bed, or when an outdoor eating area is in view of the neighbors—a screen may need to be erected. On the bubble diagram, thick lines can represent screens between functions.

Site qualities should also be indicated on the diagram. A noisy street might be represented with a jagged edge, while a pleasing view that should be preserved may be defined with an angular shape directed in the direction of the view. A north arrow helps to locate the shadier and the sunnier sections of the garden. Diversely shaped arrows may represent where uncomfortable drafts play a role (curved to indicate direction; thicker or thinner to indicate amount of air). Problem areas, such as ones requiring improved drainage or spots where the soil is especially soft and muddy in the rainy season, should be noted as well. All of these factors will determine what measures are needed to make the garden an enjoyable and useful place.

The Base Plan

Now it's time to take stock of just what you have to work with. Measure the garden, and, on a sheet of tracing paper, draw to scale an accurate representation of the garden area, such that each point in the garden has a precise location on the plan and relative sizes of specific garden areas are correct. Locate existing trees, shrubs, and other important features, and place them on the plan in relationship to the property lines and house. It is also important in the base plan to indicate the locations of windows and house entrances.

Keep the base plan simple and clear: it is just a design aid. Use thick marks (felt-tip pen) to render important lines such as the perimeter of a building. A circle with a dot in the middle is enough to represent trees. Color need not be used, except to lend greater clarity.

Rough Drafts of a Design Plan

Using a second piece of tracing paper laid on top of the base plan (a technique that allows unlimited trial-and-error work), draw a rough sketch to try out ideas for possible features and spaces. Use as many pieces of tracing paper as you need—this is the time to sort through the choices and trade-offs and the variety of ways that the interests of family members might be accommodated. Indicate with contrasting textures and colors all important proposed garden elements, such as trees, plant screens, annual beds, and perennial borders. Where, for instance, might diverse elements like a vegetable garden, flower beds, trees, patios, and shade structures go, and how might paths connect different garden areas? It is worth taking the time to cut out scaled pattern pieces of furniture, fruit trees, or other elements proposed for the garden, so that they can be moved quickly around the plan view.

You can also use tracing paper to get a three-dimensional impression of the effect certain design elements will have. Say you're considering a planting screen of trees or shrubs. Just lay a piece of tracing paper on a photograph of your house and sketch what you have in mind. This is a very simple way to get an idea of how your design will work.

Soon several competing plans will have taken shape. These must be examined thoughtfully one at a time, and then compared. Referring to the base plan, draw to scale one of the proposed plans in terms of garden "rooms"—a layout of small, large, and open spaces, or spaces that are to be enclosed overhead—using colors to differentiate each type of space. In addition to defining the garden rooms, draw in screens, trees, large shrubs, benches, water features, and other garden elements. Repeat this process for each design under consideration.

Look closely at how well each plan serves intended garden functions. Does the patio or main seating area in a particular design work connected to the living room exit, or might it be more effective elsewhere in the garden? Test new ideas by making new plans. Perhaps moving the seating area improves views within the garden or makes better use of sun and shade patterns. Is the geometry of the garden design varied enough? If round shapes dominate, for example, you might try a new version with diagonal shapes to form garden paths or flower beds.

Including some garden elements in one design and leaving them out in

When developing our prototype garden designs at the Strybing Arboretum in 1993, we engaged in a collaborative process with such professionals as Patrick Miller and Robert Kourik (with Andreas Reimann).

House and garden are integrated as a whole environment in the Chainey/ Schiller Garden, Davis. (Landscape designer: Steve Chainey)

another is also a way to develop garden alternatives. One plan may have a lawn area, the other a ground cover; one may use clipped hedges as screens, the other walls or wooden fences; one may preserve a view while sacrificing some privacy, while the other ensures a secluded spot.

Conflicting goals, such as a view versus privacy, though challenging, often lead to innovation. The solution could involve building a balcony and stairs, thus providing access from a second-floor bedroom to the garden; the balcony has the view, and the garden can be enclosed. In smaller gardens, more conflicts arise because of the limited space, but you should not give up on an idea too quickly. If there is not enough room for a mature fruit tree, for example, what about growing a fruit tree against a wall or fence as an espalier? This solution not only ensures fresh fruit but also leaves space for another garden element.

Any given garden can be arranged in thousands of ways, with diverse plants, forms, styles, objects, colors, and textures. That is not to say that gardeners should develop endless design alternatives; however, it is important not to get stuck on one design concept, without considering other possibilities. Putting two or three garden designs on paper, and then discussing and comparing them, is a way of considering not only what is possible but also what is realistic.

Evaluation and Finalization

Even when you reach a point where everyone involved is certain about what they want and where they want it, it is useful to spend some time looking carefully at the alternative plans for weaknesses that may arise in the near and long term. For example, plants may eventually be too tall or wide for their space, or a planting area that needs partial shade might need to be moved closer to a tree. Perhaps a low hedge will need to be included to direct children past, rather than through, a kitchen garden. A plant screen or overhead vine in one area may obliterate the view from another without constant maintenance, or a pond might be in a location where water runoff from a neighbor's yard will carry unwanted nitrogen fertilizers into it.

It can be helpful to show other people the designs and get their comments. They may, based on their own gardening experience, spot a problem that you have overlooked or offer encouragement about some feature you are reluctant to build.

Once this evaluation process is complete and all the alternatives have been reviewed, you should be able to sit down and draw up a final design: your garden master plan. Check it again against the original goals for the garden, recognizing that even at this stage a design plan can be changed if it does not meet your real needs. Go over it, too, to see if there are changes that could be made to simplify construction.

Now the project becomes more concrete as the actual materials and building methods are decided on, perhaps in consultation with friends or professionals. The design will likely need to be adjusted further once construction costs and schedules are assessed.

FROM PAPER TO GARDEN SITE

As you begin to make concrete decisions about garden elements and materials, it is very helpful to go sit at the garden site with the design schematic. By using everyday objects as surrogates, you can fairly easily imagine the effect planned elements will have. For instance, a garden hose can delineate the precise edges of planting beds, paths, patios, or a pond. Once a particular object is defined, pour a trail of talcum powder or household flour to mark the area it fills. Cardboard or plywood may help you envision how screens will form a garden space, in terms of size, orientation, light, and views. Poles can stand in for trees. And so forth.

Evaluating a design on site can mean discovering pleasing forms and unexpected functions (like little niches for plants) as you respond intuitively to the physical setting itself. It is also an opportunity to fine-tune the design plan by figuring out ways in which native plants and local building materials

Landscape architect Ron Lutsko Jr. adapted patterns found in the local landscape in his design for the Greene Garden in St. Helena. (Ron Lutsko Jr.)

can be put to use as they become available. One beauty of the California landscape garden is that it evolves out of its environment and is amenable to being crafted in stages, once the larger design elements that shape the garden's form and function are in place.

SUSTAINABLE DESIGN ELEMENTS

Creating a Microclimate

The garden's microclimate can be easily manipulated through design, in turn benefiting the home in terms of heating and cooling needs. Ambient air temperature, for example, can be controlled through the use of arbors, shade trees, and the orientation of sitting areas relative to the sun, and air flow can be manipulated by means of wind screens. Influencing sunlight and wind also affects the ambient humidity. These atmospheric aspects play an important role in the choice and location of plants and garden activities.

Windscreens, in particular, are a useful addition to almost any garden. Not only do they help define outdoor spaces, or "rooms," but in their ability to divert wind they also affect the microclimate of the home. This makes the garden more comfortable, both for people and for small wildlife that may appreciate the shelter provided, such as butterflies and songbirds. In addition, shielding a building from the wind can have a significant savings effect on energy consumption: a conventional wood-frame building, for example, can be made as much as 10 to 15 percent more energy-efficient simply by protecting it from the wind. In areas where summers are hot, trees and large shrubs, which transpire more heavily than smaller plantings, may be relatively cool on their lee side when a summer breeze blows past or through them. A screen of vegetation can also help to purify the air of dust and pollutants by simple filtration and by reducing wind speed, allowing suspended particles to drop out.[3]

Diverting the force of wind can be a science in itself, since different screens produce different results. Dense barriers like a wall block the wind efficiently, but their effect is confined to the immediate vicinity and they create turbulence downwind. Thickly planted vegetation, such as a grouping of coniferous trees, doesn't completely block the wind, but it effectively reduces wind speed over a distance of several tree lengths, and it produces less turbulence by allowing a portion of the air to pass through.

Although major cooling winter winds in California generally blow from a northwesterly direction, a region's topography can create diverse local effects. The garden site must be evaluated carefully in this regard, with hedges or other garden wind screens oriented in the direction of the strongest winds that buffet the area.

Choosing Surface Materials

Pavement certainly has advantages, especially in high-use areas of the garden, since it does not need to be watered and is fairly easy to take care of. A combination of paving and drought-tolerant shrubs and ground covers offers great versatility to meet design goals: the pavement organizes the garden and allows for movement, and the plants add sensory elements of texture and contrast. Several environmentally friendly paving materials exist, allowing a range of functional and aesthetic effects. These include adobe pavers, mulched garden refuse, and broken concrete.

An alternative to pavement in areas of the garden with moderate to low foot traffic is bare earth, possibly amended with sand or decomposed granite. Some trees, like eucalyptus and Monterey cypress, do not allow plants to grow nearby; this suppression of other species by the release of toxic substances, a process called allelopathy, leads to a bare surface and open views under such plants, which may be a desirable design aspect. An accent element, such as a hanging basket with stag fern or displayed art, can nicely set off the spacious simplicity of allelopathic plants.

Mulch, often generated by the plants themselves, is an effective, even beautiful, surface under trees and large shrubs, and in many cases is perfectly adapted for passive activities such as picnics. Where foot traffic over mulched surfaces is necessary, the area can be stabilized with gravel, sand, or decomposed granite.

Ground Sculpting with Blocks

Spaces can be defined quite effectively by changes in elevation. A sunken square of adobe or brick with steps leading down to it, for example, provides an inviting seating area and puts surrounding flowers closer to eye level. An elevated patio with a wide, spacious step leading up to it, or a raised bed of herbs in the back of the garden, can make even a small garden look elegantly distinctive. Retaining walls of various heights add interesting topographical detail and, in combination with paths, steps, arbors, or other features, can create a strong focal point for the garden. Planting beds that are placed higher than access paths can be enjoyed more easily and are more convenient to care for. A change in levels may also set off a planting bed from the lawn area.

Multiple levels may be organized in a variety of geometrical orientations. For example, instead of relying on a straightforward square layout, you might place a retaining wall at an angle to the house, or build one with a curve to it. Such unusual orientations and shapes lead to a more diversified spatial arrangement, lending added interest to the garden as a whole.

Large adobe block is an especially adaptable and environmentally sound building material for low retaining walls, patios, and steps. If the changing levels do not exceed two to three feet, the blocks can be laid dry (without concrete mortar); this allows flexibility in layout when, for instance, a larger patio or a larger planting bed is desired. It is also possible to combine adobe blocks with other building materials such as brick or recycled concrete or bottles. A gravel and sand base under the adobe pavers provides a level, stable foundation and helps ensure good drainage.

Construction with Rustic Poles

Imagine accessing the garden from your living room via a spacious patio overhung with a grid of rustic wood or bamboo poles that supports lush, fragrant vines. Natural textures, aromas, colors, and contrasts all invite you to go outdoors. Tied together as fencing or used to support a plant screen, rustic poles offer both function and character as they form appealing gateways into garden spaces, create privacy or shade, provide an architectural accent, frame a view, or mark an edge of a flower bed. Along similar lines, a beanpole teepee can give children a place to organize their outdoor playthings or drape wet play clothes.

Like all organic material, rustic wood and bamboo poles decompose over time and need to be replaced periodically—as often as every ten years in a moist climate, depending on the type of wood used and whether the poles are able to dry out between damp periods. Although protecting untreated wood from moisture will help to preserve it (keeping the entire structure above ground, for example), the design of any rustic wood framework should allow for periodic replacement of individual components. Bamboo is an especially useful material for a standing structure if the structure is designed with replacement in mind. The hollow bamboo is simply slipped over pipe or steel posts secured in the ground; when it comes time for replacement, the poles can just be pulled off their supports.

Plants and pole structures can create garden rooms and provide shade.

If rustic poles are being used to build a shade structure, another strategy for their eventual replacement would be to simultaneously plant young trees. When the stability of the poles begins to wane, the trees will likely be large enough to take over the job of providing shade.

Poles can be attached to each other and to the ground in various ways. Wire ties are a straightforward method, and practical as well: when tied rather than nailed, the poles are able to shrink, twist, and turn as they dry. Larger poles, say four to five inches in diameter, can be bound with annealed iron wire (no. 9), which is then retied after the poles have shrunk. To attach a bundle of small-diameter poles to the ground, simply tie them to a bracket that is embedded in a concrete base.

Young eucalyptus saplings make useful and attractive poles if they are worked while they are still green; the bark is left in place so that the poles dry slowly and evenly. After the wood has dried, however, it is very hard—so much so that it is difficult to use nails for construction. Also, as the wood dries it can twist quite severely, forming deep cracks. These drying problems are

Willow branches can take root and make a creative play space for children.

less serious with saplings two to four inches in diameter. An attachment method appropriate for unruly eucalyptus poles is to fasten two members with a rebar hook that is driven through drilled holes.

Living Structures

Nature can do some of the work in the garden if plants are placed strategically or trained to make a living structure. Green garden rooms can be defined by placing trees or woody shrubs around their perimeters. Trees planted in a circle, in rows, or in a grid, by making a regular, formal pattern, might replace an architectural screen, shade structure, or entryway; they may also contrast beautifully in color, texture, and form with the hard surfaces of adjacent paving, walls, or buildings.

Some of the most effective garden designs are based on tree- or shrub-lined vistas that may, for instance, dramatize the entrance into a front yard. Planting two rows of shrubs or small trees and tying the upper branches together to form a sequence of arches, with openings for views and patterns of light and shade, gives the effect of a tree alley in a small garden.

Woody vines open up an entire realm of possibilities for the creation of living structures. For example, around the periphery of a dome-shaped structure constructed with long slender branches—which on its own would last only five to ten years—can be planted a series of vines that develop thick woody stems, such as grapevines. As the vines grow and are trained to twine through the structure, they eventually support themselves, and soon *they* are the structure.

Trailing plants can also be used in gazebos, pavilions, and trellises; only a frame need be built, for the plants themselves create the walls or ceiling. Once a simple structure is dominated by a screen of green vegetation, small ornamental details give the entire composition great aesthetic appeal. Medieval European gardens, as seen in sketches from those days, provide especially good examples of the masterful inclusion of classical accents in living structures.

Construction with Metal

The properties of metal—strength, durability, and versatility—make this material highly appropriate for use in garden structures ranging from delicate hanging plant stands to heavy, overhead archways. You can find salvaged or commercially available metal in a variety of forms and sizes, including sheets, bars, and square or angled shafts that can be bolted or welded together. A fun

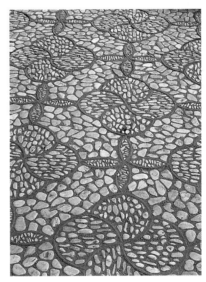

Left: *Metal structures create shadow and drama in the Randall/Denny Garden in Marin County. (Landscape architect: Topher Delaney, of Delaney, Cochran & Castillo; photograph by Topher Delaney)*

Below: *Stone pebbles found locally create an eye-catching paving pattern in the garden.*

and easy project to make with metal shafts is an archway or gate, where trailing plants provide much of the texture and color in the arrangement. The use of a metal archway to mark an entryway or a place where paths cross, as in a vegetable garden, can be especially appealing.

Ceramic and Pebble Mosaics

Collections of broken pieces of ceramic, colored plastic, shells, or rocks can be composed into striking and original garden surfaces, either on the ground or embedded as mosaics in stucco or plaster walls. Salvaged and collected materials bring added personal and environmental meaning, but if you are in a hurry you can also obtain remnants from tile installers and stores that sell floor coverings.

A particularly inspirational example of mosaic art can be seen at Watts Towers in Los Angeles, which was constructed over several decades by an Italian immigrant, Simon Rodia. He used salvaged pipe, steel, concrete, shells, rejected tiles, and bottles to construct an incredible assortment of walls, wall openings, passages, and delicately ribbed towers.

More subtle mosaics employing small stones are a traditional art form in many Asian and Mediterranean cultures. Pebbles, abundant in many soils and along waterways, are set on end, slightly higher than the finished surface will be, in a wet mixture of clay and sand or on decomposed granite; they are then pressed evenly with a board. The pattern may be geometrically formal or more organic and undulating. Pebbles can also easily be combined with brick, broken concrete, or flagstone to form bold, dynamic patterns.

THE EVOLVING CALIFORNIA LANDSCAPE GARDEN

One of the most powerful elements of a garden is the way it reflects human activities and inputs, which, of course, change with time. Seeing evidence of people's evolving interests or hobbies—healthy vegetables growing, a comfortable chair by a table with an open book, or a water spray for birds—makes a garden seem more alive.

Time acts on the garden itself as well. Certain plants, and the surface patina of some materials, may become more beautiful with age. On the other hand, planting beds can also become overfilled and scruffy looking, as favorite plants are crowded out and garden objects grow rusty and cracked. The salvaged materials and other found objects that were placed so carefully begin to seem more like clutter than like special treasures.

The time will come when you will want to get rid of lackluster objects and spruce things up. The children may appreciate clearing an area under a tree or helping to prune the tree, making it easier to climb. Or perhaps the children are grown and a play area that is no longer used needs to be refurbished. The original goals of any garden will inevitably change. It is important to revisit those goals occasionally and make appropriate adjustments.

Time also affects our knowledge of how the bioregional landscape garden functions as a natural system. As gardeners observe their designs in action and interact with other gardeners, they acquire new insights and information—about the availability and needs of native plants, about ways of encouraging beneficial garden insects, about new building materials for sustainable designs. Such practical knowledge can be put to use in a garden over the years to improve its ecological potential.

All of this is to say that a well-loved, well-used landscape garden is dynamic, never static; it evolves together with the needs of a family and the specific characteristics of the site more than any other type of garden. It is never "finished." The relationship between a gardener and this special place is ongoing. Keeping this in mind, you would do well to review the garden's base plan periodically and make a new overlay, noting changes that might improve the way the garden meets your needs and responds to the natural region around you. For at the end of the day, nature has the last word on design, and it is a lifetime pursuit to stay attentive to the meaning of what we see around us.

> Nature is already, in its forms and tendencies, describing its own design. Let us interrogate the great apparition that shines so peacefully around us. Let us inquire, to what end is nature?
>
> Ralph Waldo Emerson, *Nature*

CHAPTER FIVE

PLANTING THE LANDSCAPE GARDEN

Arcadia, if we may speak broadly, is a place where human beings cooperate with nature to produce a richness of ecological variety that would not otherwise exist. . . . Perhaps it is a country of the mind only, but we can see traces of it in the hills of Tuscany, the hedgerow and beech landscape of the Cotswolds, the savannas of Africa.

Frederick Turner, "A Field Guide to the Synthetic Landscape"

The greatest inspiration for the landscape garden is found, as we have seen, in the spiritual, multicultural, technological, and ecological mosaic that is the larger garden called California. We have seen how each native habitat—a home that meets the multiple needs of a particular community of plants and wildlife—has been crafted historically from local natural conditions. We have also seen how human impacts have fragmented what was once a statewide biosystem that supported an astounding diversity of life. The clock cannot be turned back; we must instead learn how to move forward, garden by garden,

Plants create habitat for people and other living things. (Landscape designer: David Buchanan)

and reknit habitats. The building blocks of this new landscape garden are soil, climate, site, and especially plants.

Native plants that have declined in or disappeared from a region are potentially among the most meaningful elements of the garden. In addition to providing a rich aesthetic, native plants can help tie together remaining fragments of natural habitat in a conservation "patch" or "corridor." According to Dennis Murphy, director of the Center for Conservation Biology at Stanford University, the restoration of natural landscape elements in urban and suburban neighborhoods that are now dominated by introduced species may be the single greatest contribution to conservation an individual can make.

Informed gardeners working together can pool their influence in the area of resource conservation. The California landscape garden aims to restore an equilibrium between people and nature, relying on native and certain naturalized species that have proven their worth in terms of both wildlife and human values.

Trees evoke a sense of place and restore habitat in the Strybing Arboretum, San Francisco. (Landscape architect: Ron Lutsko Jr.)

CALIFORNIA'S FLORA

Some facts and figures about California's floristic community will provide clues about how to bring more of wild nature into our own backyards. In Chapter 3 we discussed the importance of regional vegetation in defining the appropriate character of a landscape garden. The term *vegetation* refers to a general vegetative cover, such as dense forest, grassland, or oak woodland. The term *flora,* on the other hand, refers to the plant species of a region. For example, the flora of Kern County comprises about 1,700 species of plants, while the vegetation of Kern County includes grassland, pine forest, and freshwater marsh—the descriptive names of which also point to a dominant type of

Plants can connect the garden—visually, historically, and naturally—with the larger landscape, as at Stoney Hill Ranch. (Landscape architect: Ron Lutsko Jr.; photograph by Lutsko Associates)

plant (grass, pine, reed). The vegetation of two regions might be the same, but their floras are likely to be quite different, from the dominant species on down. In the pine forest of the Point Reyes peninsula, for instance, the dominant species is the Bishop pine, while in the northern Sierra it is the whitebark pine, and the associated plant species accordingly vary considerably. The point is, it is worthwhile to pay attention not only to the general type of local vegetation but also to regionally native species when planning your garden.

The ten bioregions of California contain nearly one thousand distinctive plant communities, with slightly more than five thousand named species of native vascular plants (including ferns, conifers, and flowering plants).[1] About 40 percent of these species are restricted to a specific locality or habitat, generally because of exacting soil or climate needs.

One-third of California's native plants are found nowhere else in the world. Currently, moreover, more than 850 plant species in California are classified as rare and endangered, while 34 others are known to have become extinct between the Spanish mission period and modern times. The dynamic plant communities that once consisted solely of native species now include an estimated 975 introduced weedy species. Such changes have had a profound impact on natural systems and resulted in a loss of wildlife diversity.

The widespread disappearance of plants, butterflies, frogs, and other wildlife from the California landscape is a dire indicator of the decline in the native habitats that once supported them. This loss of biodiversity is of grave environmental concern generally. Yet it is in this realm that a gardener can make a difference. The following discussion briefly introduces some important considerations regarding plants in the California landscape garden: the meaning of plant names, planting design principles, how plants are selected and placed in the garden, and how they are cultivated within a garden habitat.

PLANT NAMES

Native Americans thought that by naming a thing—whether plant, animal, or inanimate object—humans could know the spirit of that thing. Names were descriptive, often having a geographical component, and were intended to reveal relationships. Today, the names we have given California's bioregions, habitats, and plants have much the same functions. Through taxonomy, the science of classification (from the Greek *taxis,* "arrangement," and *nomos,* "law"), much can be understood about the plants living in a particular area. Learning the scientific and common names of plants makes them all the more familiar and valued.

A study of the Latin names of even a couple of species will quickly illustrate just how much can be learned about an organism's unique character. For instance, the California fan palm, native to the deserts of southern California, is called *Washingtonia filifera;* the species name, *filifera,* describes the fibrous appearance of its much-folded leaves, which are torn nearly to the middle. In the case of the picturesque California sycamore, the genus name, *Platanus* (from the Greek *platýs,* "flat"), refers to the wide growth habit and the broad radial leaf, while the species name, *racemosa,* describes the unique ball-like clusters that are distributed along a slender, pendulous stalk.

The systematic nomenclature begins with grouping the biotic world into five kingdoms: Animalia, Plantae, Monera (bacteria), Fungi, and Protista (mainly one-celled plants and animals). Six hierarchical steps, from more inclusive to very specific, follow: phylum (or, for plants, division), class, order, family, genus, and species, the latter referring to a group of like individuals. Generally we pay attention only to the binomial combination of genus and

Learning the names of plants makes them all the more familiar and interesting.

species (as in *Washingtonia filifera* and *Platanus racemosa* above), which, like a person's first and last name, reveals shared botanical characteristics and clues to family relationships that are important for choosing plants for the garden.

Hybridization illustrates why it is important to understand something of plant taxonomy. In this naturally occurring process, plants respond to environmental changes, stresses, and competition by cross-pollinating, thus ensuring the continuation of genetic stock. When humans intervene, however, a new dimension is added. Certain native plants—manzanita, ceanothus, and oak, for example—hybridize readily. These genera, moreover, often have distinct regional species, such as coast manzanita and valley foothill manzanita. If brought into proximity with each other, these species will cross-pollinate to form hybrids with characteristics of both parent plants; the result is plants that are less adapted to local conditions and less useful to native wildlife. By moving plants from one location to another, in short, people can inadvertently erode the original character and value of the well-adapted native.

Plants are often deliberately hybridized as well, usually to encourage a desirable characteristic—especially colorful blossoms, unusual form, or disease resistance, for example. Such plants need to be propagated vegetatively (by cuttings) so they don't lose their specific characteristics. They can be easily recognized in a nursery by their third, varietal, name, such as *Ceanothus griseus* var. 'Monterey'.

PLANTING DESIGN

Plant selection and composition are part of a larger design process in which the general layout and organization of the garden comes into play, including its use areas, pathways, and planting beds.[2] One of the first steps in this process involves selecting compatible plant species with which to compose the entire garden scene—much as an artist chooses a color palette before beginning to paint. In this way a natural-looking setting, even with some added formal design elements, can be achieved (see "Mary Wattis Brown Garden," below).

As discussed in Chapter 3, a valuable approach to successful planting design lies in observing native plant communities and following nature's cues. Along the coast, for example, you might get ideas from walking through low-growing, moundlike coastal sage communities or, in more inland areas, from chaparral or streamside vegetative communities. In a high mountain

Rather than being hidden out of sight, the vegetable patch can be a central feature of the landscape garden. (Landscape architects: Patrick and Jane Miller, 2M Associates; photograph by Jane Miller)

MARY WATTIS BROWN GARDEN

The Mary Wattis Brown Garden at the University Arboretum, University of California, Davis, is the focal point of the extensive native plant collection at the UC Davis Arboretum. It serves as a demonstration garden for plants native to California's Central Valley, featuring water-conserving, drought-tolerant, and low-maintenance design strategies. It is also a research collection and study area for the arboretum staff and a place for landscape architecture and plant science students to learn native plant taxonomy. The garden is divided into several areas, including a Mid-Elevation Garden, a Silver and Red Garden, a Dark Wood Shrub Island, and a Shady Grove area under oaks. Designed by landscape architect Cheryl Mihalko in the early 1990s, this accessible public garden is an excellent place to gain inspiration for the use of native plants in a home garden.

The Wolfe Garden exemplifies effective planting design. (Landscape architect: Topher Delaney, of Delaney, Cochran & Castillo; photograph by Topher Delaney)

region, inspiration might come from montane meadows and alpine fell-fields, while at intermediate elevations sagebrush scrub, Joshua tree woodland, and creosote bush scrub communities may spark your imagination. Pay attention to soil and moisture needs as well as to plant associations, growth habits, and colors and textures.

The scale of the natural environment will of course not match your garden scale. When making final selections, carefully assess each plant's size, in relationship both to other plants and to the garden itself. On a traced copy of your final garden plan, sketch in the proposed plant choices, using a size equivalent to two-thirds of the plant's mature growth. By doing this, you will avoid large problems and smaller disappointments. Small plants, for example, often tend to be placed where they are easily overlooked and have little effect. A sketch will make such potential problems apparent and help you identify alternative design options, such as a rock garden, which, intended to be admired up close, is ideal for showcasing smaller specimens.

It is critical to keep the basic design elements of color, line, texture,

The purpose of design is to create places of activity and enjoyment.

composition, and form in mind when planning a landscape garden. The colors, forms, and textures of plants can be made to work together to create contrast in the garden composition, making it readable. Plants of similar texture and color range, for example, may be massed, with one or two contrasting elements—such as grasses, brightly colored stems, or the stark forms of agaves—providing an accent. Or you might juxtapose dark green with light green foliage, or smooth or feathery foliage with coarse or statuesque plants. Plants with gray-green foliage or large, variegated leaves help make shady gardens lighter and more visually inviting. Unusual bark, branches, or seed capsules can also be used to lend interest and structure to the overall composition.

Seasonal changes can be taken advantage of to give the garden year-round appeal. The bright green, gray-green, and especially silver foliage of so many coastal natives, for instance, stands out in ever altering hues through periods of spring growth, bloom, maturing of fruit or capsules, and dropping of leaves. For inland gardens the inclusion of dark green shrubs affords an attractive contrast to the beautiful tans and golds that develop during the summer dormancy of grasses.

Composition also sets the stage for special sensory effects that will draw people into the garden again and again. Feathery grasses in an open area that sparkle with morning dew or catch the afternoon breeze; a vine trained on a breezeway trellis providing both shade and fragrance—such effects catch the attention and enhance peaceful enjoyment. Light can be used to create surprising visual effects and natural art. A simple way to achieve an intense experience of color is to position plants with thin leaves or translucent flowers so that they are between a viewer and the sun. When light shines through the autumn leaves of vine maple or the petals of western azalea, for example, they appear to glow with radiant color, like a stained-glass window.

PLANT SELECTION

When selecting plants for the California landscape garden, several factors must be considered, including climate zones, wildlife value, and plant conservation. You can learn about plants that might work well in your yard—their needs for space, light, and water and their aesthetic potential—by visiting a nursery that specializes in native species. Do not forget to consider seasonal changes that will affect the plants' form and appearance. Also, keep your own interests in mind, such as bird or butterfly watching, plant breeding and propagation, the cultivation of medicinal or culinary herbs, and maintaining a supply of cut or dried flowers, fruits, nuts, or craft materials.

Regional Climatic Zones

Geographic features such as topography, altitude, proximity to the coast, and latitude to a certain extent define a local area's weather patterns—the typical range of temperature, moisture, available light, prevailing winds—and hence the local environment for plant growth. For example, California's outer Coast Ranges (next to the Pacific Ocean) receive much more fog, and therefore extra moisture and cooling, than the middle Coast Ranges, which receive intermittent fog, and the inner Coast Ranges (the foothills bounding the Central Valley on the west), which lack coastal fog entirely. In addition, strong summer winds prevail along the outer Coast Ranges and are absent from the inner ranges. These significant differences in climate as one travels the relatively short distance between the ocean and the Central Valley are reflected by significant differences in plant communities, which serve as a reliable guide to narrowing plant choices for a landscape garden in any given locale.[3]

Plants with Wildlife Value

Native plants and a number of naturalized plants have great potential in home landscapes in part because of their importance for local wildlife. Wildlife-attracting plants have one or more of three key characteristics: they produce food, such as nectar, pollen, seeds, or fruit; they provide cover for nesting, perching, roosting, or hiding; and they host a diversity of insects for insect-foraging vertebrates like birds. A foundation plant such as a sage (*Salvia* spp.) or rose (*Rosa* spp.), placed in a sunny location, will meet all three criteria and almost certainly will be visited by an assortment of local butterflies and birds.

A diverse selection of wildlife-attracting plants will supply food year round by coming into season at various times. Deciduous plants offer an abundance of tender new growth in spring, and even the decaying parts (including fruit) of both deciduous and evergreen plants can provide sustenance for many forms of wildlife throughout the year.

The table on the following page lists an assortment of native trees, shrubs, perennials, annuals, and grasses that supply one or more of the necessary amenities for attracting wildlife to the garden. The list includes widely distributed species with various forms; where only a genus is mentioned, it is useful to survey local growing conditions and garden characteristics and consider whether the plants are native to your region before deciding which species will work best in your garden. Most of these species are susceptible to root rot with overwatering and require good drainage (see Chapter 6 for advice on amending clay soils or using planting mounds to improve drainage).

The Garden Conservationist

County historical sources can help you identify species that may be candidates for conservation in a landscape garden. A good place to start is the California Native Plant Society (CNPS) in Sacramento, which can furnish you with a list of regional natural history publications and the phone number of the CNPS chapter nearest your home. Nurseries that specialize in native plants can also help you determine which native plants are still common in your area, as well as which ones are no longer common and may even be endangered. A garden planted with relatively common natives creates links within the larger landscape by decreasing the isolation of species still resident in the area.

Trees

Aesculus californica. CALIFORNIA BUCKEYE. The California buckeye, one of the showiest small native trees of California's Mediterranean-climate regions, has an overall broad shape and blooms in showy, fragrant clusters 6–10 inches long at the ends of its branches. The California buckeye is dormant from late summer to winter; during this period, pear-shaped seed capsules give sculptural effects and supply a favorite element for fall flower arrangements. It is a very significant late-spring nectar source for many butterflies and a larval host for some. Hummingbirds and a good variety of other interesting insects are also attracted to the flowers. Flower buds are relished by gray squirrels.

Alnus rhombifolia. WHITE ALDER. This fast-growing deciduous native tree grows along rivers and perennial streams throughout California. It is especially effective planted in groups. Its seeds attract goldfinches and pine siskins, and numerous other birds forage for insects in its foliage. The white alder adds nitrogen to the soil through its nitrogen-rich leaves, which decay quickly.

Arbutus menziesii. MADRONE. This native tree, distinguished by its attractive reddish-brown bark, is common in central to northern coastal regions. The early-spring flowers are a choice nectar source for hummingbirds, and the early-fall berries are very popular with cedar waxwings, mockingbirds, acorn woodpeckers, Steller's jays, towhees, flickers, and a variety of other birds. The madrone is also host to a variety of mushrooms, which in turn are a food source for many creatures.

Heteromeles arbutifolia. TOYON. A handsome native evergreen shrub or small tree, common on brushy slopes in California, the toyon has conspicuous red or orange berries in winter. The flowers attract a good number and variety of insects. Many birds favor the fruits, including robins, thrushes, bluebirds, titmice, wrentits, and red-breasted sapsuckers.

Pinus spp. PINE. California is home to a large variety of native pines, and they have tremendous wildlife value. Many birds, such as jays, mourning doves, pine siskins, juncos, and nuthatches, eat the pine nuts. Gray squirrels and chipmunks also eat both the pine seed and the mush-rooms that grow in association with the trees. Other plant parts and sap are also consumed. Pines are preferred foraging and nesting trees for many birds.

Quercus spp. OAK. Native California oaks are often mentioned for their outstanding habitat value. Along with their leaves and acorns, the associated mushrooms, galls, lichens, and mistletoe all support wildlife. More than 250 species of birds in California use these trees for food, cover, and nesting. The many types of insects associated with the tree and its litter feed every insect-eating creature. Gray squirrels, gophers, ground squirrels, raccoons, and deer are commonly seen in and around oak woodlands. The leaves of oak trees are larval hosts for some of the most spectacular California butterflies. One of them is the blue and yellow California sister, which returns to a favorite perch after patrolling the area.

Salix spp. WILLOW. Native willows make up a diverse group of fast-growing and easy-to-care-for deciduous shrubs and trees. Willows are popular with birds for perching, nesting, and foraging for insects. The young buds and unripe seed capsules are readily eaten by goldfinches, warblers, thrushes, flycatchers, and other birds. Native willows host a great diversity of insects, including interesting gall-forming insects and beautiful butterflies, such as the large yellow and black western tiger swallowtail. The very early flowers of willows are rich in nectar, attracting bees and other insects. The abundant spring growth and consequent quantity of leaf litter provide a habitat for a diverse community of microorganisms.

Shrubs

Arctostaphylos spp. MANZANITA. These attractive native shrubs and ground covers offer excellent cover for wildlife. A variety of birds, such as quail, mockingbirds, thrushes, towhees, jays, wrentits, and acorn woodpeckers, also visit manzanita to forage for insects or eat the bell-shaped flowers or fruit that looks like tiny apples.

Baccharis pilularis. COYOTE BRUSH. These native shrubs (also known as dwarf chaparral broom), familiar in many California biotic communities, are excellent cover plants with dense foliage that are useful in difficult growing situations. The fluffy flowers of the female plant attract butterflies (for instance, the distinctive buckeye butterfly, marked by a large and a small eyespot on each wing), skippers, bees, and other insects. Coyote brush can be started from seed if female plants are unavailable. Cutting back the coyote brush every second or third year improves its appearance and vitality.

Berberis spp. MAHONIA. This handsome low shrub provides excellent wildlife cover, and many birds eat the fruit. The genus includes species that thrive in either moist or dry areas and range in height from low ground cover to small tree.

Ceanothus spp. WILD LILAC. One of the most attractive and well known of native California shrubs, the ceanothus is also a superb nectar plant and larval host plant for butterflies, including the California tortoiseshell, an orange butterfly with black lining and spots. The flowers are also very attractive to bees, more so than other plants. Birds such as wrentits, thrushes, sparrows, towhees, finches, and juncos forage for insects in the litter beneath the wild lilac.

Cornus sericea and *C. glabrata.* DOGWOOD. These tall, deciduous native shrubs of California foothills grow in moist locations along drainage ways. Small white flowers and fruit attract many birds, including flickers, black-headed grosbeaks, Swainson's thrushes, orioles, vireos, and woodpeckers. Some birds select dogwoods also for insect foraging and nesting. Dogwoods grow fast and tolerate garden watering and shade, but they fruit best in sunny locations.

Eriogonum spp. BUCKWHEAT. Native buckwheats adapt well as sculptural small shrubs in gardens. The nectar-rich blooms are magnets to visiting butterflies, beetles, and other interesting insects. Different species of native buckwheat serve as the single host plant for some of California's endangered butterflies.

Holodiscus discolor. CREAM BUSH. This deciduous native occurs on moist hillsides or canyons from Los Angeles County to British Columbia, including inland foothills. It is very handsome when the creamy-white flower clusters cover the shrub in late spring. The mass of flowers as well as the soft deciduous foliage attracts insects, followed by chickadees, warblers, wrens, and other birds. Hummingbirds visit the flowers as well. The cream bush is also a larval host for butterflies, such as the beautiful

pale swallowtail, which is sometimes seen flying around the summits of exposed hills.

Lonicera involucrata and *L. subspicata.* TWINBERRY and CHAPARRAL HONEYSUCKLE. These vinelike deciduous shrubs, both native to California, provide preferred nesting sites for birds, and the berries are favored by many birds as well.

Rhamnus californica. COFFEEBERRY. Birds like to forage for insects in and near these native evergreen shrubs typical of the California chaparral. Many other birds like to eat the fruit, which turns from green to red to black with age. There are several varieties of coffeeberry, varying in foliage, height, and form.

Rhamnus crocea. REDBERRY. This smaller relative of the coffeeberry, a native to the Coast Ranges, is also a useful plant for birds. It has short, spiny branches and is an adaptable garden plant.

Ribes spp. WILD GOOSEBERRIES and CURRANTS. All *Ribes* species furnish nectar for hummingbirds, while their berries and sometimes flowers are eaten by many birds, including quail, robins, goldfinches, flickers, and chickadees. California has thirty-one native species, divided nearly equally between those that grow in dry places and those that do best in moist habitat.

Rosa californica. CALIFORNIA ROSE. This native plant makes good wildlife cover. The attractive hips are relished by pine siskins, goldfinches, vireos, thrushes, California quail, and other birds.

Salvia spp. SAGE. All salvias provide nectar for hummingbirds, especially *S. spathacea,* hummingbird sage, native to the central and southern coastal mountains of California. Other birds may visit to eat the seeds. Native creeping sage *(S. sonomensis)* is very effective combined with lupine and native bulbs in semi-dry borders.

Sambucus mexicana. BLUE ELDERBERRY. The blue fruit clusters are a favorite food source for many birds, and the flowers are showy and fragrant. In addition, this upright native shrub provides excellent cover and nesting opportunities and hosts a diversity of interesting insects.

Perennials

Achillea millefolium. COMMON YARROW. This popular garden plant with fernlike leaves and flat white flower heads is readily visited by many beetles and butterflies. One of the more successful garden varieties is *A. millefolium* 'Fire King', which has gray foliage and dark reddish flowers.

Asclepias spp. MILKWEED. The common milkweeds are interesting additions to mixed borders. They have elongated leaves, and some have showy white to purple flowers. Milkweed is an excellent nectar source for bees, bumblebees, butterflies, a variety of wasps, and many other insects, and it is the host plant for the monarch butterfly. *A. californica*, *A. cordifolia*, and *A. speciosa* are especially useful for the California garden.

Aster lentus. CHILEAN ASTER. This native perennial with purple flowers is especially valuable in wet borders as a late-summer and fall source of nectar, though any small-flowered aster is a good nectar source. Birds also like the seeds.

Heracleum lanatum. COW PARSNIP. A sculptural flower stalk that, though not native to California, attracts a tremendous number and variety of insects, especially beetles.

Monardella spp. MONARDELLA. Twenty species of monardella are native to California, and about half of these are evergreen. Coyote mint *(M. villosa)* is a favorite among gardeners, with low, fragrant mounds and delicate flower stems that attract bees and butterflies.

Perideridia spp. YAMPAH. *Yampah* is the Native American term for a plant that forms edible root-tubers, shoots, and flowers. This little-known plant, which grows in heavy clay, is graceful and has the advantage of being late flowering. Doubtless it is edible by many creatures besides humans.

Sidalcea malvaeflora. CHECKER HOLLYHOCK. This handsome low perennial for borders or rock gardens is a larval host to several California butterflies, including the pretty West Coast lady.

Solanum umbelliferum. BLUE WITCH. Part of the nightshade family, blue witch can be used in a sunny perennial border and produces an abundance of small fruit that are relished by many birds. A warning: the berries are poisonous to humans.

Solidago californica. CALIFORNIA GOLDENROD. The showy yellow plumes of goldenrods are excellent additions to any sunny perennial border. They are a superb source of nectar and highly attractive to butterflies.

Urtica holosericea. NETTLE. Nettles, while not spectacular, are very important larval hosts for a variety of butterflies, including the red admiral, satyr angelwing, Milbert's tortoiseshell, and painted lady. Nettles like nitrogen-rich soil and some moisture, so they may be just right for the out-of-the-way compost corner.

Annuals

Many California annuals supply nectar, pollen, and seeds for birds and insects. They include California poppy, tidy tips, *Linanthus* spp., miner's lettuce, Chinese houses, columbines, and *Phacelia* spp. In addition, most members of the sunflower family, such as cosmos, black-eyed Susan, bachelors' buttons, *Coreopsis* spp., and marigolds, are useful nonnative additions in the habitat garden.

Grasses

Bunchgrasses are popular intermixed among other perennials and shrubs in the garden. Both leaves and seeds are quite edible and thus attractive to wildlife. Grass tufts also provide excellent cover. Moreover, the fibrous root systems of grasses build up the soil, feeding many creatures beneath the soil's surface. Like many other native plants, native grasses support California communities of butterflies and other interesting insects. The native bunchgrasses also offer better-quality foliage and produce less seed than the introduced annuals, thus favoring voles and harvest mice rather than ground squirrels, which are mostly seed eaters.

(SOURCE: Compiled from Hickman 1993 with the help of Jeff Caldwell)

Mediterranean and native plants depend on an extensive root system to survive long dry periods. This characteristic causes them to become easily root-bound in pots: if circles of roots fill the bottom of the pot, that means the plant has been forced to grow too long or too fast in the container and it will likely not do well in the garden. When selecting nursery plants, therefore, it is best to lean toward plants that look too small for the pot they're in. Exceptions include many perennials, which often rejuvenate quickly after constriction in a nursery container.

The Right Tree for the Right Spot

Tree planting is an investment in the future. The right kind of tree planted in the right location is a long-term asset that provides a great many human and wildlife amenities. The opposite, however, is also true. It is tragic when a ten-year-old tree, just entering its prime, has to be torn out because it was planted where its roots interfere with a sidewalk, foundation, or sewer line or its branches obstruct overhead utility wires. Another common problem that also typically is solved by tree removal is the leaf, flower, fruit, or pollen litter of many trees when they are planted too near a use area. Some of these problems can be avoided if trees are planted at least ten feet from a building and ten feet away from walls and other permanent structures. In addition, it is important to make sure that the tree's cultural requirements—fertilizer and water—are compatible with nearby plants and structures.

The shade that a tree will eventually broadcast can influence the growth or even survival of other plants in the garden as well as garden activities. Often, however, shade poses little problem. Indeed, dappled shade is perfectly suited to many use areas, such as decks and patios, and even deep shade makes no difference in utility areas such as driveways or garbage can storage areas. In warm climates, moreover, shade for the house and parts of the garden can save on cooling costs, and it makes the garden inviting during hot afternoons.

The smaller the garden, the more important it is to consider the placement of trees carefully. All of the problems mentioned above are exacerbated when a tree is too large for its space, and one other problem is posed as well: planting a tree that causes unwanted shade, litter, or roots on a neighbor's property can lead to serious, even legal, disputes.

Native trees are used for a dramatic sense of entry (Landscape architect: Ann Christoph).

California's nature offers from several up to dozens of native trees that are suitable for any garden below the high Sierra tree line. Within each genus, moreover, shrublike forms and even ground covers can be found that make good companion plants for their larger relatives. Of these natives, oaks are especially appealing, in part because of their ability to create a truly Californian sense of place (see table, opposite, and "A Family's Woodland Garden," pp. 128–129). For example, huckleberry oak *(Quercus vaccinifolia)*, a low, spreading evergreen shrub; scrub oak *(Q. dumosa)*, an evergreen shrub three to ten feet tall; and black oak *(Q. kelloggii)*, a deciduous tree thirty to eighty feet tall, are often planted together in wild gardens of the foothills and mountains for both erosion control and aesthetic compatibility.

For oak seedlings to grow successfully, it is important to reduce the competition from nearby plants. A deep mulch of organic litter helps to control weeds such as annual grasses while supplying the seedling with necessary nutrients. In addition, care must be taken not to overwater. Although seedlings require consistent moisture in porous soil, at least for the first few years, like mature trees they are susceptible to root rot with overwatering. For that reason, water-hungry flowers should not be planted around an oak. Instead you might consider such natives as manzanita, ceanothus, sage, and currants and gooseberries.[4]

In two or three years an oak seedling may be six feet tall. Most oaks grow straight up in the first few decades and spread later on. Blue, interior live, and valley oaks can achieve a canopy width of from seventy to one hundred feet within fifty years. Ideally an oak should be placed so that its canopy will stay within property boundaries. Because the backyards of many new homes are shallow or narrow, the front yard may provide the best opportunity for planting an oak. For these reasons, it is important to consider carefully the space you have available.

A Matrix of Shrubs

Shrubs help structure the garden in ways that increase its experiential and operational qualities, by framing and directing views and by supplying engaging detail. A matrix of shrubs can also provide privacy for a favorite spot in the garden, give wind protection, screen undesirable views, or serve as a backdrop for other plants. Last but not least, shrubs are welcome habitat for small birds in search of food and cover.

The native botanical resources of California provide abundant models for diverse shrub formations and themes. For instance, coastal sage scrub might

CALIFORNIA OAKS (*Quercus* spp.)

Common Name	Species	Height (in feet)	Evergreen/ Deciduous	Characteristics
TREE OAKS				
black oak	*Q. kelloggii*	30–80	D	spring and fall color, glossy green in summer
blue oak	*Q. douglasii*	50	D	dry, hot locations; fall color; wide-spreading
canyon oak	*Q. chrysolepis*	20–60	E	round head; leaves shiny green above, light below
coast live oak	*Q. agrifolia*	20–70	E	round, wide-spreading; dense foliage; greedy roots
Engelmann oak	*Q. engelmannii*	40	E	wide-spreading; leaves oval, smooth; native to southern California
interior live oak	*Q. wislizenii*	30–75	E	wide-spreading, dense crown; glossy green leaves
island oak	*Q. tomentella*	25–40	E	round canopy; best in ocean-moderated locales
Oregon oak	*Q. garryana*	40–90	D	wide-spreading round crown; twisted branches; glossy leaves
valley oak	*Q. lobata*	70	D	mightiest oak; lobed leaves; tolerates high heat
SHRUB OAKS				
Brewer oak	*Q. garryana* var. *breweri*	15	D	usually grows in thickets; shiny green leaves
coastal scrub oak	*Q. dumosa*	3–10	E	shiny green leaves; good for erosion control; drought tolerant
deer oak	*Q. sadleriana*	3–6	E	conical, vase-shaped canopy; native to northern California mountains
desert scrub oak	*Q. turbinella*	10	E	grows in thickets; small, yellowish-green, toothed leaves
huckleberry oak	*Q. vaccinifolia*	2–4	E	gray-green leaves; suitable for wild, rock, or mountain gardens
island scrub oak	*Q. parvula*	6–12	E	native to maritime chaparral; similar in character to interior live oak
leather oak	*Q. durata*	3–10	E	dull green, hairy leaves; good for erosion control; drought tolerant
Muller oak	*Q. cornelius-mulleri*	<6	E	similar in character to coastal and desert scrub oaks
Palmer oak	*Q. palmeri*	10	E	chaparral shrub; gray-green, spiny leaves
scrub oak	*Q. bereridifolia*	6–15	E	grows in thickets; leaves green on top, gray underneath
shin oak	*Q. garryana* var. *semota*	3–6	D	shrubby; native to the southern Sierra and Transverse Ranges
shrub interior live oak	*Q. wislizenii* var. *frutescens*	3–6	E	flat, shiny green leaves; tall, densely branched
HYBRID OAKS				
Alvord oak	*Q. X alvordiana*	3–6	—	cross of blue oak and desert scrub oak; large shrub
Chase oak	*Q. X chasei*	3–6	—	cross of black oak and coast live oak; similar in character to oracle oak
Epling oak	*Q. X eplingii*	3–6	D	cross of blue oak and Oregon oak; compact tree
MacDonald oak	*Q. X macdonaldii*	30	D	cross of scrub oak and valley oak or subspecies.; round crown
oracle oak	*Q. X morehus*	25–40	D	cross of black oak and interior live oak; yellow fall color

(SOURCES: Pavlik et al. 1991; Hogan 1994)

A curved-seat wall, a small fountain, and citrus trees form a small sitting area (see item 9, opposite).

A FAMILY'S WOODLAND GARDEN

The roughly half-acre woodland wildlife-oriented design for a California landscape garden in Redlands creates habitat, conserves natural resources, and serves the needs of a family with young children. Everywhere the garden is linked with the surrounding bioregion through the use of native plants, adobe, tree branches, artfully used salvaged materials, and harvested rainwater.

Four large native oak trees, many smaller native and edible tree varieties, a downed-wood sculpture, a small meadow, and ample native vegetation provide many wildlife amenities. In addition, rainwater and graywater from the house are channeled to a pond with shallow edges, which is largely covered with aquatic plants. There is plenty of garden shade, as there should be in a region with a hot summer climate; this contributes to the site's energy efficiency and creates inviting areas for summer play and relaxation. Year-round functionality is achieved by orienting entertainment areas and much of the front toward the direct sunlight, which also allows sun-loving, showier plants to be grown.

Form, function, and lasting appeal were key considerations in the aesthetic design of this garden. The large front patio provides sharp contrasts among water, plantings, and diverse hard-surface materials (rubble, adobe, sand, gravel, and stone). Underneath the oaks is an area of more subtle design, consisting mostly of grasses and tree duff; small sculptures and birdhouses provide visual accents. Meanwhile, the children find many places to play on the front patio, in the buffalo grass meadow, and in overgrown places throughout the garden.

inspire a richly contrasting composition of plants that includes sage, coyote brush or lemonade berry, bright monkey flowers, yellow yarrow, canyon lupine, and buckwheat, with its rusty masses of dried flower stalks. Bold forms of agave are also typical in coastal sage scrub of the southland and can provide excellent texture.

The dense growth of chaparral, found in higher elevations near the coast or in inland foothills, is ideal for the formation of garden rooms. You might consider, for example, such handsome plants as the reliable ceanothus, an assortment of manzanitas, coffeeberry, toyon (adorned with red berries in winter), chamise, and scrub oaks, along with varieties of buckwheat. On northern slopes, which offer more moisture, the evergreen oaks, bigleaf maple, California bay, flowering ash, redberry, and flowering gooseberry might join the shrubby expanse.

Woodland Garden

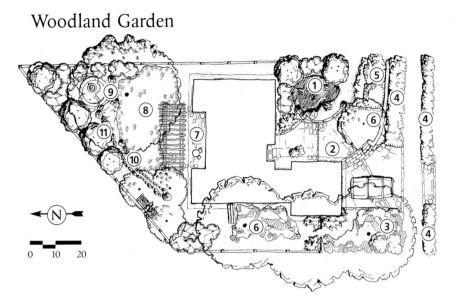

1. Pond
2. Entry court with adobe block
3. Shade-tolerant native grasses
4. Colorful ground cover
5. Old-fashioned shrub roses
6. Oaks with birdhouses
7. Patio with trellis and adobe block
8. Unmowed buffalo grass meadow
9. Seating area with citrus trees (see drawing on page 128)
10. Seasonal creekbed with boulders and rocks
11. Willows

PLANT LIST FOR WOODLANDS GARDEN

TREES
Coulter pine *(Pinus coulterii)*
California sycamore *(Platanus racemosa)*
coast live oak *(Quercus agrifolia)*

SHRUBS
ceanothus *(Ceanothus* spp.)
toyon *(Heteromeles arbutifolia)*

California shrub oak *(Quercus dumosa)*
coffeeberry *(Rhamnus californica)*
sugar bush *(Rhus ovata)*

SHADE
coastal wood fern *(Drypteris arguta)*

UNDERSTORY
island alum root *(Heuchera maxima)*

iris *(Iris* spp.)
scarlet sage *(Salvia spathacea)*

GROUND COVER
wild buckwheat *(Eriogonum* spp.)
festuca *(Festuca* spp.)
beard tongue *(Penstemon* spp.)
sage *(Salvia* spp.)

Because native shrubs have evolved techniques for dealing with dry conditions, including small, usually leathery leaves that lose little moisture, light-colored foliage, and succulence, they do not need to be watered or pruned often. It may be useful, however, to mulch heavily around native shrubs; think about using local materials for mulch, such as grape skins that remain after the crush, rice hulls, or sawdust.

A California Perennial Border

The familiar perennial border is quite appropriate in a landscape garden: it supplies colorful and textural diversity, can be made to keep pace with the seasons, and possesses habitat value. In a border, plants—including herbaceous perennials, low woody plants, and annuals for accent—are situated along the edge of a path, perhaps backed by contrasting shrubs or a fence. A

Native shrubs can be used to screen a front garden from traffic. (Landscape architect: Ron Lutsko Jr.)

border that uses well-adapted native perennials is referred to in garden books as a dry perennial border, since it has reduced water requirements (see the table on pages 132–133 for a sampling of suitable plants). It has the advantage of being relatively self-sufficient, requiring only occasional watering, weeding, mulching, and pruning. Advanced soil preparation may be necessary, however, because most drought-tolerant plants require excellent drainage.

To look attractive year round, a dry border requires plants that either stay green in summer or provide contrast through sculptural forms in the summer season, when colors are more subdued and some plants are dormant. Among native species, such choices as penstemons, sages, woolly blue curl, and California goldenrod yield a long succession of flowers to enhance the color scheme of a dry border; lupines, woolly sunflowers, buckwheat, and monkey flowers give supplemental effects, such as varying height and form. Naturalized plants from the Mediterranean climate zones are appropriate for added contrast as well. In addition, adaptable native bulbs, such as leopard lilies, fawn lilies, and wild onions, can be planted in open areas where the semiarid conditions of a mature dry perennial border will suit their requirements.[5]

A Bed of Annuals

Colorful annuals are California's "pioneer plants," the first to occupy bare soils under poor conditions, such as areas ravaged by fire or landslide. Under nat-

Shade plants and pavers surrounded by grass or ground cover make an inviting sitting area in the garden (Landscape architect: Ann Christoph).

ural conditions, as they die off annuals form a natural compost, improving the soil and paving the way for other plants like shrubs or trees that need better conditions to get started—a process known as succession. Before the arrival of Europeans in California, these pioneer plants were by and large native spring wildflowers. Today, aggressive exotic annuals like wild mustards and oats have taken over the pioneer function; they do not, however, perform the same role as wildflowers in establishing succession. Wildflowers have been unable to reclaim many areas, in part because they cannot withstand the competition.

In the landscape garden, annuals are useful in areas with infertile, well-drained soils, where competition from weed species is not so intense. The same aggressive weeds that have taken over much of California often defeat the attempt to establish wildflowers. Also, garden soils tend to be relatively rich, which makes the native annuals leggy. Despite these difficulties, native flowering annuals can be used successfully in flower beds along with other annuals and perennials.

Native perennial bunchgrasses (which also have been overwhelmed by exotic annual grasses) are good candidates for the California landscape garden, both because of their beauty and because, once established in weed-free areas, they allow native flowering annuals and the seedlings of woody plants to grow. In other words, in a bed intended for annuals they become the pioneer plants and allow for the succession of annual wildflowers. Like annual

NATIVE PERENNIALS FOR A DRY BORDER

Low Plants (<1 ft.)

Abronia latifolia, A. maritima, A. umbellata	sand verbenas
Antennaria spp.	pussytoes
Armeria maritima	sea thrift
Asclepias californica	California milkweed
Brodiaea spp.	brodiaeas
Calystegia malacophyllus, C. subacaulis, *C. soldanella*	low-growing morning glories
Camissonia ovata, C. cheiranthifolia	suncups
Castilleja wightii, C. latifolia	coast paintbrushes
Chrysopsis villosa	golden aster
Corethrogyne californica	dune aster
Dodecatheon spp.	shooting stars
Eriastrum densifolium	sapphire flower
Erigeron cernuus	Siskiyou daisy
Eriogonum parvifolium	small-leafed buckwheat
Eriophyllum confertiflorum, E. lanatum, *E. stachaedifolium*	woolly sunflowers
Erysimum spp.	wallflowers
Fragaria chiloensis	coast strawberry
Grindelia stricata, G. latifolia	gumweeds
Helianthemum scoparium	sunrose
Horkelia spp.	horkelias
Ivesia unguiculata	rock potentilla
Lasthenia macrantha	bluff goldfields
Linanthus nuttallii	perennial linanthus
Lotus nevadensis	Sierra lotus
Lupinus breweri	Brewer's lupine
Lupinus lyallii	Lyall lupine
Mirabilis bigelovii, M. greenei, *M. froebellii, M. laevis*	four o'clocks
Penstemon davidsonii	alpine penstemon
Penstemon newberryi	mountain pride penstemon
Phacelia californica	California phacelia
Phlox spp.	phloxes
Polygonum paronychia	dune knotweed
Salvia sonomensis	Sonoma sage
Scutellaria spp.	skullcaps
Sidalcea malvaeflora	checkerbloom
Sisyrinchium bellum	blue-eyed grass
Solanum parishii	mountain nightshade
Solidago spathulata	coast goldenrod
Viola douglasii	Douglas's violet

Medium Plants (1–3 ft.)

Achillea spp.	yarrows
Anaphalis margaritacea	pearly everlasting
Asclepias speciosa	showy milkweed
Balsamorhiza macrolepis, B. hookeri	balsamroots

Bloomeria crocea	golden stars
Calochrotus spp.	Mariposa tulips
Castilleja affinis, C. chromosa, C. foliolosa	Indian paintbrushes
Coreopsis maritima	sea dahlia
Delphinium spp.	western larkspurs
Dichelostemma capitatum, D. congestum, D. multiflorum	wild hyacinths
Erigeron glaucus	seaside daisy
E. inornatus	rayless aster
Eriogonum spp.	buckwheats
Erysimum capitatum	foothill wallflower
Eschscholzia californica	California poppy
Eupatorium occidentalis	western thoroughwort
Franseria chamissonis	beach bursage
Fritillaria spp.	adobe lilies
Ipomopsis aggregata	sky rocket
Linum lewisii	blue flax
Lupinus spp.	lupines
Monardella spp.	coyote mints
Oenothera deltoides howellii	Antioch dunes evening primrose
Penstemon azureus, P. heterophyllus, P. labrosus	penstemons
Scrophularia villosa	shaggy bee plant
Senecio blochmanae	Blochman's senecio
Senecio douglasii	Douglas's senecio
Solanum umbelliferum, S. xantii	blue nightshades
Solidago californica	California goldenrod
Sphaeralcea ambigua	apricot mallow
Stephanomeria cichoriacea	wandflower
Triteleia laxa, T. hyacinthina	milk lilies
Wyethia spp.	mule's ears
Zauschneria californica, Z. cana	hummingbird fuchsias

Tall Plants (3–6 ft.)

Argemone munita	prickly poppy
Calystegia cyclostegius, C. macrostegius, C. occidentalis	wild morning glories (vines)
Coreopsis gigantea	tree coreopsis
Dicentra chrysantha	golden eardrops
D. ochrolecua	creamy eardrops
Eriogonum arborescens	Santa Cruz Island buckwheat
Eriogonum giganteum	St. Catherine's lace
Helianthus californicus	California sunflower
Lilium rubescens	chaparral lily
Lilium washingtonianum	Washington lily
Mentzelia laevicaulis	blazing star
Oenothera hookeri	Hooker's evening primrose
Romneya coulteri	Matilija poppy
Xerophyllum tenax	beargrass

(SOURCE: Keator 1990)

weeds, bunchgrasses spread by broadcasting seeds; however, they are much less invasive, concentrating vegetative growth around individual tufts rather than forming a solid ground cover. The drift of a parent plant of bunchgrass can be controlled by thinning it into tidy clumps. An alternative is to plant already established bunchgrasses in open groups with space in between for seasonal wildflowers.

If your goal is to grow wildflowers every year, you will still need to be diligent about weeding and perhaps turn the soil every few years to reduce accumulated tannins. The more robust native annuals, such as the California poppy and a few *Clarkia* species, will continue to seed themselves year after year. Others, which depend on specific pollinating insects at just the right time to ensure fertility, will need to be reseeded every few years. Although Nature broadcasts her seeds in summer, for the gardener it may be more prudent to wait until the onset of winter rains. By lightly raking the seeds in after the rains begin, you will better ensure their germination and eventual bloom. (If simply broadcast on top of the soil, they are likely to dry out or be eaten by birds.)

Small annual beds that are cultivated every few years and in which aggressive weeds can be kept under control are the most practical option for most gardeners. Small beds are also less noticeable during the necessary summer dormancy. To enhance their attractiveness during this time, you can incorporate large rocks, statues, or colorful clay pots, as well as perennials, such as bunchgrasses and shrubs. Some of these perennials may also go dormant, while others will look robust all summer long.

If you have a lot of space, beautiful effects can be achieved by allowing wildflowers to naturalize out in a meadow or under large deciduous trees.

Container Gardening

In the small spaces of courtyards and roof gardens, it is quite possible to attract butterflies and other nectar-seeking wildlife through the use of container plants. California Dutchman's pipe, for example, is but one example of a native deciduous vine that can bring life to a balcony space and at the same time give certain butterflies a place to lay their eggs.

Containers can be used to create tiny water gardens or to display large, sculptural reeds. A box might exhibit the golden forms of summer dormancy as if in a dried-flower arrangement. Even the smallest of spaces can hold a prairie of wildflowers; in fact, the most reliable and least labor-intensive way to enjoy a burst of spring color is to plant wildflower seeds in a container, per-

Bunchgrasses can be combined with annuals to create natural beauty.

haps surrounding a central sculpture of tufted bunchgrass. A sea bluff might be represented by succulents, or forest undergrowth by an iris clump and ferns. Planters also serve as a decorative accent for paved surfaces, along walkways, or at terrace edges in gardens of any size. A further advantage of containers is that when their show is complete they can be moved offstage and allowed to recover. For this reason it is useful to have a small nursery area in a landscape

SOME NATIVE WOODY PLANTS FOR CONTAINER GARDENING

Adenostoma fasciculatum	chamise
Arctostaphylos edmundsii	Little Sur manzanita
Cupressus governiana pygmacea	pygmy cypress
Eriogonum giganteum	St. Catherine's lace
Fallugia paradoxa	Apache plume
Mimulus aurantiacus	bush monkey flower
Quercus durata	leather oak
Romneya coulteri	Matilija poppy
Salvia leucophylla	purple sage
Sphaeralcea ambigua	apricot mallow
Vaccinium ovatum	California huckleberry

(SOURCE: Lacey, *Growing Native Newsletter,* May/June 1991)

garden where plants can rest and be propagated. Leftover areas, such as in side yards or behind garages, are ideal for such plant maintenance activities.

Many California native perennials do well in containers because of the lack of competition and the good drainage (see the table above for some native woody plants you might consider for this purpose). However, a more diligent watering schedule is called for than with in-ground planting beds because containers dry out more quickly. Installation of a simple drip irrigation system for potted plants may save a great deal of time in the long run.

SOME PLANTING ISSUES

Some issues to keep in mind when developing a planting design and selecting plant materials are water requirements, plant propagation, weed control, fire suppression, and ongoing maintenance.

Water Requirements of Native Plants

Gardeners unfamiliar with native California plants may find that their water requirements take some getting used to. Many natives require little or no summer watering and indeed may die from root rot (caused by fungi and molds in the soil) if too much irrigation is applied. In general, the plants most susceptible to root rot are those adapted to sunny, dry slopes, such as the chaparral shrubs and native oaks.

However, the *judicious* use of summer water in well-drained soils can create optimum conditions not found in nature, stimulating root systems to develop faster and foliage to fill out more attractively. Glenn Keator gives the following guide for applying water to California natives in the summer:[6]

1. Seedlings and cuttings need constant moisture to stimulate root growth.
2. Most natives, even if planted during the rainy season, need some summer water their first year to establish deep roots.
3. Most native perennials look better if they receive occasional deep watering during the summer.
4. Natives from bogs, marshes, and wet meadows *must* have summer water.
5. Natives from the higher mountains planted at lower elevations may need summer water.
6. Natives from redwood forests and other coastal forests planted outside their native range may need some summer water.
7. Natives planted in sandy soils require some summer water if they do not grow naturally in sandy soils.
8. Coastal natives when planted inland may need some summer water.

Native Plant Propagation

Nowadays California native plants can be obtained at specialized nurseries, from seed companies, and in plant sales sponsored by local arboreta, botanical gardens, or chapters of the California Native Plant Society; nevertheless, their availability remains limited. If you cannot locate a desired species, propagation may be your best bet. Fortunately, most native plants are easy to grow from seed or by plant division, layering, or cuttings. Information about which propagation method is most appropriate for which species and how to find plants at the right stage to collect seeds or cuttings may be found in books such as Marjorie Schmidt's *Growing California Native Plants* and the Saratoga Horticultural Foundation's *California Native Plants with Commercial Sources*. Periodicals also supply information on the propagation of native plants, including tips from readers.

To remove cuttings or rooted stock from public property, a state collecting permit may be required; removal of a plant or any part of a plant from protected wildlife areas is forbidden. On private lands, permission from an owner is necessary, but that should pose little problem: landowners, glad to learn about the plants on their land, tend to be quite generous about requests for plant materials.

A word of caution: borrowing native plants from their natural habitat can damage particularly fragile plant populations. One way to avoid unwittingly doing harm to existing ecosystems is to coordinate collection activity among local chapters of the California Native Plant Society.

Weed Control

California's vegetation has been significantly altered by invasive exotic species such as wild oat, ryegrass, and mustard. Most weeds were introduced through agriculture, either intentionally or unintentionally. Some seeds were transported to California entangled in livestock hides and hooves, for example; others were brought in deliberately as grazing fodder; while others, including iceplant, pampas grass, and French broom, were introduced for decorative purposes.

In a garden weeds can be rampant and unattractive; the real reason to discourage them, though, is that they compete with cultivated plants, in various stages of development, that require the available nutrients. A deep layer of mulch around newly planted shrubs, trees, and perennials can give these desired plants a competitive advantage over invasive weeds. For greatest effectiveness, make sure the area is entirely weed free before applying the mulch; that way no new weeds can grow from established roots.

The summer dormancy of many California native plants offers an advantage when it comes to controlling weeds. Without water, weeds like crabgrass, bermuda grass, and purslane stop growing. As cultivated plants mature and spread they may form a solid cover that discourages weeds by robbing them of light. Areas that remain open, such as beds of annuals, need more aggressive weed control and therefore should be restricted in size so that they can be maintained regularly.

The easiest way to rid an area of weeds is to remove any invader before it sets and scatters its seed. After that point, any disturbance of the soil encourages new weed growth by bringing seeds to the surface. One effective method for eliminating weeds is soil solarization: sheets of black plastic are placed over the treatment area for four to six weeks during warm weather, raising the soil's temperature and killing both plants and seeds. Diligent hand weeding is another option, especially for smaller areas or where the

A planting scheme of well-adapted perennials interspersed with leaf litter creates a pleasing, low-maintenance cover under trees. (Landscape architect: Rick Fisher)

weeds have not taken over entirely. An area subsequently seeded with annuals can usually be kept weed free with light maintenance.

Although isolated application of an herbicide may be tempting to get at an especially troublesome weed, the use of poisons is not recommended in the home garden. It is difficult to treat a weed without injuring its neighbors or affecting plants that will grow in that spot next. Moreover, no poison should be used in a garden that provides food for humans or wildlife without a careful understanding of its immediate and residual effects. For all the time, expense, and care needed to use herbicides, digging a weed out by hand is, in the end, the most efficient method of control.

Certain weedy species have considerable habitat value, providing nectar, seeds, and other foods for insects and serving as foraging grounds for birds. In addition, some weeds—malva, for example, fennel, thistles other than the noxious yellow star thistle, and legumes such as vetch and clover—are an important larval food source for several butterfly species.

Combustible Vegetation and Fire Prevention

Every summer and fall in California, fires dramatically sweep through chaparral, coastal sage, and other shrubby habitats. Because human settlement has increasingly claimed these once isolated areas, fires have been suppressed and fuel loads have been allowed to build up. Hence, when fires do occur, they are devastating.

A small front pond adds a habitat area (see item 1, opposite).

A VALLEY HERITAGE GARDEN

A century ago the Great Central Valley was characterized by vast riparian areas and golden grasslands dotted with the gray-green foliage of native oaks. A reflection of this heritage valley landscape can be found in the front yard design for a home in Chico.

A rainwater-fed pond stands at the center of this garden's riparian zone. As in nature, the summertime water level of this pond is low relative to that during the rainy season. In the nearby grassland, some flowering color accents are always in evidence, but otherwise the dry season is allowed to do its natural work, leading to a dormant, golden landscape. The west side of the house is lined with valley oaks that provide both summer shade and valuable habitat for wildlife.

The backyard garden, through which a rustic walkway meanders, is designed as a low-maintenance refuge, a place to enjoy flowers, homegrown fruit, and pleasant fragrances—all the small details that nature sets out seasonally for close viewing. A spa provides the perfect spot for gazing at the starry sky and enjoying the nighttime sounds and smells.

The special challenges that needed to be resolved with this design included the property's heavy clay soils and the limited amount of time the homeowner has to do yard work. Construction materials included natural valley products or by-products such as adobe block, tree and shrub branches, almond shells, and mulch. Photovoltaic cells on a south-facing roof collect solar energy to power an urban vehicle and heat the spa.

Ecologists view this fire danger in a somewhat different light than do homeowners. Scientific study of plant succession in these habitats has shown that fire is critical for ecological balance: it clears away ground herbs, allowing plants to become established on bare dirt, and in many cases fire is necessary for seeds to germinate.

A balance can be achieved between restoring these habitats with their naturally combustible vegetation and reducing the fire threat to homeowners. The main precaution involves clearing out some undergrowth and creating open areas in the landscape. Not only is this sound ecologically, but a habitat mosaic of trees, wet areas, and open spaces is more inviting for wildlife.

The central issue in reducing fire danger is reducing the combustible load of vegetation—wood fuels such as trees and shrubs—especially near buildings. If a fire does break out, a greater vegetative mass generally drives both the traveling speed and the intensity of fire. In areas of high fire danger,

Valley Heritage Garden

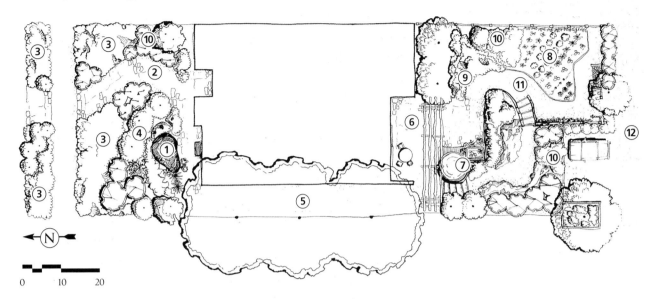

0   10   20

1. Pond with recirculating water feature (see illustration, opposite)
2. Entryway with local adobe blocks
3. Grassland habitat
4. Riparian vegetation including willows, native roses, and wild grapes
5. Valley oaks
6. Patio with trellis and adobe blocks
7. Spa
8. Vegetable garden with twig woven fences
9. Cut-flower garden
10. Habitat-enhancing shrubs
11. Walk made of almond shells
12. Alleyway

therefore, it is especially important to thin out dense plantings of shrubs and trees. Fortunately, most plants, particularly chaparral plants, benefit from being pruned back periodically; it keeps them dense and healthy. Seasonal vegetation such as bunchgrasses or annuals should also be trimmed back during the summer dormancy period. In the vicinity of homes and outbuildings, the perimeter should be planted with a broken pattern of perennials and low ground covers, lightly interspersed with trees and shrubs. Immediately around a house stones and paved areas can provide a noncombustible buffer zone.

LOOKING FORWARD: A PLACE TO ENJOY

Perhaps by now a landscape garden image is taking shape in your mind. Many aspects of garden design have been covered already, and we will soon

Regional California native plants can be used effectively in ways similar to more typical, imported species, as here in this Soka University, Malibu, garden. (Envicom Corp. and Toyon Design; photographer: K. Patey)

explore a few more. But now let us take stock once again of what the garden might someday be and what it might represent for you.

Imagine sitting on a deck near a small grove of live oaks or redbuds, which, with their richly textured trunks, contrast with the grayish leaves of purple sage planted in a mixed border close by. Manzanita, tall native bunch-grasses, and large rocks screen you from the main part of the garden. As leaves and debris fall, they are swept off the deck and allowed to age beautifully as a low-maintenance mulch and ground cover. Little terra-cotta sculptures, some found objects readapted as garden art, and a cotton hammock add a touch of handiwork and personality. This is a peaceful spot, a place to read, to daydream, and to share with others.

Design allows us to have a garden that is beautiful from within (see "A Valley Heritage Garden," pp. 140–141), not a sterile garden covered with plastic, rock, or bark to keep weeds down. There should be no hurry to tidy up here, since so many lovely details are worth lingering over. This place requires no flowers when it is not the proper time for them; a striking vase, even if somewhat weatherbeaten, is just as welcome an impression for the eye. In this garden, shrubs aren't clipped much; they have been positioned such that if they want to extend energetic boughs high into the sky, they can. A successful old tree that offers prime habitat for wildlife might be allowed to crack and raise a walk to some degree. By all accounts, even Eden was not perfect.

In the California landscape garden, the shapes and patterns of the surrounding bioregion are admired. The plants that invite you to learn their stories, the textures and colors, are all from the vicinity. Design allows a garden to grow from within, simply, into a living composition.

CHAPTER SIX

LIVING WITH SUSTAINABLE RESOURCES

The home [garden] should grow and reflect the increased richness of our experience, reminding us of our history and friends, our loves and interests, our own unique identity. Any room that has grown like this through a lifetime will show the richness of the owner's personality.

David Pearson, *The Natural House Book*

A California landscape garden is inspired by its surroundings, by local landforms and resources that at one time had a sustainable natural order. It is not just *in* California; it is also *of* California. Its plants, vegetation schemes, and other habitat values help to sustain California's nature.

Any natural system requires resources to maintain balance and support life itself. Gardens can be designed to reflect this balance of local conditions by relying on means of construction and upkeep that are sustainable. Renewable local resources such as water, soil, and building materials are important ingredients for the landscape garden, both in its own right and as part of a larger environment. Through reliance on and conservation of local natural resources—including sunlight—the need to import nonrenewable resources is spared.

THE CONCEPT OF SUSTAINABILITY

The idea of sustainability is based on an understanding of resources not as commodities to be produced and sold, bought and used, but as complex systems that must, through judicious management, be kept in a state of equilibrium. Like any business, large or small, a system that sustains a net drain on its resources cannot hope to survive for very long. In sustainable forest management, for instance, this means that within a given period of time the biomass of trees harvested must be essentially equal to the biomass growth of remaining or newly planted trees. Because of environmental legislation—or public pressure in lieu of legislation—accounting for overall costs of the system now also includes the costs of mitigating environmental impacts. For example, harvesting wood by clear-cutting damages regional watersheds by polluting creeks, causing soil erosion, and reducing the diversity of plants and animals, which are all part of the forest-watershed system. Mitigation involves not just replanting the trees that have been cut down, but also implementing projects that reverse pollution and erosion and rebuild wildlife diversity.

Issues of sustainability and environmental accountability now constitute a form of political pressure. The Institute for Sustainable Forestry, an organization in northern California, certifies wood products that are harvested with these objectives in mind, so that a consumer can select products harvested by sustainable methods. When enough consumers—in conjunction with activists, lobbying groups, and, often, ensuing legislation—insist on systematic, environmental accounting on the part of the producers, resources tend to be conserved because the cost of doing otherwise becomes prohibitive. One very important component of this consumer pressure is the notion that private and state or federal businesses that capitalize on air, land, and water resources should be regulated for the long-term public interest.

The concept of sustainability has more recently been applied to human landscapes, which are seen as complex consortiums of private and public interests. The late landscape architect John Lyle, in his book *Regenerative Design for Sustainable Development,* visualizes the city optimally as a system of balanced inputs and outputs. The unsustainable city, in contrast, is one in which primary resources such as water, food, minerals, wood, paper, and petroleum products are simply absorbed, not recycled, and in which the primary products are sewage, garbage, toxic waste, pollution, heavy storm runoff, and noise.

Lyle argues that we must institute regenerative systems in the urban landscape that sustain and renew themselves over time—the sustainable city should be a place that produces clean water, reusable forms of nitrogen and heat, and reclaimable waste. One of the links to the sustainable city is the private garden; indeed, the California landscape garden is itself a steady-state, sustainable system of inputs and outputs, in which local resources are conserved and products that reenergize the system result from natural processes of weathering, decay, and regrowth (see "California Wash Garden," p. 148).

In this chapter we explore these links between the garden, the community, and the bioregion. We begin by examining the basic raw materials from which the California landscape garden is created: sunlight, water, and soil, as well as local building materials such as straw, clay, and stone. The fundamental ecological premise that nothing goes to waste in a natural system also encourages inclusion of recycled and salvaged materials, such as wood and plastic.

In the last part of this chapter we return to the overlooked natural resource of wildlife to consider how, by reflecting California's natural state, the garden can encourage multiple species (including people) to coexist. Although a comprehensive look at wildlife is beyond the scope of this book, the stories presented here reiterate a key fact: habitat restoration, resource use, and the fate of wildlife are intimately related issues, all of which can be addressed in the home landscape. We consider here not only the common birds and butterflies that, for the time being at least, are still part of the everyday experience of many people, but also species whose fate depends on the choices we make as Californians. Some of these species are threatened only by our lack of understanding; if we learn to supply garden spaces with usable habitat, they will surely return. Others have been displaced by urban sprawl, and with habitat loss their numbers have plummeted. These losses illuminate the real costs of fragmented ecosystems and wasted resources. By opting against sterile or exotic home landscapes and instead striving to connect restored habitats with the larger bioregion, we can nurture diversity and enrich our own experience.

Landscape architect John Lyle used locally found materials in his home garden in southern California. (John Lyle)

CALIFORNIA WASH GARDEN

Landscape architect John Lyle is one of the leading advocates and theorists of sustainable landscape design and planning. He has written the definitive book on the subject, *Regenerative Design for Sustainable Development,* and incorporated his ideas into his own garden on the outskirts of urban Los Angeles. He tells this story of his garden in his book:

> The garden derives from the larger landscape of which it is part. The effort here is to embrace and distill ecological processes and their complexity and to give them visible expression.
>
> The setting is at the base of the San Gabriel Mountains, a dramatically rugged range on the edge of the southern California urban area. This mountain interface zone is the setting of a dramatic and dynamic set of ecological processes at the transition between mountain and valley.
>
> Some of the most active of these occur where water collects and moves. Under natural conditions, when water from mountain rainfall pours out of the canyons at the mountain's edge, it spreads out and flows at a slower pace over a broad depression called a wash. Washes are important nodes for dissipating floodwaters and recharging groundwater. They are covered with rocks and dotted with plants struggling to take hold.
>
> The analogous washes in my garden play a similar role, holding water and allowing it to percolate. The basic material—rock— is the same as that of a natural wash, but it is used in a controlled way at a scale related to home garden dimensions. Thus the form of the garden wash does not mimic the natural wash, but recalls its process in human terms related to the human environment.[1]

A GARDEN'S SUSTAINABLE RESOURCES

Diverse resources go into the ongoing care and maintenance of a garden. Water, fertilizers, and insect controls are all necessary to garden upkeep. We must learn to use these resources responsibly, and also to tap into naturally occurring resources, such as solar power and rain. By being aware of natural processes and paying attention to the ecological needs of our gardens, we can live more lightly on the land. Design plays an important role in this endeavor.

Passive Solar Design

Sun and shade patterns can greatly affect the heating and cooling needs of a house. By maximizing the effects of solar heat in the winter and taking advantage of shade patterns in summer, not only will you make the garden more hospitable, for you and for your plants, but you can also substantially reduce your home's energy requirements. The energy savings of shade alone, for example, can be considerable: up to 60 to 65 percent on hot summer days, according to one study of mobile homes using air conditioning.[2] The money thus saved can offset other costs of the garden system.

Deciduous plants large and small are the key tools in achieving optimal patterns of garden shade and sun throughout the year: combinations of dense and dappled shade can be created where needed during hot weather, and when the foliage drops maximum radiant exposure is available during cold weather.

Peak energy demands in most of the United States—including much of California—occur in the summer during late afternoon, when approximately three-quarters of total heat gain in the home comes through the windows as a result of direct sun exposure. Therefore, it is important to shade windows during the mornings and afternoons, when the sun is lower in the sky. Proper placement of trees and shrubs can respond to the location and changing angle of the sun. Deciduous shade for surfaces that tend to absorb heat, such as dark pavement, is also useful. In winter, south-facing houses need to be as unobstructed as possible to allow the sun to penetrate windows and heat the walls of the house. Local utility companies can provide information about placing trees and shrubs in the landscape for maximal energy efficiency.

A home's architectural features can be combined with plantings to conserve energy as well. Although an overhang may be sufficient to protect south-facing windows and walls from direct solar heat during hot months and yet allow sun exposure during winter, the addition of an open trellislike structure supporting a deciduous vine can increase control over radiant exposure (and, perhaps, increase the garden's usable space if included as a substitute for energy-conserving shrubs and trees).

Water Conservation

Urban water conservation is important for California's ecology and economy. On the local scale, residential water meters are increasingly a fact of life and make gardeners more cognizant of water use. Water savings can be effected in part by determining a yard's "hydrozones," where the space is divided into

A trellis with deciduous vines provides passive solar shade in the summer while allowing sun to warm the house in the winter.

areas of heavy human activity and areas of primarily visual importance; high-use parts of the garden, such as a lawn for ball play or children's use, are slated to receive heavier applications of water, while areas that are used infrequently or not at all receive less water.[3] Plants and ground covers are selected according to which hydrozone they will be placed in.

Thanks largely to the efforts of landscape architects, landscape contractors, and government agencies in California, a 25 to 90 percent reduction in water use for landscape plantings has been achieved in specific projects, mainly through the installation of drought-tolerant landscapes, more efficient irrigation practices, and changes in maintenance techniques. The replacement of lawn with any of a variety of ground covers can by itself reduce water use by 50 percent or more—benefiting not only the environment but the home gardener as well, who has less upkeep to worry about. Where lawns are left in place, fine-tuning the irrigation schedule via application rates, controllers, and moisture sensors accounts for a 30 to 50 percent savings over the average turf irrigation requirements.[4]

Water Harvesting Graywater and rainwater harvesting with open-channel drainage and on-site detention ponds is a new and innovative way to reuse water in the home landscape. Recycled graywater (that is, water that has not come in contact with toilet waste, soiled diapers, or sewage), properly collected, carries few if any harmful organisms. Many local municipalities are recognizing the benefits of recycling for certain purposes and adopting ordinances that allow water reuse at the residential level.

Appropriate sources for a graywater system include kitchen or bathroom sinks, bathtubs, showers, washing machines, and outdoor hoses. Contrary to popular belief, the biodegradable phosphates from household soaps contained in recycled water can actually benefit the soil and plants. Oil and grease, however, should not be discharged in large concentrations into graywater destined for the garden. Open-channel drainage can be used to let rainwater flow into low areas of the garden, where it seeps into the soil and creates seasonal wet spots. In addition to helping water percolation, open-channel drainage can partly eliminate the need for costly subsurface storm drainage systems. Locating plants in areas where surface water collects also eliminates the need for extensive irrigation.

Rainwater harvesting systems provide a strikingly different visual and environmental landscape image by creating riparian habitats within an urban setting (see "Garden Catch Basins," next page). Throughout the year these

GARDEN CATCH BASINS

Rain is a welcome event in California's arid regions, where, at seasonal streams, vernal pools, and large portions of wetlands, it means life and new activity. All the more reason, then, to celebrate it as a visual element in a garden. By making rainwater visible, a catch basin system of open drainage with sandy areas, rocks, and vegetation becomes a spontaneous, active point of interest in the garden. With sufficient space, a more extensive riparian habitat can be created. In gardens with a small perennial stream, for example, low spots along the waterway may be planted with vegetation whose roots are adapted to temporary submersion in water, while an adjacent catch basin holds overflow water during rainy periods.

dynamic areas illustrate seasonal processes, attract wildlife, and make fun and safe places for children to play.

Drip Irrigation   The manner in which water is applied to the garden can spell the difference between waste and conservation of that precious resource. Fortunately, advances in both technology and horticultural practice make it easier than ever for the home gardener to use water responsibly. Computerized drip irrigation technology is now accessible and affordable to most home gardeners, and it comes with every conceivable feature, including rain and soil moisture sensors that will override irrigation programs to reduce unnecessary watering.

The estimated water savings from drip irrigation is 30 to 50 percent of the amount used in conventional methods of irrigation.[5] Any planting for which a heavy layer of mulch is appropriate is a good candidate for a drip system. Drip systems are also ideal for shrubs or large areas of perennial plantings because the drip line can be placed in between and around the plants. For beds of annuals and smaller perennials, however, which need to be watered in total and fairly often, a sprinkler system still does a better job.

The advantages of drip irrigation are multiple for the garden, the gardener, and the environment. Water is delivered directly to the roots of plants rather than to the foliage, and the very slow rate of application ensures that there is no water runoff and that little water is lost through evaporation. Gardeners benefit because building codes allow the low-pressure irrigation lines used for drip systems to be placed on the surface rather than deeply buried, thereby eliminating considerable installation costs compared to in-ground sprinkler systems.

Maintenance of a drip system that is installed on the ground can be reduced through the use of heavy-gauge tubing with built-in emitters so they do not get constantly broken off. In areas of hard water, clogging is a problem because flows are low, so water filters may be necessary as well as an occasional flushing of the lines.

Soil and the Value of Good Drainage

In the garden, nature's complex web of life begins with the soil. Experts in soil biology estimate that the combined total of microorganisms such as fungi, bacteria, nematodes, and protozoa per cubic centimeter of fertile soil ranges in the billions. These organisms help decompose organic matter, form symbiotic relationships with the roots of plants to fix nitrogen, make minerals and iron available to plants and other animals, and keep each other's populations in check through an intricate soil-based food web.

A little higher on the food web are earthworms, ants, millipedes, termites, insect larvae, springtails, midges, and mollusks, which digest plant material, microorganisms, and each other. Larger organisms such as earthworms perform a major ecological service in loosening the soil for greater water and nutrient penetration. At the same time these organisms encourage microbial development with their fecal material.

A robust soil biology depends largely on the availability of organic matter. Compost is invaluable in the garden to improve both soil structure and nutrient content. Parts of the garden, however, should remain lean—without added organic matter or nitrogen fertilizers—to accommodate California native plants, many of which cannot survive in rich soils. This lean soil requirement explains why, for instance, many wildflowers do not self-propagate in gardens that have been fertilized for many years.

Soil Types   The two soil extremes found in California are clay, composed of closely packed microscopic particles, and sand, composed of the largest soil particles. Clay soils are hard to work, are slow to drain, and have poor aeration. Sandy soils have excellent drainage but dry quickly and usually lack available minerals for plants. Loam, a soil in between sandy and clay types, generally works better than either extreme for plant cultivation.

Adding compost and organic material over the years can improve a soil for many native plants that are part of the successional stages of a region. As layers of leaf litter and other organic matter decompose on top of the soil year after year, the sandy extreme begins to hold water and the clay extreme has better aeration. Although any organic material can be used to enrich the soil, wood chips, bark, and sawdust tend to tie up nitrogen, making it necessary to add back this essential nutrient. Incorporating gypsum or lime into heavy soils adds important minerals and also improves their ability to form "crumbs," that is, larger soil clusters, which improve soil aeration and drainage. Good aeration further increases the bacterial activity in the soil.

Many California native perennials and shrubs evolved on exposed, dry, rocky hillsides with lean soils that cannot hold water for very long. These plants therefore rarely do well in heavy clay soils, which limit growth and health more than does the searing summer heat. Overwatering plants that thrive in the arid conditions of summer, moreover, usually causes root rot, which is the main reason plants need good drainage in the garden. In clay conditions, most shrubs and perennials benefit from being planted on a small mound where the soil has been amended to improve drainage.

Good drainage, in addition to preventing root rot, allows plant roots to grow faster. Plants then develop more vigor, which better prepares them for dry weather. Perennials in general invest a lot of their growth energy in the root system, which means that a gardener may not see much above-ground growth until the second or third year—that is, until the root system has developed.

Soil Chemistry   Besides particle size, soils differ greatly in their chemistry. Acidic soils (marked by a pH less than 7) exist primarily in areas with a lot of rain, organic litter, and cool temperatures. Alkaline soils (with a pH above 7) generally occur in areas with little rainfall. Simple and inexpensive soil pH kits are available in local nurseries and hardware stores for testing garden soil.

Just as in nature, acidic soil can be induced in the garden by means of raw wood amendments and by leaching with water. The addition of lime reduces soil acidity, while coniferous bark used as a mulch acidifies the soil. Plants that are adapted to acidic conditions, such as many plants of the forest floor, seldom grow well in alkaline conditions.

Mulching   Mulches, organic dressings placed on soil, have many uses in the garden. For one thing, they significantly reduce the water needs of the landscape by keeping the soil temperature cool, which slows evaporation. By maintaining a relatively consistent level of soil moisture, mulches help ensure plants' health. As an added bonus, mulches over four inches deep are very effective weed suppressants (though care must be taken not to cover the bases of the plants, which can smother the crown). Mulches also help reduce soil compaction, which is important not only to enable healthy root development but also to protect against water runoff and erosion. Finally, mulches often give a tidier look to areas landscaped with annuals, perennials, and woody shrubs.

Organic mulches are more versatile than crushed rock used as a mulch because they improve the structure of the soil as they decompose, adding nutrients and thus supporting the biological activity of soil insects and microorganisms. Like compost, as mulch breaks down it helps improve soil texture, especially of the upper layers. Nutrients from decomposed mulch enrich the topsoil and then permeate down to root areas.

About one-fifth of municipal solid waste in the United States, ending up in landfills, is garden waste. By creating mulches and compost from your garden refuse you not only minimize nonlocal inputs into the garden but also spare the environment.

Fertilizers, Pesticides, and Other Garden Chemicals

American home gardeners typically use more pesticides and fertilizers per acre than farmers in the United States apply to cropland. This contributes significantly to wide-scale ecological problems as fertilizers, entering the aquatic system, nitrify creeks, ponds, and lakes, which leads to algal blooms. Pesticides, meanwhile, are too often used routinely or for cosmetic reasons only. Many yards in urban and suburban neighborhoods are deserts to insect-eating songbirds because of the heavy use of pesticides.

Although a slow-release fertilizer may benefit a plant during its first year in the ground by helping it to grow more vigorously, native or well-adapted plants generally do not require nitrogen-rich fertilizers after they have established a sound root system; high-nitrogen fertilizers may even reduce the life span of a plant. By choosing plants appropriate to a site, employing responsible horticultural methods, and cultivating realistic expectations, we can make a big difference in the way home gardens affect the environment.

Where garden pests do need to be controlled, a number of environmentally safe products, such as insecticidal soaps, may do the job just fine, making chemicals unnecessary. In addition, various services exist statewide to help the home gardener find biological alternatives to chemicals. Integrated Pest Management, administered through county University of California

Cooperative Extension offices, and the nonprofit Bio-Integral Resource Center (BIRC) in Berkeley are two such programs, providing public education on garden pest management and publishing informational pamphlets, such as BIRC's "Commonsense Pest Control." In addition, most UC Cooperative Extension county offices coordinate a volunteer Master Gardener Program that provides information to gardeners over the telephone and through free or low-cost publications. In the final analysis, when steps must be taken to control pests, good organic alternatives make the use of chemicals in the garden increasingly unnecessary.

Garden Maintenance

Most gardens require more attention in their first few years, especially with a weeding and watering regimen, than after they are established. California landscape gardens are no different in this respect; indeed, initially they may require more time and effort than a traditional garden, as locally available plants and materials are tested and proven for their horticultural value. Once established, however, the California landscape garden tends to be less maintenance-intensive than a traditional garden as spontaneous natural processes take over.

CRAFTING A LANDSCAPE GARDEN WITH REGIONAL MATERIALS

By using materials in the home garden that reflect the surrounding natural environment we achieve a certain simple elegance and a pleasing aesthetic. Natural materials such as wood, branches, reeds, and live plants and inorganic materials like rocks and earth have a high degree of integrity. They have evolved in the local region and are part of a natural cycle of production, decomposition, and rebirth. They do not pollute when they are spent, but rather find new applications within the ecological cycle.

Working with locally harvested materials, the gardener gains a relationship with the full life of the region by understanding where things come from, how they grow or evolve, and what becomes of them when they die. Wood, for instance, provides habitat for mosses, fungi, and a large variety of insects before it completely decomposes into soil nutrients. Earthen substances such as adobe blocks and even stone return to nature as elemental forms as well, in ways that are observable and understandable.

Right: *Locally available natural resources make a useful and beautiful building material, as seen in this garden screen made of recycled branches.*

Below: *Detail of branch screen construction.*

Environmental Costs of Building Materials

Owen Dell, an ecologically minded landscape architect who has practiced in Santa Barbara since 1972, has evaluated the environmental impacts of common materials used in landscape construction, such as imported topsoil versus compost and brick versus adobe block pavers.[6] He finds the least desirable construction materials, from an environmental point of view, to be high-input materials such as lumber, concrete, flagstone (especially from outside California), tile, brick, decomposed granite (which is often a by-product of mining operations), redwood bark, and topsoil, in that order. The most renewable and lowest-impact landscaping materials are wood chips from local urban trees, broken concrete, adobe block, rammed earth, straw bales, gravel, and local stone.

When one of the low-input materials does not suffice and a choice has to be made among the high-input materials, criteria such as durability and function come into play. To create a durable surface, for example, decomposed granite might be the best choice, since it is produced with fewer environmental impacts than brick or tile. Water conservation is another important criterion. Although brick, concrete, and turf are all highly resilient surfaces that require high energy inputs during their manufacture and installation, turf in particular must be maintained with considerable inputs of water, as well as pesticides, fertilizers, and machinery.[7] This fact may make paving materials much more desirable.

In general, in the spirit of sustainability, the use of high-input surfaces should be concentrated in areas of intensive garden activity, such as entertainment and recreation areas. Conversely, for low-intensity or passive-use areas, surfaces such as drought-tolerant vegetation or mulch may be the most appropriate choices. Low-maintenance trees, shrubs, and ground covers at the same time serve a multiplicity of purposes, functioning as screens, defining outdoor rooms, guiding people's movement through the garden, directing views, reducing wind exposure, and creating wildlife habitat. This is not to say that no nonrenewable resources can be used in the ecological garden; some features, such as a fountain with an electric pump, may well enhance a focal spot in the overall layout. However, a well-planned garden will rely only minimally on complex technology, making use instead of naturally available materials to the extent possible.

Painted tree branches make a creative play structure for children. (Play structure design by Baile Oakes)

Local and Accessible Construction Materials

There are many innovative ways to utilize locally available resources as elements of design and organization in the California landscape garden.[8] Leaf

Right: *Concrete can easily be recycled in the garden as pavers or as material for retaining walls. (Designer: Marcia Donahue)*

Below, top figure: *Locally found stones create a focal point in this Santa Barbara garden. (Landscape architect: Owen Dell)*

Below, bottom figure: *A collection of stones is a major feature in the Stamper Garden. (Landscape architects: Delaney, Cochran & Castillo; photograph by Topher Delaney)*

litter left in place functions first as a mulch and eventually as a compost; smaller branches that have been pruned can be shredded into a ground cover; larger branches can be woven into fences or plant trellises. Branches, reeds, rocks, and earth, salvaged wood, brick, and concrete, are examples of accessible materials that can prompt an imaginative approach to building.

Local materials also tend to be inexpensive, and many—such as pavers crafted from smooth river rock and walls made from rammed earth or adobe and adorned with earth pigments—have timeless applications, having been used throughout history.[9] The choice of materials depends on their presence and abundance, which vary from one region to another. For example, adobe blocks may be the most appropriate paving choice in California's deep-soil valleys, while in the rocky California foothills locally abundant stone is a natural choice.

Recycled and Found Materials   Salvaged or recycled materials—natural items such as branches and rocks, leftover industrial products such as pipes and paint, wood and tiling—can be very appropriate for the garden, allowing surprising forms of expression and function. Consider, for example, a mortarless retaining wall made of common recyclables, in which bottles and concrete pieces are substituted for stones or bricks. Similarly, concrete rubble, bottles, rocks, and salvaged bricks may be put together in pleasing, naturalistic patterns to emulate rocks that have been acted on by geologic forces. The aesthetic appeal is similar with any of these materials.

The creative use of recycled or found materials involves a process of dis-

Found objects displayed in the garden express cultural and personal meaning.

covery. The sculptor Andy Goldsworthy is an inspiring practitioner in this regard: by recognizing the aesthetic qualities of color and texture in everyday, found materials, he creates beautiful objects of great simplicity.

Found objects that may be on their way to the scrap heap can be given new life in the garden, perhaps through the crafting of a sculptural or architectural composition of contrasting color and texture. For example, a sculpture of a person made with salvaged pieces of metal can add a charming accent in the garden. Artists tend to be the most avid collectors of discarded, seemingly useless trinkets. Finding a treasure trove of unusual objects—such as a dozen bowling balls—can make a gardener into an artist willy-nilly. The results are likely to be interesting, refreshingly original, even humorous.

Dan Knapp of Berkeley has built a thriving business out of reclaiming the useless. He cofounded a profitable salvaging operation called Urban Ore, which annually diverts five thousand tons of materials from landfills. People drop off all sorts of objects, from old doors and metal scraps to bed frames and bath tubs, which are then sold at a minimal price. One person's junk is

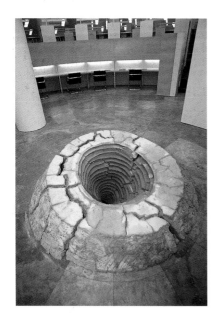

The artist Andy Goldsworthy bases his art on nature and natural processes. (Getty Museum, Los Angeles; photograph by Marc Schenker)

potential art to another, and Urban Ore is a supplier *par excellence* for artists seeking low-end materials. Tapping into the same creative urges, gardeners too may discover new uses for discarded objects available at places like Urban Ore.

Recycled objects also give the garden a sense of integrity, of continuity in use and process. Bricks or stones may be used to construct a path, then, a generation later when the path needs to be changed, they may be moved to another place in the garden. Some precautions need to be taken with materials that contain toxic substances, however, such as railroad ties or other preserved wood pieces.

Weaving a screen with long, pruned cuttings or shaping a plaster relief mural does not require expertise, just curiosity and an enjoyment of working with readily available materials. Hands-on projects such as embedding broken ceramic pieces in a fresh stucco wall or making a path of pebbles set in sand mixed with clay are direct and uncomplicated means of creating meaning and expression in the garden.

Part of the challenge and fun of incorporating salvaged materials into the landscape is to find aesthetically pleasing ways to use them constructively. Discarded automobile tires, for example, may be cut in half or in smaller sections with a skilsaw and used as long-lasting bed edgings; a little paint or the simplicity of draped, green plants may be all that is needed to make them attractive. Old automobile tires can also be filled with earth, stacked, and then covered with plaster as a wall, and they are useful for stabilizing a steep bank. Placing tires in undulating patterns, rather than forcing straight or angular patterns, takes advantage of their own curved shape and is more attractive.

Salvaged materials lend themselves especially to humorous and surprising garden features. An S-shaped drainpipe painted to look like a dragon that spews red-colored springs; a pergola of metal mattress supports supporting a dense covering of vines; an old door that now serves as a bench; a painted iron pipe with a T-valve on top to support a plant—these are just a few salvaged materials that provide fun but practical accents in the garden. Not only that, but such playfulness encourages us to keep our vision fresh and to realize that things are not always what they seem.

Rustic Wood   Certainly, milled wood from a lumberyard, available in standardized sizes and grades, is well adapted for many garden projects. Historically, however, before milled wood became the norm, rough poles, logs, and branches were employed for many useful structures, and it makes sense now

A POSTAGE STAMP GARDEN

Good things come in small packages, and this tiny garden in San Jose proves that there is always room for a flood of sunlight, the fragrance of herbs, the beauty of flowers, and the sounds of birds. It also demonstrates that the smallest of gardens can contribute to protecting California's natural resources. Here, for example, rainwater is harvested in a small pool that is used to irrigate a fruit tree, shrubbery, and a perennial bed filled with plants that attract small wildlife.

Above: *A small wooden gazebo is a focal element in the Postage Stamp Garden.*

1. Patio with adobe paving
2. Trellis with hanging vines
3. Water basin
4. Gazebo (see drawing)
5. Insect-attracting perennials and shrubs
6. Fruit tree
7. Compost
8. Greenhouse

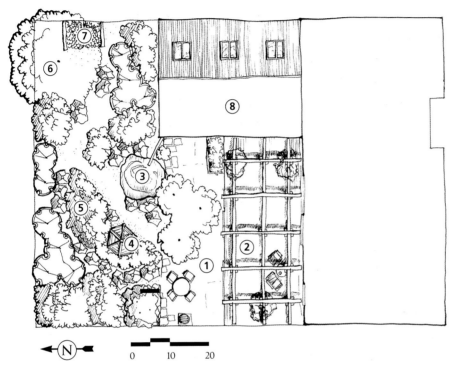

to consider these rustic alternatives for use in the sustainable landscape garden. Such wood can be purchased, or it may be gathered directly from the land; in any case, use of such wood need not involve the commercial harvesting methods that have damaged woodland ecosystems throughout California.

Indeed, removing small trees and shrubs from a dense copse for a yield of garden rails or poles has a certain advantage. By thinning vegetation, the harvester reduces fire danger and helps preserve the overall character and diversity of the healthy forest mosaic. Remaining trees have a greater proportion of available resources, including space, nutrients, sunlight, and water; and soil quality, vegetative cycles, and habitat values for the biological community are enhanced.

Rustic poles also require substantially less energy in terms of production. Not only is little sawing required, but the log can also be much smaller in diameter than a tree that will be milled into lumber with the same strength.

Many plant communities yield usable wood for small-diameter logs and poles; you might even find suitable trees and larger woody plants in your own neighborhood. Moist areas universally produce fast-growing woody plant materials, even in desert regions. If a sustainable source of building materials is your goal, you can create a small, moist spot that supports luscious woody growth year round by allowing roof runoff or graywater to collect in a water sink (see "A Postage Stamp Garden," p. 161). Traditional European gardens often had a boggy place with willows or hazels that were periodically harvested. In California, native hazel and willow, which form straight, long rods within just a few years, can take the place of the European varieties.

Rough logs and branches are very useful for garden projects and lend a simple beauty as well. Don Weber of Mendocino is a versatile furniture maker and blacksmith interested especially in old English arts and trades. He crafts fences, overhead trellises and archways, and fine furniture out of branches harvested from the local forest using a low-impact method called coppicing. When severely cut back on a regular basis (every year or two), many woody plants, such as willows, alders, and redbuds, are rejuvenated and put out strong, long, straight growth that is especially useful as a craft material. Native peoples practiced this coppicing method to procure materials for construction and tools such as hunting bows. Weber likewise relies on coppicing for supple lengths of wood; in addition, he uses odds and ends of logs or thicker branches, which he cleaves along the grain with a wedge or an ax. From materials that most people would use only for firewood, Weber creates beautifully crafted chairs.

Going out into the woods to harvest or plant is at once both labor and spiritual stimulation. Says Weber, "I become aware of the forest growth patterns and identify individual species, even from a distance. It's different than going to a lumberyard to buy wood. I find little treasures like mushrooms or lady slippers along the way. Technology has removed us from the mystery of our natural environment."[10]

Branches, Bamboo, and Reeds   Branches and twigs pruned from fast-growing trees, harvested from coppiced trees, or even collected from commercial vineyards and orchards can be used in many ways: tied together, they make effective windscreens, panels for an overhead lattice, or fences, in a variety of styles and forms; or they might support a vine espalier, or serve simply as a wall ornament. Long, straight, thin branches that are tied into bundles to compound their strength can be bent to form graceful garden arches or domes, possibly defining the entry into a garden space. Artful arrangement—weaving the branches together, perhaps, or orienting them diagonally to the frame—can lend additional interest to the already attractive natural material.

Bamboo is another versatile garden building material. The strength of bamboo rivals that of most wood, but at the same time it is very lightweight, making it ideal for construction—as many gardens in both the Far East and multicultural California attest (see "Bamboo and Rainwater," p. 164). Not only is bamboo strong and light, but it is also extremely fast growing. Within a few years of planting, once a dense root mass and rhizome base is established, individual bamboo shoots may grow sixteen inches per day. Some species of timber bamboo grow to their full height of sixty feet in just a few months.

A fence made of recycled poles.

Earth and Adobe   Earth has been a common building material since the dawn of civilization. Adobe is mud of clay and sand, often reinforced with straw, that is molded into blocks and then baked in the sun. In the modern marketplace, one can find adobe blocks that are impermeable to water thanks to a petroleum resin that is added to the adobe mixture before it dries, making the blocks more permanent. Construction can also be done with rammed earth, in which a coarse, wet soil blend is tamped into a form made of plywood or metal and allowed to dry in place. Fine sand and clay can also be combined to make mud plaster, which is often used as a protective cover for adobe or rammed-earth structures.

In the southwestern United States, Native Americans still construct their pueblos with sun-baked bricks, which are then covered with a protective layer of plaster. Over the centuries, generations of Europeans used wattle and daub to construct entire villages—homes, barns, commercial buildings, and public structures. In this technique, which is similar to modern lath and plaster, branches are woven together to form a frame (wattle), against which earth plaster (daub) is applied.

African and Middle Eastern earth constructions offer especially rich inspiration for garden structures, featuring a play of shadows in recessed motifs and perforated, sculpted walls with diverse geometrical patterns. Besides

BAMBOO AND RAINWATER

In thinking about the design for a large shared garden, the patriarch of an extended family from Indonesia considered two things especially important: he wanted the children to experience the mystery of nature as he did when he was a boy, and he wanted plenty of bamboo, just as in the old country.

The garden site in Santa Cruz just two blocks from the beach made a coastal habitat theme a natural choice. Sandy soil, wind, and salt spray would be the site's special challenges, but at the same time these conditions supported the cultivation of bamboo, which would serve as a major building material for the garden, in addition to bringing in a little extra income.

To create a riparian area in which bamboo is grown as both a cash crop and a source of construction materials, rainwater is harvested with a roof drainage collector, which channels the water down through a trellis that simultaneously provides shade. The water feeds the pond and tule bogs during the rainy season; in summer, the water level is reduced and the bog humidity supple-mented with graywater, a source of both moisture and nutrients for the bamboo. A meditative water gurgle may be added during dry weather through an egg-beater wind pump, which also aerates the pond water.

The water-collecting trellis, a fence, and side-yard vine holders, all made from bamboo, provide a novel contrast to the native trees and shrubs, which are grouped in plantings with similar needs and so require little maintenance. Low maintenance was also desired in the front garden, where aesthetic appeal is heightened by the accent of a flowering ground cover. In the back-yard, a glass hothouse is used to cultivate heat-loving vegetables and other plants.

Altogether, these natural and cultural elements give the children a sense of participation with the weather, biological cycles, bird migrations, and family culture. Bamboo cultivation also provides them with a rustic play area, a place they share with the family's chickens, which are allowed to wander freely and scavenge for food.

German artist Peter Strum fabricates outdoor structures from a multitude of local plant materials, such as willow branches. (Peter Strum)

being artful, the perforations admit air and light. The walls of buildings also provide a surface for murals painted with brightly contrasting earth plaster.

Many Californians have discovered that homes made with rammed earth maintain an even indoor temperature and are long lasting. David Easton, an architect who integrates modern techniques with traditional building methods, has built many rammed-earth homes in northern California with a time-saving technique he developed, in which the soil mixture is shot from a hose and left to harden.

Walls can be constructed from adobe blocks (bought or homemade) laid on top of each other dry or with adobe mortar between the blocks. For structural integrity, an adobe wall may require buttresses, a broader base, a concrete or stone foundation, or a wood or concrete bonding beam at the top. Beams strapped by metal bands to such a bonding beam can be used to support a trellis. T-bolts embedded in an adobe wall will support ledges or frames for other construction.

While earth constructions lend themselves naturally to the California mission revival style of architecture, adobe and rammed earth are at the same time universal building materials that complement most garden designs. The soft, organic character of earth structures is hard to match and harmonizes well with other garden elements. Decisions on how to shape the earth can be made on the spot, without prior planning, as children and adults alike leave an imprint of their own creativity while the project is under way.

Adobe especially lends itself to imaginative experimentation, being a firm yet workable substance that can take a degree of sculpting (see "Earth and Plaster Fantasies," p. 166). You might make a niche in a thick adobe wall to display an art object, for example, or decorate a wall with carved relief designs. An elaborate stucco facade can be added to adobe walls using stucco netting.

Because rammed earth is less flexible than adobe, some planning is required. Niches and depressions, for example, need to be embedded within the casing before the earth is tamped in. Styrofoam can be used for this purpose and is easily removed when the form is released. Rammed earth, though, lends itself to an altogether different type of design than adobe, such as multiple strata made from different colors and textures of earth.

Prior to using garden soil for earth constructions, it is important to evaluate it aesthetically and structurally by making a test block. Earth used for making adobe should be composed mostly of sand, with just enough clay (10 to 30 percent) to bind the sand particles together. If there is too much clay, the block will crack and admit water, which will ruin its structural integrity. With too much sand, the binding quality of the earth is compromised and may crumble under pressure. Dry fibrous material such as hay is often mixed into adobe to offset such problems. The soil for rammed-earth constructions may contain gravel and requires only small amounts of clay. No organic binding material is necessary, since structural integrity is achieved by ramming the loose material into a tight composition that stands on its own.

The "jar test" can give a rough idea of a soil's composition: place soil from the test site in a jar of water, shake it, and allow it to settle. Larger soil particles (sand and gravel) will settle at the bottom, with finer clay silt on top. If there is too much clay or sand, the composition can be easily adjusted. Clay is found near creeks; it is slick and firm when wet. Remove rocks and other debris by soaking the clay in water; again, heavier particles will sink to

Patterns in a rammed earth wall lend visual interest to the garden.

EARTH AND PLASTER FANTASIES

Ornamentation has long been an important element in gardens. Any sculptural shape tends to enhance the garden setting through contrast with the irregular textures and forms of vegetation. Such contrast can help to give order and definition.

The eaves of historic buildings, the ornate ceilings of state capitols and luxurious mansions, and antique Victorian furniture all have eye-catching details crafted by artisans of bygone eras. These forms offer inspiration for the garden that can be enjoyed long after historic buildings are torn down.

Hand-crafted ornaments, most often made of plaster, find many uses in the garden: small reliefs worked into a wall or bench; a small sculpture set among potted plants; decorative parapets or pedestals, perhaps placed in combination with gates or steps; and ornamental basins and birdbaths all create a pleasing focus of interest. The relief themes adorning such elements are often stylized interpretations of nature, such as vines, flowers, pinecones, fruit, or shells. Simple geometric shapes—spheres, pyramids, and spirals, for instance—are also popular.

Take a family field trip to the library to scout for ornamental patterns—classical, traditional, or modern—such as can be found in the illustrations of old books and magazines. These often inspire artistic expression that will eventually beautify the garden. Materials and methods are simple enough. Plaster, found at any crafts store, is poured into a sand mold and imprinted or carved when it reaches a semisoft stage. Another ornamental material is adobe, which can be purchased as large, stabilized blocks and shaped with a file or a hatchet, cut with a masonry blade attached to a skilsaw, or shaved with a straight-edged shovel. Rustic adobe sculptures may then be given finer detail with plaster.

the bottom and lightweight organic debris will float to the top. Because humus compromises the integrity of both adobe and rammed earth, it is important to scrape away the top layers of organic material to get at the firmer, subsurface layers before collecting large amounts of soil.

Straw Bales The simple elegance of bale construction has caught people's attention in recent years, prompting numerous publications and workshops.

The best hay for building is harvested in the late fall when it is tough and woody—and cheap. Straw bales are ideal for building stout garden walls and benches that, like adobe, are then covered with plaster. The stacked bales must be punctured with rods to stabilize the structure, after which stucco wire or chicken wire is stapled onto stakes that are driven into the side of the straw wall, and stucco or plaster is applied.

WILDLIFE AS A NATURAL RESOURCE

In our efforts to work with local natural resources, California's vanishing wildlife presents a singular, and difficult, challenge. Some of the habitat-building measures discussed in Chapter 3, for instance, may in the short run favor already abundant species that thrive in and around urban environments, such as nonnative cowbirds, house sparrows, and ground squirrels. Any increase in their populations may work at cross-purposes to the agricultural sector's desire to be rid of them or to the preservation of other, threatened, species, such as songbirds. Until such time as enough naturalized, accessible habitat is restored throughout California to allow more vulnerable wildlife species to regain healthy population levels, the twin problems of habitat loss and intense competition from dominant, imported wildlife species will continue to vex us. Yet by providing more space for the common, we may encourage the uncommon. That is the hope, and it appears to be a reasonable one in light of the significant potential gardens have both for increasing acreage that might attract wildlife and for raising environmental awareness.

The idea of enhanced wildlife experiences in your own garden may sound better in theory than in practice. Aesthetic values projected onto wildlife are slippery, particularly when a species shows up that is neither amusing nor enjoyable. At the same time, a Disneyesque perception of the value of the creatures of the natural world will certainly not inspire the earnest and committed public support required to stem wildlife losses. What is needed instead is a recognition that each species of native wildlife is uniquely evolved, a working member of a complex biological system that is now fragmented and therefore dysfunctional in key ways. Ecological balance must be the guiding principle for protecting wildlife, restoring habitat, and welcoming native creatures into the home landscape. They are, after all, as natural a resource as water, soil, and sunlight.[11]

Many of the species discussed here will not be found in every garden, or even be possible in many gardens; however, by being aware of them we can lift our sights to new opportunities to value California's nature. Unlike some of the more familiar birds and butterflies that please us, moreover, some of these species are not necessarily lovable. Nevertheless, we can respect them by appreciating the process that designed them, the details of that design, and the many unique adaptations animals have made to coexist with us.

Making Habitat Accessible

In Chapter 3 we discussed the need for wildlife corridors in and around urban areas, which allow wildlife to find food, shelter, and mates more easily. Gardens in the vicinity of wild or naturalized areas, particularly riparian corridors, can extend habitat by means of native plants and other wildlife amenities.

For earthbound wildlife, however, a major problem remains: fences. Fences by design create a controlled space at a homesite, especially in the backyard, ensuring privacy and keeping small children and pets in while excluding uninvited visitors. If a garden has a pool or other water feature more than a few inches deep, a fence is imperative for child safety. Still, a gardener has choices about what will be permitted entry, choices that may call deeply rooted attitudes about wildlife into question.

At first glance, fences are a practical matter. Asking a gardener with a deer problem to take down an eight-foot-high fence designed to exclude these animals from the property may seem ludicrous, unless the garden is redesigned to harmonize with its natural surroundings. Deer are attracted to the lush foliage of gardens seasonally, particularly in summer, when naturally available food sources are limited. A California landscape garden, in step for the most part with its surroundings by relying on native plants, which experience summer dormancy, would need a deer barrier only where a warm-season vegetable garden or perennial herb garden is planted. Native shrubs such as manzanita, sage, and ceanothus can withstand some pruning by deer once they are established. Some beautiful nonnative herbs are reliably deer proof as well, including rosemary, lavender, thyme, and certain salvias.

Fences, in addition to being practical measures, are symbolic of mental barriers to wildlife, for they represent attitudes about perceived or possible risks. Throughout history nature has been demonized, romanticized, and, more recently, rationalized—interpretations that one sees encoded in myriad cultural outlets, including art, fairy tales, architecture, and gardens.[12] Rather than working in successive stages, these perceptions tend to be layered, such that the demons in nature are never entirely banished but rather are reconstructed in a less threatening light.

Rachel Carson was one of the first environmentalists to awaken the public to the idea that humans, as a species, live in an interdependent web with all other inhabitants of the earth. Her elaboration of the prospect of a "silent spring" defined a clear turning point in people's perception of nature.[13] What affects wildlife affects us, though that fact is not always obvious in the short term. Now, as we look ahead, concern about the very survival of *Homo sapiens* as a species moves us to embrace nature more closely, even as we recall some of the very real fears that led our ancestors to push it away—to "civilize" it—in times gone by.

There is no question that nature can be annoying and even dangerous; plants, animals, insects, and microbes all can pose a danger to people and pets. Reports about tick-borne Lyme disease, chipmunks transmitting bubonic plague, skunks and bats infected with rabies, and mosquitoes carrying encephalitis confirm real fears about allowing nature to come too close. Although such reports are localized or infrequent, they cannot be dismissed out of hand.

Risk management is a familiar concept these days, whereby the benefits and risks of an endeavor are weighed and an action decided on accordingly. Allowing wildlife to approach human settlements always requires careful consideration, but generally the benefits outweigh the risks, as most people realize from their own experience. For example, although honeybee stings cause more human fatalities than the bites and stings of all other venomous insects, spiders, and vertebrates combined, gardeners welcome honeybees because of the important role they play in pollination. A basic familiarity with their habits—particularly the simple need to give them space—usually suffices to bring about peaceful coexistence.

Any species of wildlife that presents an unacceptable risk, of course, must be excluded from the garden. Landscape gardeners can exert some control over visitors by erecting relatively impermeable barriers and by withdrawing amenities. It goes without saying that venomous snakes and spiders, not to mention pesky mosquitoes, are not welcome, and they can be controlled to some extent by, for example, removing stacked piles of wood and standing water. However, other animals can be of great interest, acting as important links in the ecological scheme of the bioregion, whether as part of the food web or in their capacity as pollinators. When designing the garden, therefore, risk management assessment—done with an open mind and, if needed, a certain amount of research—is key. For in the end, education is the best tool for stripping away our fears.

Snakes Regardless of your views about snakes, it is comforting to know that they are very rarely seen in urban or suburban gardens that are not directly associated with farmland or a natural area. Many of California's thirty-eight species of lizards and thirty-seven species of snakes, all in the order Squamata, are well adapted to the arid West (the few exceptions live in moist riparian habitats). Their local abundance, however, has been greatly affected by land development and other modes of habitat destruction. The harmless coast horned lizard, for example, is now generally restricted to remnant populations in the foothills, and water-loving species of garter snakes, like other riparian wildlife, are threatened by severe habitat loss. Three species in southern California (the barefoot banded gecko, Coachella Valley fringe-toed lizard, and southern rubber boa) and five species in other parts of the state (the blunt-nosed leopard lizard, island night lizard, Alameda whipsnake, San Francisco garter snake, and giant garter snake) are on the federal list of threatened and endangered species.

Although the booming sales of exotic reptiles as pets would seem to indicate a certain fascination with these descendants of dinosaurs, that enthusiasm apparently does not extend to wild snakes, which are almost universally reviled—primarily as a result of misinformation and misunderstanding. And this loathing has serious repercussions. People's fear of rattlesnakes, for example, which account for three of the four venomous snakes found in California, has made life very difficult for the gopher snake. The gopher snake is indeed similar in size—up to six feet—and markings to the diamondback rattler, and it doesn't help its cause by shaking its tail when alarmed. However, not only do the ranges of these two snakes differ, but gopher snakes are easily distinguished by their pointed tail and slender head; the rattler's triangular head, in contrast, is twice as wide as its neck. Also often misidentified is the kingsnake, which, because of its pattern of white bands (common kingsnake) or yellow and red bands (mountain kingsnake) with black, tends to be mistaken for the fourth venomous species in California, the coral snake, even though that snake is limited to the southeastern corner of California, near the Imperial Valley.

Study of the habits and physical form of snakes—such as the adaptive features of their eyes and head—reveals important clues to the workings of natural selection. The endangered Alameda whipsnake makes a good example. Most snakes have poor depth perception because their eyes are mounted on the sides of their head. The whipsnake compensates for this disadvantage by means of two characteristics, one behavioral, the other morphological: by moving its head from side to side, it can apparently better judge striking distance; and thin, dark grooves on each side of its head running from eye to mouth give it a hunting edge by functioning like sights on a gun barrel.[14]

In terms of reducing our fear of them, it is perhaps most comforting to know that when frightened, snakes retreat if they can, seeking cover under brush or a rock, in a wood pile, or in a rodent burrow. Indeed, the vast majority of snakes in California present no risk to humans.

Restoring Garden Food Webs

If television commercials for bug sprays and fumigation services are any indication, homeowners would prefer to have all insects eliminated from house and garden. It is a daunting prospect. Measured in terms of biomass or number of species, insects and other small invertebrates make up 95 percent or more of terrestrial animal life. In California alone, compared to approximately five hundred vertebrate species—birds, mammals, amphibians, and reptiles—there are upward of twenty-seven thousand species of insects.[15] This abundance is good, because insects are critical to a healthy, balanced environment.

Along with plants and soil organisms, insects form one of three legs of a system on which the entire global food web is based. Not only do they serve as food themselves, but insects, by distribution and numbers, are also the most important plant pollinators, together with bats and birds. Without pollinators, our diets would contain no food with which we are now familiar. As E. O. Wilson, a noted biologist and expert on ants, comments in a Xerces Society brochure, "Quite simply, the terrestrial world is turned by insects and a few other invertebrate groups: the living world would probably survive the demise of all vertebrates, in greatly altered form of course, but life on land and in the sea would collapse down to a few simple plants and microorganisms without invertebrates."

Insects are prolific breeders—an excellent survival strategy. However, insects survive only as a habitat allows them to survive; they are low on the food web and are kept in check if diverse species are present. Insects feast on each other, and reptiles, amphibians, birds, bats, and other small mammals all rely on consuming the egg, larval, or adult forms of insects to survive. Aphids, for example, are an important food source for the beneficial insects every gardener wants to encourage, such as ladybugs (both larval and adult), lacewings, and hover flies. The latter, one of the most important flower pollinators, synchronizes its life cycle with that of aphids.[16]

Beetles   The order Coleoptera (meaning "sheath-winged"), to which beetles and weevils with brittle, armorlike wings belong, is so large and diverse that it accounts for 40 percent of all known insect species. Beetles have adapted to almost every niche imaginable, on all continents except Antarctica. Whirligigs, for instance, the small, round skaters seen twirling on water surfaces, feed on water insects and their larvae. They are perfectly adapted to search for their prey, having eyes that are divided so that one half sees above the water and the other half below.

The order includes some of the worst agricultural pests known to humankind, but it also includes some of the most ecologically beneficial, like the familiar orange and black ladybird beetles and the many decomposers, janitorial beetles that recycle dung or clean animal carcasses to the bone, thereby enriching the nutrient content of soil. Pollen-feeding beetles such as checkered and long-horned beetles with vivid colors are easily spotted on the flowers of many native plants. Nocturnal predaceous ground beetles, of which there are nearly eight hundred species in California alone, and their larvae prey on other ground-dwelling insects. Turn over a piece of wood or debris during the daytime, and you're likely to see a member of this family.

As eminently successful as this order is, it does have a cautionary tale to tell. The delta green ground beetle, which evolved with California's vernal pools, is in immediate danger of extinction owing to habitat loss. Currently, as far as we know, it is found only at Olcott Lake, in the Nature Conservancy's Jepson Prairie Preserve in Solano County.

Both larval and adult forms of ladybird beetles are voracious aphid hunters; after hatching from an orange egg laid near a mass of aphids, a single larva can eat several thousand aphids, during which time it molts several times. Ladybird larvae look like tiny alligators and are often mistaken for pests before they develop into the familiar shiny, round form. As winter approaches, several species of this common little beetle (there are more than 125 species of ladybird beetles in California alone) undertake an amazing migration to the canyons and hills of the coastal ranges and Sierra Nevada, where they find each other through a keen sense of smell and begin hibernating in massive groups, surviving even winter snows.

No other beetle enjoys the same esteem as ladybirds do. However, because of the newsworthy villains that destroy agricultural crops, such as the Japanese beetle, which is threatening to push its way into California from its stronghold in eastern states, all are suspect, and many are killed. Simply observing where a beetle is and what it is doing tells a great deal about whether it is a serious pest—and most are not.

Bee Flies and Hover Flies   Many flies of the order Diptera—meaning "two-winged"—mimic bees but can be distinguished from them by their wings (bees have two pairs of wings, while flies have only one pair); by their agility, which they demonstrate through speed, sudden changes of direction, and instantaneous reaction times (by comparison, bees are quite cumbersome fliers); by their ability to hover in a stationary position; and by their resting position (bees fold their wings over their backs, while flies hold them slightly out to the side). Bee flies and hover flies also come in many different colors and forms. The larvae of some species of bee flies prey on the eggs and young of grasshoppers and beetles. Hover flies feed on nectar, pollen, and aphid "honeydew." Next to bees, these flies are among the most important pollinators, visiting garden flowers on regular routes three to five times an hour.[17]

Parasitic Wasps   Parasitic wasps of the genus *Trichogramma* play a very important role in the biological control of farm and garden pests. If you see a dried-out caterpillar cocoon with a small hole drilled in it, one of these tiny wasps may well have made it. The hole is where newly hatched wasps, which started out life as eggs laid on the caterpillar just before it pupated, emerged after they finished a leisurely meal. Although these wasps parasitize some desirable caterpillars, such as the one that becomes the beautiful anise swallowtail, they prey on many more that are unwelcome pests.

To encourage parasitic wasps, avoid routine use of insecticides and include in your garden a variety of food plants that offer pollen and nectar for the adult wasps. Species that have a long bloom and those that produce small flowers with accessible pollen and nectar for the tiny wasps (four or five of which fit on the head of a pin) will probably provide the most benefit.[18]

Bats   Compared to birds and butterflies, bats receive scant notice in wildlife gardening literature, which is surprising because bats readily adapt to human settlement and they help control insect populations. Part of the reason may be that bats are a known vector for rabies; however, less than 0.5 percent of bats ever acquire rabies, and the chances of their transmitting the disease to humans are even slimmer. The more significant reason that bats are reviled may be their association with the occult in the West. Contrast this with attitudes in the Orient, where bats are often considered symbols of good luck, long life, and happiness.

The nine hundred–odd species of bats in the order Chiroptera (meaning "hand-winged") are the only mammals to have achieved true flight, which explains why they have their very own order with no other members. Most species of bat orient their flight and forage by means of echolocation, the production of short, high-pitched sound pulses far beyond the range of human hearing that are reflected from objects in the vicinity. It is a fascinating evolutionary achievement, especially considering the fact that the target of bat sonar is often no larger than a mosquito. Bats, forty species of which are known in the United States, are divided into two groups: one family of principally visually oriented bats and another seventeen families that are acoustically oriented (though most members of these families also have excellent vision).

In California, the two species of bats that are most commonly seen are the guano bat (wingspan of about eight inches) and the hoary bat (wingspan of about sixteen inches); both are nocturnal and voracious insectivores. The guano bat used to be called the Mexican free-tailed bat; its new common name reflects the commercial value of the rich fertilizer it deposits in copious quantities at its roosting sites. This bat prefers to roost in caves, in attics, and on the walls of buildings. In the winter it migrates to escape cold weather and a declining supply of insects. In the twilight of a warm summer evening, the small dark shadow that flits about in a seemingly erratic pattern is very likely the guano bat getting a fix on the location of mosquitoes, moths, and other insects. The hoary bat gets its name from the silver-tipped hair on its back, which gives it an aged appearance. Its wings are uniquely engineered for controlled flight, and it is a graceful insect hunter. It prefers to roost in trees, where it sleeps hanging upside down during the day. In the fall it migrates to coastal areas.

Bats reproduce very slowly, giving birth to only one offspring per year on average. Like cavity-nesting birds, many will accept boxes for nesting and raising their young, which then typically return to their birthplace year after year. Increased use of insecticides has placed bats on endangered lists throughout the world, and they have also suffered the same losses of habitat that have reduced the populations of much of California's other wildlife.

A simple way to encourage bats to take up residence in your garden is to provide a roost: wrap a piece of tarpaper around a tree trunk at least ten feet above the ground, attaching it in such a way as to leave a loose, wide, bell-shaped opening at the bottom.

Songbirds: A Special Concern

Many native birds as well as visitors that spend part of their life cycle here are facing extreme pressures as they try to find appropriate nesting sites and raise their broods. The western bluebird is a case in point. This bird breeds in the open woodlands of foothills, especially among oaks or deciduous trees lining creek corridors, where it seeks out a tree cavity, preferably overlooking an open area with low vegetative cover, for its nest. This type of edge habitat, particularly with the amenity of a nest cavity, is now scarce. Only 2 to 5 percent of California's presettlement riparian woodland is left, yet more than 135 native bird species depend on it for all or part of their life cycle, making competition extreme.[19]

The problem is magnified by aggressive imported birds such as European starlings and house sparrows (formerly called English sparrows), which out-compete native birds for the available nest sites. Native birds that do manage to find nest sites are further challenged by brown-headed cowbirds. This sturdy, resourceful bird, originally a companion of the Great Plains buffalo herds, has managed to expand its range tremendously. As the buffalo declined in number, cowbirds followed the arriving settlers, who cleared the land for cattle and other grazing animals. Cowbirds lay their eggs in the nests of more than 200 species of North American birds and then leave them to be cared for by the surrogate parents; this clever ploy allowed adult cowbirds to constantly move with the buffalo herds and still produce as many as forty eggs a year for other birds to incubate. The larger, more aggressive cowbird chicks hatch sooner and dominate the food resources provided by the foster parents, which decreases the survival rate of the smaller, younger non-cowbird hatchlings. This practice, known as cowbird parasitism, has led to a significant drop in the reproductive rates of California's native birds and of migrants that nest here.

Loss of riparian habitat and other pressures that depress reproductive rates have forced state agencies to accord such species as the Bell's vireo, yellow-billed cuckoo, and willow flycatcher protected status, and nonprofit private groups concerned with the well-being of prized songbirds like the bluebird have launched such projects as the California Bluebird Recovery Program under the auspices of the National Audubon Society. Other initiatives such as California Partners in Flight represent coalitions of public agencies and private organizations hoping to stem population declines among migratory songbirds.[20]

Turning a backyard garden into a bird refuge requires that multiple needs be addressed simultaneously. For example, food must be provided in conjunction with cover, for the birds' safety. In many cases, nest boxes remedy the housing shortage that has become so acute; however, care must be taken that the box is properly designed and placed for the target bird population, lest you inadvertently invite undesirable birds to take up residence (see "Providing Nest Sites and Materials for Birds," pp. 76–77).

Neotropical Migratory Songbirds   Migration is a great mystery of life, and we still understand but poorly just why animals as diverse as birds, whales, and butterflies travel so far—often thousands of miles—from feeding areas to specific breeding grounds. Nevertheless, Californians have been entrusted by nature with a responsibility to preserve migrant songbirds that breed and nest here.

Every autumn like clockwork, neotropical migrants (*neo-* referring to the New World) depart California for wintering grounds in the tropics and then in the spring fly north again to breed near the spot where they were born. How do they do it? The easy answer is that they teach one another the route. That is part of the story for some species, but not all of it. Consider an inexperienced blackpoll warbler, for example. A young bird on its own migrates from western Alaska to Venezuela by crossing Canada to New England and then heading due south over the western Atlantic. By itself that is a marvelous, perilous feat, but perhaps even more notable is the fact that it returns home via another route: over the Caribbean to land, then diagonally across the North American continent.[21]

A complex relationship between genetic (evolutionary) and external (environmental) cues drives and modifies migratory behavior. The evolutionary mechanisms that enable a bird to migrate include the ability to orient itself to the sun, the stars, the earth's magnetic field, and polarized light and interpret these as a journey's itinerary. A clear indication of the influence of environment is the fact that some birds don't necessarily migrate; local conditions of adequate winter food and low snowfall can induce dark-eyed juncos, for example, to overwinter in an area.

The fact that these beautiful singers manage to survive such long, arduous journeys—locating food and water along the way, avoiding predators, finding places to rest—in a world that becomes more inhospitable with each passing year would seem to suggest that they are tough enough to adapt when they return to find that their nesting areas have been bulldozed, but field studies show otherwise. The mounting pressures on embattled songbird populations from loss of nesting sites, loss of habitat along migratory routes, pesticide use, and the onslaught of exotic species such as cowbirds have been manifested in the past two decades by a 50 percent decline in migratory flocks.[22] As their numbers have dropped, other, more aggressive species such as crows, jays, and starlings have thrived and now prey on the eggs and young of songbirds. In addition, each year in prime nesting areas feral cats kill enormous numbers of migratory songbirds—a source of heated conflict between cat lovers and those who want to save the songbirds.

Although we know why overall reproductive rates among songbirds are in decline, there are no fast or easy remedies. For most species, information about just what is affecting which part of a specific bird's life cycle is lacking. For instance, cowbird parasitism is devastating warbler, tanager, flycatcher, and vireo populations, but not other species; for these others the greater problem seems to be low shrub diversity, which means that predators can find them more easily.

Any gardener wishing to attract migrant songbirds that breed and nest locally would need to learn about those species' preferences in habitat, food, ground cover, and nesting sites. In general, upon arrival songbirds look for a place that offers insects (caterpillars especially) for their young, nest materials or nest sites not already occupied by competing birds, and sufficient safety from cats and other predators. Experts also suggest that restoring native plant species may help, especially oak trees and native grasses in former oak savannas, or native cottonwoods, willows, and diverse shrubs in areas once covered in riparian vegetation.[23]

California's Vanishing Amphibians

Amphibians (from the Greek, "living in two ways") depend on water to reproduce and require a moist environment during adult life. Certainly habitat loss, but also perhaps insecticide use and stream pollution, has caused salamander, frog, and toad populations throughout California to either disappear from or be drastically reduced in areas that have long sustained them. Seven species of salamanders face extinction, and there is special concern for the California newt. Habitat restoration or mitigation is of little use to species like the California newt, which must, like salmon, return to the place where it was spawned in order to mate and reproduce.

The enemies of these creatures appear to be legion. An unnerving number of amphibians in supposedly pristine environmental niches exhibit the gross skeletal abnormalities seen in colonies of laboratory animals exposed to mutagens. Like the canary in the mine, whose demise signaled the presence of lethal gases, the unprecedented and largely unexplainable losses among California's twenty-three species of frogs and toads and twenty-six species of salamanders have led many researchers to hypothesize that an ecological collapse is in the making. As a result, the effects of increased exposure to environmental pollutants and ultraviolet light (via ozone depletion), to which amphibians' skin is highly sensitive, are receiving keen attention. In addition, frogs such as the western spadefoot have become much rarer in California since the introduction of the bullfrog, a large predator from the East Coast. Once bullfrogs find their way into a pond, the population of other frogs and aquatic inhabitants rapidly declines. Habitat loss, however, is perhaps the biggest concern—both actual wetland loss and increased car traffic, which affects these animals particularly as they set off on their seasonal migrations to and from their breeding grounds.

Because the amphibian life cycle is tied to water, these species do not disperse widely and often form rather isolated populations, which is a disadvantage in terms of survival. This vulnerability is counterbalanced, however, by their not having to spend energy on warming their bodies, which allows them to live on proportionately less food than warm-blooded animals. Most birds, for instance, consume one to two times their body weight in food every day; to meet that need generally requires wide-range, constant foraging. Amphibians, in contrast, can meet their needs locally, which may make it easier to provide habitat for them in a garden (see "A Toad-Friendly Garden," opposite).

Gardens in the vicinity of a moist environment or wildlife corridor may be especially suited to attracting and sheltering amphibians, such as the western toad or the small, bright green Pacific treefrog, the most common amphibian in California, which likes to hide in low vegetation and seeks out permanent or temporary pools. In coastal mountains and valleys, and foothills west of the Sierra Nevada, the red-legged frog might also be drawn to a garden habitat that supplies an abundance of insects.

Frogs and Toads   Frogs and toads, members of the order Anura, share many characteristics. They all breed and lay their eggs in aquatic environments,

A TOAD-FRIENDLY GARDEN

Charles Goldman, a specialist in the study of freshwater bodies renowned for his efforts to save Lake Tahoe, and a professor of ecology at the University of California, Davis, has long advocated preserving toads in the urban landscape. He recently convinced the city of Davis to build a "toad tunnel" under a new highway overpass to reconnect them to their pond habitat. He also has developed a practical approach to attracting toads to his own garden in Davis.

Goldman outlines a few principles for making a toad-friendly garden. First, he says, these nocturnal animals need several cool, damp hiding places for their daytime siesta (this is especially important in areas with hot summers) as well as a ready, safe water supply in which to "tank up" each night. The latter can be easily provided by digging a depression in which a shallow plastic dish can rest. Goldman says that potted plant saucers, eight to twelve inches in diameter with an inch-and-a-half rim, are ideal; these are available at most hardware or garden stores. Since toads tend to work along fences at night, locating the water hole along a fence line is most effective. Place the dish under a heavy bush, dug in level with the ground, in the coolest, shadiest part of the garden, where it can be topped up when evaporation and toad tanking deplete the water supply. One or more "toad holes" are also necessary, giving the toad daytime shelter. These can be made under cement stepping stones, where a depression is hollowed out and a small entrance dug. The soil around and under the stepping stones should be kept damp but not muddy. In the hot Davis summer. Goldman notes, the toad holes must be insulated by placing a thin, damp board under the stepping stone and providing some shade so that solar radiation does not overheat the animals. Come fall, Goldman loosens the earth beneath the stones so that the toads can dig themselves well into the ground for further insulation and moisture during the months of hibernation.

If cover is sparse in the garden and insects are in short supply, hunting access to the surrounding area should be provided under a gate or through a small opening dug under a fence, so they can range out at night to forage in the greenbelt or in neighboring gardens. Goldman has noticed that toads tend to leave their burrows if they dry out and return if they are wetted down. Locating the watering holes near vegetable gardens also works well, since these areas tend to attract insects, which the toads will eat, especially spiders, earwigs, and sow bugs. They also eat various ground beetles and tomato worms. (Toads do not, however, seem to care for snails or slugs, in Goldman's experience.)

Goldman says toads add an interesting, living dimension to an urban garden. He has two in regular residence as well as two frequent visitors that leave for days at a time but return after patrolling the surrounding area. By inviting toads into the garden, he adds meaning and diversity of life. He also expresses his larger environmental concerns in his own backyard.

including naturalized garden ponds with aquatic vegetation. Egg clusters, usually deposited on underwater stems, hatch within a few days into tadpoles, which in turn are readily consumed by birds, fish, and dragonfly larvae, among others; they therefore, especially in a small body of water, need adequate protective vegetation. Adult toads spend much more of their time on land than frogs, often at a fair distance from the water in which they lay their

Amphibians need only a relatively small habitat in the garden, as long as there is ample water nearby.

eggs. Outside of breeding season both frogs and toads may hide in vegetation or under rotting logs or burrow into a moist niche during the day, becoming active at dusk. During the winter they often hibernate in holes or in mud at the bottom of a pond; toads also may hibernate during extremely hot weather. Frogs and toads eat a variety of foods, including insects, insect larvae, slugs, and earthworms.

Salamanders These rare creatures and their relatives the newts are members of the order Caudata. They resemble lizards in form but instead of a scaly skin they have a smooth, absorptive skin, sometimes adorned with red or yellow spots or stripes, which must remain moist. Because they need a consistently damp habitat, they live in close association with vernal pools and foothill streams, where, as in the case of newts and the California tiger salamander, they may also breed. The California slender salamander, a lungless species that requires a thin coating of moisture on its skin for oxygen absorption, deposits its eggs in moist cavities. Temperature and humidity sensors regulate their seasonal activities, compelling them in spring to abandon their solitary lives and congregate for the courtship dance. Outside of breeding season, these creatures spend most of their time underground in the burrows of ground squirrels and gophers, where they hunt worms, spiders, sow bugs, and a variety of insect larvae. Some species do come out on cloudy or rainy days, which is the best time to look for them.

COMING FULL CIRCLE

California, as viewed from space, has no abstract boundaries of city, county, or state. Rather, California is part of a continent, which is surrounded by ocean, which together are part of a planet, and so on. Similarly, the original garden design that nature crafted here was not rigid, with straight lines and tidy borders, but was a dynamic place where ecological processes operated and natural wonders evolved. California was a place of movement, where plant species found new niches when conditions changed and wildlife traversed the state following the cues of the seasons.

California viewed up close now, whether over a backyard fence or from a freeway, is a different matter. Everywhere there are boundaries, barriers, and exclusions to California's native fauna and flora that jeopardize their existence. Air quality, water availability, and habitats crafted by nature from local resources, all once part of a successful ecological system that evolved over millennia, have been changed by human activities.

With descriptions and stories of these resources, beginning with habitat and ending with wildlife, we have illustrated how people can interact with the California landscape, not as users, but as participants who can make a difference literally in their own backyards. The power of the process that arrested millennia of ecological achievement in just over a century, exploiting it for human advancement, can, we suggest, be used just as well to set things right. That power is codified in our very name as a species, *Homo sapiens*, Latin for "wise man." This cognitive ability to derive meaning sets us apart as a species; though it sometimes leads us to do wrong, it also defines our best quality. Cognitive ability is deeply biological in nature. It arises from what today we view as a joint venture between "mind" and "body," and yet native peoples knew that these aspects are, in the end, indistinguishable. Native Californians, indeed, preserved the link between the cerebral and the visceral in all aspects of their community lives. A sensual knowledge of the earth was the key to understanding, and benefiting from, ecological processes. It was productive of a worldview that was essentially biocratic. This is the goal of the California landscape garden as well.

A seasonal creekbed serves as a small habitat corridor in this Oceanside garden. (Landscape designer: David Buchanan)

HEALING
LANDSCAPES

We are returning to our native place after a long absence, meeting once again
with our kin in the earth community.

Thomas Berry, *Dream of the Earth*

The simple phrase *healing landscapes* carries a dual meaning. In one sense, it
signifies the therapeutic power of the garden to heal the physical and emo-
tional distresses of people.[1] This book, however, has focused on the comple-
mentary sense: how we, as gardeners, can help to restore the nature of California in our personal terrain. In the end, of course, both these meanings
belong to an unending circle. For as we work in our own gardens to heal the
larger California garden, we are ourselves healed and restored by a personal
habitat that is full of life and ecologically robust, in which nature itself provides deep and lasting meaning.

The California landscape is essentially a healing landscape. (Jane Miller)

This relationship underscores the reality that it is easier for plants and gardens to heal people than it is for us to heal ecosystems. As we move away from an attitude of dominance over nature, it is no less arrogant to think that ecosystems that took eons to create can be fully restored by human intervention or that restoration of native habitats, plants, and wildlife can in fact "heal the planet." We do not know, for example, how to "fix" critical natural processes, such as the carbon and nitrogen cycles. These cycles require the systematic work of members from all the biological kingdoms over long periods of time. They perform for the planet what the major organ systems, including the immune system, perform for the human body: sustain life by digesting, metabolizing, purifying, and recycling organic material. Only the earth knows how to do that for itself; as Thomas Berry observes:

> We need to realize that the ultimate custody of the earth belongs to the earth. The issues we are considering are fundamental earth issues that need to be dealt with in some direct manner by the earth itself. As humans we need to recognize the limitations in our capacity to deal with these compre-

It is in the interaction between people and the environment that healing occurs. (Robin Moore)

hensive issues of the earth's functioning. So long as we are under the illusion that we know best what is good for the earth and for ourselves, then we will continue our present course, with its devastating consequences on the entire earth community. . . . The earth will solve its problems, and possibly our own, if we will let the earth function in its own ways. We need only listen to what the earth is telling us.[2]

A NEW VOCABULARY

In the spirit of cooperation, what we can do is take first steps. Wherever it is still possible, we must put nature's things and its life-supporting processes back where they once were. Then, we must watch and listen. The vocabulary used in this book—ecology, bioregion, habitat, plant community, biodiversity, genus and species, seasonal process, sustainable resource—will help us to accomplish this: to understand nature, communicate with each other, and seek out the knowledge required to return to a garden site its natural endowment.

A systematic understanding of California's nature that speaks to the mind is crucial, but just as important is an imaginative understanding that speaks to the spirit. The most direct route to the imagination is through the senses, and throughout these chapters we have described imaginative impulses that embody garden colors, sounds, smells, and textures. To say that a native

Ecologically healthy gardens help us to be in touch with nature and, in a personal way, to heal the earth.

grassland habitat in the Sacramento Valley bioregion contains a plant community of the valley oak, *Quercus lobata,* and species within the *Stipa, Poa,* and *Aristida* genera of bunchgrasses is one thing. It is another thing to love that landscape, and that does not happen until one can imagine the teeming life it supports, the beauty of gray-green oaken foliage suspended over golden fields, and the herbal perfume of dried grasses and wildflowers. Until the venerable age of such a landscape can be comprehended, along with its place at the center of the valley's ecological life and in nature as a whole, it will not be essential to us. By nurturing a small patch of native-inspired habitat in our own yards, perhaps we can begin to regain that life-giving presence.

KNOWING WITH EXPERIENCE

The vanishing oak has long been regarded by naturalists and landscape designers alike as a symbol for the single most important, most fundamental aspect of California's nature: its Mediterranean climate and virtually rainless summers. Stately, resilient, beautiful, long lived, the oak thrives in arid summer conditions and in doing so helps myriad other plant and animal species to thrive as well. Its ecological impact reverberates at far distances from the tree itself, as with a pebble tossed into a pond.

There is another species that also symbolizes California's nature, and it may represent for a California landscape gardener the qualities necessary to respond to the environmental challenges we now face. It is the western fence lizard, a small creature that is fast, alert, agile, and adaptable. It is not currently endangered, and we hope to keep it that way. Sometimes called the blue-bellied lizard, the fence lizard is California's most familiar reptile and seems to do well in close proximity to people. Children prize them, though the lizards can usually evade capture by sacrificing their tail, which grows back. Whipsnakes, hawks, and other stealthy predators prize them too: the fence lizard can to some extent replace small rodents in their diets.

One of the most fascinating things about lizards is their so-called third eye, a small spot centered on top of the head. This tiny organ—actually the pineal gland, in a uniquely adapted form—like the other two larger eyes, has a pupil, cornea, lens, and retina, but it lacks an iris mechanism that would allow it to register images. This third eye, it turns out, senses light and temperature, somehow keeping track of how much heat and light a lizard is exposed to and cueing the pituitary and thyroid glands accordingly. By this means, potentially deceptive environmental cues, such as atypically warm weather, are interpreted correctly so that the lizard's reproductive cycle does not accelerate.[3]

The fence lizard's agile and adaptive nature even in urban environments can teach us a great deal, but it is that third eye—its sixth sense, so to speak—that is essential to its survival as a species. In similar manner, we as gardeners must develop a "sixth sense" with respect to environmental cues. Had such a sense already been in operation, the disappearance of the songbirds, butterflies, and frogs of childhood memory would have been noticed by gardeners nationwide long before a public alert was issued by the news media. Even in the day-to-day maintenance of a garden, an innate responsiveness to seasonal processes and local conditions is important. Learning how Nature gets the results she does from sometimes limited resources, such as water, requires a sensitive awareness to the natural system that is a garden. Such a sensibility is arrived at by joining knowledge with experience.

The California landscape garden reflects our culture and imagination, as in this Mexican American garden in Chula Vista.

A SENSE OF COMMUNITY

Self-reliance has long been valued in Western tradition. But of course, self-reliance is not exactly what it claims to be: it always has and always will be predicated on a deep reliance on nature. Settlers up to the present day have taken what they could from the natural bounty of California in order to survive and prosper. What is clear now is that there are limits to California's nature; the mythologized perceptions of inexhaustible riches and infinite space simply do not hold true. The notion that humans by birthright and ability can and should subdue the earth becomes more and more problematic as the struggle to prosper in this place intensifies among people from many cultures. Caught up in that struggle are all the native species that increasingly have no place at all in this finite landscape.

The point here is not that the idea of self-reliance should be abandoned; rather, the creativity and ingenuity that foster that concept must be redirected from self-interest to shared common interests. The notion of a shared biological community that includes native plants and animals as well as people is not a philosophical abstraction but a fact of nature. The wise use of local and recycled resources is therefore the crux of self-reliance. The pace at which California's ecosystems are being dismantled and wildlife eliminated cannot be sustained without serious consequences to the mammal species that sits at the top of the food web—*Homo sapiens*. What we are leisurely indifferent to

The garden is ultimately a setting for personal expression and renewal. (Designer: Marcia Donahue)

in the near term we will pay for in the long term. This rational fear about an uncertain future is what our arcadian myths have always tried to suppress yet our knowledge now inevitably confirms.

Nature has much to teach us, and the first hard lesson appears to be that as a species we are well within the sphere of ecological rules by which species rise and fall, not outside the natural system as we have long imagined. A restored alliance among people, plants, wildlife, and place is a win-win situation: nature is recognized for its gift of life and accorded more respect, while people secure a place for future generations. Rather than creating new myths to shore up the ones that no longer work, such as those centered on technological fixes, we must change course by means of knowledge and empathy. Allowing the intelligent design of the original California landscape once again to shine through is what it means to regain an authentic sense of place.

MOVING FROM AN AGE OF EXTINCTION TO AN AGE OF RESTORATION

According to E. O. Wilson, even such a valued human quality as altruism has genetic roots in natural selection. In this light, the desire to help others—or in the context of this book, to preserve California's biodiversity—though manifested as benevolence or empathy, is evolved from principles of survival

of the fittest. It is in our own best interests that we protect the interests of *all* life forms. Native peoples knew this from long experience living under nature's sovereignty. Local resources were used efficiently and judiciously, and giving-away ceremonies of highly valued commodities encoded the knowledge that to give was to receive.

Biodiversity is the means by which nature crafts new solutions for changing environmental circumstances. It is how life became distributed among the known biological kingdoms, how new species still arise, and how old species adapt to changed conditions. Within biodiversity is harbored a treasure trove of genetic resources that have allowed humans to derive new medicines, foods, and materials to enhance the quality of our lives. It is biodiversity that the California landscape garden and gardener nurture. With the third eye of a lizard we know why we must let the healing begin. E.O. Wilson perhaps states it best:

> We should judge every scrap of biodiversity as priceless while we learn to use it and come to understand what it means to humanity. We should not knowingly allow any species or race to go extinct. And let us go beyond mere salvage to begin the restoration of natural environments, in order to enlarge wild populations and stanch the hemorrhaging of biological wealth. There can be no purpose more inspiriting than to begin the age of restoration, reweaving the wondrous diversity of life that still surrounds us.[4]

APPENDIX: SOME USEFUL SOURCES

To aid in creating a landscape garden we include here some resources that the ecological gardener or garden designer may find useful, including horticultural and native plant organizations, some leading landscape architects and designers, locations of nurseries specializing in native and drought-tolerant plants, and books on various specialized topics. While not comprehensive, this section is intended as a starting point for people wanting more information on issues raised in this book. In addition to these resources, there is a vast library of material on the World Wide Web, accessible through most search engines.

GENERAL INFORMATION AND ADVICE

Information and advice can be found in a variety of places. Most newspapers, for example, have a regular gardening column, and often the columnist welcomes readers' questions. Local nurseries, especially ones that specialize in drought-tolerant or native plants, are excellent resources as well.

University of California Cooperative Extension, administered by the UC Division of Agriculture and Natural Resources (DANR), is an invaluable resource for horticultural and agricultural questions of all kinds. The service also publishes a wide variety of pamphlets on specialized topics, including fire suppression in the home landscape and oak-compatible plants. Local offices are listed in the phone book under County Government, Cooperative Extension. For further information, access the DANR web site at http://danr.ucop.edu; or contact the Division of Agriculture and Natural Resources, University of California, 300 Lakeside Drive, Oakland, CA 94612-3550, tel.: (510) 987-0060.

The California Native Plant Society (1722 J St., Suite 17, Sacramento, CA 95814; 916-447-2677; http://www.calpoly.edu/~dchippin/cnps_main.html) is the place to turn for questions regarding California natives. The society publishes a wide assortment of informative and beautiful books, and local chapters can be good sources of both information and, in annual sales, plants.

On the World Wide Web, *Urban Agriculture Notes,* published in Vancouver, B.C. (http://www.cityfarmer.org), provides much valuable information on such topics as composting, worm composting, water management, and organic farming, with links to associated sites worldwide. Two other useful garden web sites are the Bay Area Gardener (http://www.gardens.com), with helpful contacts to clubs, societies, and horticultural exhibits in the San Francisco Bay Area; and the Gardener's Gate (http://www.prairienet.org/ag/garden/homepage.htm), which likewise provides much useful information and myriad links.

PERIODICALS

There are many gardening magazines, including on-line versions. Listed below are a few of the ones that we have found useful in the areas of ecological gardening and garden design.

Arboriculture On-Line (International
    Society of Arboriculture)
http://www.ag.uiuc.edu/~isa/

American Horticulturalist
American Horticultural Society
7931 East Boulevard Dr.
Alexandria, VA 22308-1300
(703) 768-5700
http://www.ahs.org/

Avant Gardener
Horticultural Data Processors
P.O. Box 489
New York, NY 10028

Taunton Press, Inc., *Fine Gardening*
63 S. Main St., P.O. Box 5506
Newtown, CT 06470-5506
(203) 426-8171
http://www.taunton.com/fg/

Garden Design
P.O. Box 55458
Boulder, CO 20008-2302

Growing Native
P.O. Box 489
Berkeley, CA 94701
(510) 232-9865

Historical Gardener
1910 North 35th Pl.
Mount Vernon, WA 98273
(360) 424-3154

Horticulture
P.O. Box 53879
Boulder, CO 80321
http://www.hortmag.com/

Landscape Architecture
American Society of Landscape
  Architects
636 Eye St., N.W.
Washington, DC 20078-0103
http://www.asla.org/

National Gardening
P.O. Box 52874
Boulder, CO 80322-2874
(800) 727-9097
http://www2.garden.org/nga/

Organic Gardening
Rodale Press
33 E. Minor St.
Emmaus, PA 18098
(215) 967-5171
http://www.organicgardening.com/

Pacific Horticulture
Pacific Horticulture
P.O. Box 485
Berkeley, CA 94701
http://www.support.net/medit-
  plants/inprint/phhome.html

Plants and Gardens (quarterly)
Brooklyn Botanic Garden
1000 Washington Ave.
Brooklyn, NY 11225
http://www.bbg.org/

Sunset Magazine
P.O. Box 2040
Harlan, IA 51593-0003
(800) 777-0117
http://www.sunsetmag.com/

BOOKS

The Millennium Whole Earth Catalog (Reinhold, 1994) contains a wealth of useful information on sustainable gardening practices, including sections on tools, edible landscape techniques, soils, gardening techniques, biological and pest management, and sustainable conservation, to name but a few. It also lists many useful books, as well as building materials and suppliers.

AgAccess (P.O. Box 2008, Davis, CA 95617-2008; tel.: 800-540-0170 or 530-756-7177; e-mail: books@agaccess.com; web: http://www.agaccess.com) is a specialized bookstore offering a fine selection of books on ecology, gardens, and agriculture. If they do not have a book in stock, they can order it. Other on-line resources for books are Amazon Books (http://www.amazon.com) and Barnes & Noble (http://www.barnesandnoble.com), both of which can ship virtually any garden book in print, usually within a day or two.

An excellent publisher of books related to gardens and plants generally is Timber Press, based in Portland, Oregon. Access them on the web at www.timberpress.com; there you will find not only a complete on-line catalogue but also gardening advice and a complete set of web links.

Listed below are pertinent resources in various areas that are discussed in this book. (Additional sources can be found in the Reference List.)

Biodiversity and Endangered Natural Resources

Barbour, M., B. Pavlik, F. Drysdale, and S. Lindstrom. *California's Changing Landscapes.* Sacramento, CA: California Native Plant Society, 1993.

Thelander, Carl G., ed. *Life on the Edge: A Guide to California's Endangered Natural Resources—Wildlife.* Santa Cruz: Biosystems Books, 1994.

On the web, the California Environmental Resources Evaluation System (CERES; http://www.ceres.ca.gov) provides valuable environmental resource information, organized by theme, geographical area, and data type, with links to environmental law, watershed information, and so forth.

By accessing the UC Berkeley Digital Library Project's Botanical Database (http://elib.cs.berkeley.edu/calflora/botanical.html) you can view photos and distribution maps of California plants.

Birds and Butterflies

Kress, Stephen W. *The Audubon Society Guide to Attracting Birds.* New York: Charles Scribner's Sons, 1985.

Pyle, R. M. *Butterfly Gardening.* San Francisco: Sierra Club, 1990.

Tekulsky, Matthew. *The Butterfly Garden.* Boston: Harvard Common Press, 1985.

———. *The Hummingbird Garden.* New York: Crown Publishers, 1990.

Terres, John K. *The Audubon Society Encyclopedia of North American Birds.* New York: Knopf, 1991.

Also look at A Bird-Friendly Community (http://www.audubon.org/chapter/ca/pvas/bfcommun.htm), which includes informative pages on making your garden more bird, butterfly, and bat friendly.

Native Plants and Grasses

Connelly, K. *Gardener's Guide to California Wildflowers.* Sun Valley, CA: Theodore Payne Foundation for Wild Flowers and Native Plants, 1991.

Crampton, Beecher. *Grasses in California.* Berkeley: University of California Press, 1974.

Emery, Dara. *Seed Propagation of Native California Plants.* Santa Barbara, CA: Santa Barbara Botanical Garden, 1988.

Keator, Glenn. *Complete Garden Guide to the Native Perennials of California.* San Francisco: Chronicle Books, 1990.

Lenz, Lee. *California Native Trees and Shrubs, for Garden and Environmental Use in Southern California and Adjacent Areas.* Claremont: Rancho Santa Ana Botanical Garden, 1981.

———. *Native Plants for California Gardens.* Pasadena: Abbey Garden Press, 1956.

Pavlik, Bruce. *Oaks of California.* Los Olivos: Cachuma Press, 1991.

Schmidt, M. *Growing California Native Plants.* Berkeley: University of California Press, 1980.

Plant Choices and Planting Design

Chatto, B. *The Dry Garden.* Sagaponack, NY: Sagapress, 1996.

Dennis, J. V. *The Wildlife Gardener.* New York: Alfred A. Knopf, 1985.

Harper, Peter. *The Natural Garden Book.* New York: Simon & Schuster, 1994.

Henderson, C. L. *Landscaping for Wildlife.* St. Paul: Minnesota Department of Natural Resources, 1987.

Morse, Harriet. *Gardening in the Shade.* Beaverton, OR: Timber Press, 1982.

Perry, Robert. *Landscape Plants for Western Regions.* Claremont, CA: Land Design Publishing, 1992.

Stein, Sarah. *Noah's Garden: Restoring the Ecology of Our Own Backyards.* New York: Houghton Mifflin, 1993.

——. *Planting Noah's Garden.* New York: Houghton Mifflin, 1997.

Sunset. *Sunset Western Garden Book.* Menlo Park: Lane Publishing, 1997.

Waters, George W. *The Pacific Horticulture Book of Western Gardening.* Boston: David R. Godine, 1990.

Wilkinson, E., and M. Henderson. *Decorating Eden: A Comprehensive Sourcebook of Classic Garden Details.* San Francisco: Chronicle Books, 1992.

Sustainable Design and Construction

In the past few years access to sustainable materials and supplies has increased dramatically. Stores such as Smith & Hawken (800-981-9888; http://www.smith-hawken.com) and the Gardener's Supply Company (800-863-1700; http://www2.viaweb.com/gardeners/alldepts.html) sell, by mail order, useful items for environmentally responsible gardening, ranging from compost bins to benches made out of recycled plastics. Water districts provide demonstration gardens for drought-resistant landscapes and related technologies, such as drip irrigation, rainwater collection, and mulching. Adobe blocks made near Fresno are available for purchase by many suppliers of brick and stone for landscapes. Salvaged materials are obtainable from companies like Urban Ore, Inc., 1333 6th St., Berkeley, CA; tel.: (510) 559-4451. Popular yearly events are the Los Angeles and San Francisco Eco-Expos and the San Francisco Landscape Garden Show, where many environmentally sound ideas for gardens are presented.

Gilbert, O. L., and P. Anderson. *Habitat Creation and Repair.* New York: Oxford University Press, 1998.

Kourick, R. *Gray Water Use in the Landscape.* Santa Rosa, CA: Metamorphic Press, 1988.

Lyle, J. *Regenerative Design for Sustainable Development.* New York: John Wiley, 1994.

MacDonald, S. O., and M. Myhrman. *Build It with Bales.* Tucson, AZ: BIWB, 1994.

Malitz, J., and S. Malitz. *Reflecting Nature: Garden Designs from Wild Landscapes.* Portland: Timber Press, 1998.

McHarg, I. *Design with Nature.* New York: John Wiley & Sons, 1994.

McPherson, G., ed. *Energy-Conserving Site Design.* Washington, DC: American Society of Landscape Architects, 1984.

Thayer, R., Jr. *Gray World, Green Heart.* New York: John Wiley, 1994.

Tibbets, J. *The Earthbuilders' Encyclopedia.* Bosque, NM: Southwest Solaradobe School, 1989.

Van Sweden, J., and W. Oehme. *Gardening with Nature.* New York: Random House, 1997.

Pest Control

Flint, M. L. *Pests of the Garden and Small Farm: A Grower's Guide to Using Less Pesticide.* Statewide Integrated Pest Management Project, University of California Division of Agriculture and Natural Resources Publication 3332.

Common Sense Pest Control and the IPM [Integrated Pest Management] Practitioner, a pamphlet available from the Bio-Integral Resource Center (BIRC), P.O. Box 7414, Berkeley, CA 94707; (510) 524-2567.

On the web, the UC Integrated Pest Management Program has an excellent site at http://www.ipm.ucdavis.edu:80.

NATURAL HISTORY AND GARDEN ORGANIZATIONS

American Association of Botanical
Gardens and Arboreta
351 Longwood Rd.
Kennett Square, PA 19348
(610) 925-2500
http://www.mobot.org/AABGA/
aabga1.html

American Bat Conservation Society
P.O. Box 1393
Rockville, MD 20849
(301) 309-6610

American Community Gardening
  Association
100 N. 20th St., 5th Floor
Philadelphia, PA 19103-1495
(215) 988-8785
http://www.communitygarden.org/
  about/index.html

Bat Conservation International
http://www.batcon.org/

California Bluebird Recovery
  Program
2021 Ptarmigan Dr. #1
Walnut Creek, CA 94595
(510) 937-5974
http://www.scvas.org/bluebird.html

California Native Plant Society
1722 J St., Suite 17
Sacramento, CA 95814
(916) 447-2677
http://www.calpoly.edu/~dchip
  pin/cnps_main.html

California Oak Foundation
212 Broadway, Suite 81
Oakland, CA 94612
(510) 763-0282
http://www.treelink.org/connect/
  orgs/act/caoak.htm

California Releaf
3001 Redhill Ave.
Costa Mesa, CA 92626
(714) 557-2575
http://www.treelink.org/connect/
  orgs/act/carlf.htm

Lady Bird Johnson Wildflower
  Center (formerly the National
  Wildflower Research Center)
4801 La Crosse Ave.
Austin, TX
(512) 292-4100
http://www.wildflower.org

Master Gardeners Program
University of California
  Cooperative Extension
UC Fruit and Nut Research and
  Information Center
Dept. of Pomology
University of California
One Shields Ave.
Davis, CA 95616-8683
http://fruitsandnuts.ucdavis.edu/
  masgar.html

National Audubon Society
950 Third Ave.
New York, NY 10022
(212) 979-3000
http://www.audubon.com/

National Wildlife Federation
Backyard Wildlife Habitat Program
8925 Leesburg Pike
Vienna, VA 22184-0001
http://www.nwf.org/nwf/habitats/

Native Plant Society of Oregon
2584 N.W. Savier St.
Portland, OR 97210-2412
http://www.teleport.com:80/non-
  profit/npso

Point Reyes Bird Observatory–
    Partners in Flight
4990 Shoreline Hwy.
Stinson Beach, CA 94970
(415) 868-1221
http://www.prbo.org/prbo/

Sierra Club
85 Second St.
San Francisco, CA 94105-3441
(415) 977-5500
http://www.sierraclub.org

Theodore Payne Foundation
10459 Tuxford St.
Sun Valley, CA 91352
(818) 768-1802
http://www.via.net/~rferber/thp/
    thphome.html

Trust for Public Land
116 New Montgomery St., 4th Floor
San Francisco, CA 94105
(415) 495-4014
http://www.tpl.org

NATIVE PLANT NURSERIES (PARTIAL LISTING)

Berkeley Horticultural Nursery
1310 McGee Ave.
Berkeley, CA 94703
(510) 526-4704

Blue Oak Nursery
2731 Mountain Oak Ln.
Rescue, CA 95672
(916) 677-2111

Cal Flora
P.O. Box 3
Fulton, CA 95439
(707) 528-8813
wholesale and retail

Cornflower Farms
P.O. Box 896
Elk Grove, CA 95759
(916) 989-6770

Cottage Garden Growers
4040 Petaluma Blvd.
Petaluma, CA 94952
(707) 778-8025
perennials, herbs, etc.

The Dry Garden
6556 Shattuck Ave.
Oakland, CA 94909
(510) 547-3564
drought-resistant plants

Greenlee Nursery
301 E. Franklin Ave.
Pomona, CA 91766
(714) 629-9045
wholesale and retail

J. L. Hudson, Seedsman
P.O. Box 1058
Redwood City, CA 94064
mail-order seeds

Larner Seeds
P.O. Box 407
Bolinas, CA 94924
(415) 868-9407
mail-order seeds

Mockingbird Nurseries, Inc.
1670 Jackson St.
Riverside, CA 92504
(714) 780-3571

Moon Mountain
P.O. Box 725
Carpinteria, CA 93014
(805) 684-2565
mail-order seeds

Mostly Natives Nursery
27215 Highway 1
Tomales, CA 94971
(707) 878-2009

Pacific Southwest Nursery
2565 Cactus Rd.
Otay Mesa, CA
(619) 477-5333
wholesale; retail by appointment

Sierra Azul Nursery and Gardens
2660 East Lake Ave.
Watsonville, CA 95076
(831) 763-0939

Specialty Oaks, Inc.
12552 Highway 29
Lower Lake, CA 95457
(707) 995-2275
large specimen oaks

Sunny Seed Up
P.O. Box 5102
Arcata, CA 95521
mail-order seeds

Sunset Coast Nursery
2745 Tierra Way
Watsonville, CA 95077
(831) 726-1672
wholesale; retail by appointment

Tree of Life Nursery
33201 Ortega Hwy.
San Juan Capistrano, CA 92693
(714) 728-0685

Trillium Gardens
P.O. Box 803
Pleasant Hill, OR 97455
(503) 937-3073
mail-order plants

Wapumne Native Plant Nursery Co.
3807 Mt. Pleasant Rd.
Lincoln, CA 95648
(916) 645-9737

Weber Nursery
237 Seeman Dr.
Encinitas, CA 92024
(619) 753-1661

Western Hills Nursery
16250 Coleman Rd.
Occidental, CA 95465
(707) 823-3731
perennials and rock plants

Wildwood Farm
10300 Sonoma Hwy.
Kenwood, CA 95452
(707) 833-1161
wholesale and retail

Yerba Buena Nursery
19500 Skyline Blvd.
Woodside, CA 94062
(415) 851-1668
wholesale and retail

DEMONSTRATION GARDENS/ARBORETA/ PUBLIC GARDENS

These are wonderful places to visit to learn about regional native plants and plant communities. Their staff and faculty provide expertise and workshops, and they have excellent plant sales.

Huntington Botanical Garden
1151 Oxford Rd.
San Marino, CA
(818) 405-2141
http://www.cwire.com/the.hunt-
 ington/

Rancho Santa Ana Botanical Garden
1500 North College Ave.
Claremont, CA 91711-3157
(909) 625-8767
http://cgsweb.cgu.edu/inst/rsa/

Redding Arboretum/Carter House
 Natural Science Museum in
 Caldwell Park
Redding, CA
(916) 243-5457
http://tqd.advanced.org/2899/
 index.html

Santa Barbara Botanical Garden
1212 Mission Canyon Rd.
Santa Barbara, CA 93105
(805) 682-4726
http://sbbg.org/

Strybing Arboretum
Golden Gate Park
Ninth Ave. at Lincoln Way
San Francisco, CA 94122
(415) 661-1316
http://www.strybing.org/

UC Berkeley Botanical Garden
200 Centennial Dr., #5045
Berkeley, CA 94720-5045
(510) 643-2755
http://www.mip.berkeley.edu/
 garden/

UC Davis Arboretum
One Shields Ave.
Davis, CA 95616-8526
(530) 752-2498
http://arboretum.ucdavis.edu/
 Arboretum/arboretum/arbhome.
 html

UC Irvine Arboretum
Irvine, CA 92697
(714) 824-5833
http://ka.reg.uci.edu/UCI/ARBOR-
ETUM/

UC Santa Cruz Arboretum
1156 High St.
Santa Cruz, CA 95064
(831) 427-2998
http://www2.ucsc.edu/arboretum/

LANDSCAPE ARCHITECTS AND LANDSCAPE GARDEN DESIGNERS (PARTIAL LISTING)

Steve Chainey, Restoration Ecologist
Jones & Stokes
2600 V St.
Sacramento, CA 95818
(916) 737-3000

Ann Christoph, Landscape Architect
31713 Coast Hwy.
South Laguna, CA 92677
(714) 499-3574

CoDesign, Inc.
Mark Francis, Skip Mezger, and
  Rob Thayer Jr., Landscape
  Architects
231 G St.
Davis, CA 95616
(530) 756-0172

Delaney, Cochran & Castillo, Inc.
Topher Delaney and Andrea
  Cochran, Landscape Architects
156 South Park
San Francisco, CA 94107
(415) 896-2998

Owen Dell, Landscape Architect
  and Contractor
County Landscape and Design
  P.O. Box 30433
Santa Barbara, CA 93130
(805) 962-3253
http://www.owendell.com

Richard Fisher, Landscape Architect
553 E. Woodbury Rd.
Altadena, CA 91001
(818) 798-0578

Isabelle C. Greene, Landscape
  Architect
2613 De La Vina
Santa Barbara, CA 93105
(805) 569-4045

Rachel Jackson, Landscape Architect
P.O. Box 381
Mill Valley, CA 94942
(415) 388-6739

Joni L. Janecki, ASLA, Landscape
  Architect
303 Potrero, Suite 16
Santa Cruz, CA 95060
(831) 423-6040

Ron Lutsko Jr.
Lutsko Associates, Landscape
  Architects
Pier One and One Half
San Francisco, CA 94111
(415) 391-0777

Robert Perry, FASLA, Landscape
  Architect
409 Harvard Ave.
Claremont, CA 91711
(909) 621-4647

Jana Ruzicka, Landscape Designer
530 Cress St.
Laguna Beach, CA 92651
(714) 494-8871

Achva Stein, Landscape Architect
1116 Diamond Ave.
Pasadena, CA 91030
(818) 441-3693

Ron Wigginton, Landscape
  Architect
Land Studio
733 Allston Way
Berkeley, CA 94710
(510) 849-0288

James Zanetto, Architect and
  Landscape Architect
2459 Creekhollow Ln.
Davis, CA 95616
(530) 758-8801

NOTES

INTRODUCTION

1. Nash 1993, 53–57.
2. For the companion book to the television series, see Baines 1985.

CHAPTER ONE

1. An excellent introduction to the geology of California can be found in McPhee 1993.
2. Johnson, Haslam, and Dawson 1993 provides an excellent overview of the Great Central Valley.
3. On the changes that have been wrought to California's landscape over time, see Barbour et al. 1993.
4. Muir [1894] 1977, 251.
5. See Benyus 1989 for an ecological and historical overview of the oak woodland habitat; Pavlik et al. 1991 provides valuable information on the ecology of California oak lands.
6. Benyus 1989 discusses the shrinking of the oak woodland habitat.
7. For an appreciative yet sobering look at California's endangered species, including the mission blue butterfly, see Thelander 1994.

8. For a thorough presentation on lichens, including their significance to humans, see Sharnoff 1997.

9. Blackburn and Anderson 1993, 18.

10. Lee 1987, 169.

11. Personal interview with E. Roger Apodaca, February 1993.

12. Beatty 1977, 39.

13. Quoted in Streatfield 1994, 33.

14. Quoted in Beatty 1977, 41.

15. Quoted in Yoch 1992, 62.

16. Streatfield 1994, 22.

17. On Church, see Church, Hall, and Laurie 1995; on Eckbo, see Treib and Imbert 1997.

18. For more information on endangered species of wildlife and plants, see Thelander 1994; and Barbour et al. 1993.

19. Pyle 1990, 133.

20. Hough 1990, 78.

21. Thayer 1994, 38.

22. Thayer 1994, 329.

23. Berry 1988, 81.

24. Deloria 1994 presents an authentic and articulate voice about the relationship of Native Americans with their environment.

25. Berry 1995, 10.

26. Interview with Louise Lacey, September 1992.

27. Pollan 1991 provides a thorough discussion of the wilderness ethic as it relates to gardening.

28. Pollan 1991, 232.

29. Pollan 1991, 30.

30. Berry 1988, 81.

31. Waters 1993, 1.

CHAPTER TWO

1. For further reading on the meaning of place, see Francis and Hester 1990.

2. Berry 1995, 9.

3. Interview with Jana Ruzicka, 1995.

4. Armstrong 1993, 20.

5. Carney 1989, 8.

6. Berry 1988, 199.

7. Luz 1986.

CHAPTER THREE

1. For an informative article about Ron Lutsko's approach to design, see MacFadyen 1992.

2. Ecological corridors are discussed in Lyle and Quinn 1991.

3. The natural value of vacant lots is discussed in Vessel and Wong 1987.

4. Barbour et al. 1993, 203.

5. For the impact of domestic cats on wildlife, see Harrison 1992.

6. Hay 1992, 65.

7. Barbour et al. 1993, 74.

8. See Crampton 1974 for further information on native California grasses.

9. Two useful references on attracting birds to the garden are Kress 1985 and Tekulsky 1990.

10. On the success of starlings and cowbirds as invaders and as nest parasites, see Ehrlich, Dobkin, and Wheye 1988, 490–493, 619–625.

11. Further information about birdhouses can be found in Terres 1994 and McElroy 1960.

12. Blakey 1985 provides a useful guide to plants that attract butterflies in California gardens.

13. Terres 1994.

14. Ehrlich, Dobkin, and Wheye 1988, 433–435.

15. Milne and Milne 1990, 697, 533.

16. See, for example, Tekulsky 1985; Xerces Society 1990.

CHAPTER FOUR

1. Examples of the work of professional designers can be found in periodicals such as *Landscape Architecture*. The work of landscape architect Ron Lutsko Jr. is discussed in full in MacFadyen 1992.

2. Lacey, *Growing Native Newsletter,* Nov./Dec. 1991.

3. Heisler 1984 discusses using plants for wind control.

CHAPTER FIVE

1. Noss, O'Connell, and Murphy 1997.

2. For an excellent discussion of the diversity of native plant species in California, and of the losses currently being incurred, see Hickman 1993 and Barbour et al. 1993.

3. Useful references on planting design include Van Sweden and Oehme 1997; Conran and Pearson 1998; Crowe 1981; and Cox 1991.

4. Sunset 1998a includes detailed maps and descriptions of climate zones throughout the western United States.

5. A complete list of plants suitable for use under California oaks can be found in Zagory 1992.

6. Schmidt 1980 and Xerces Society 1990 offer useful information on how to create butterfly gardens.

7. Keator 1990.

CHAPTER SIX

1. Lyle 1994, 289–291.
2. McPherson 1984 provides a useful overview of the energy-conserving benefits of plants and landscape.
3. Thayer 1984 and Richman 1984 both offer a detailed guide to sustainable hydrozoning for gardens and lanscapes.
4. Thayer 1984 provides useful guidelines for water-conserving landscape design.
5. Thayer and Richman 1984.
6. See Dell 1994 for an excellent summary chart comparing the environmental impacts of different materials typically used in the garden.
7. Several chapters in McPherson 1984 provide information useful on water conservation for home gardeners.
8. Reingold 1994 and Wilkinson and Henderson 1992, 164–67, are excellent resources for sustainable approaches to garden design.
9. Streatfield 1994 provides an excellent overview of how materials have influenced the character of the California garden.
10. Interview with Weber, May 1995.
11. Dennis 1985; Henderson 1987.
12. See Schama 1995 for a thorough account of the role of landscape in cultural expression.
13. Carson 1962 was one of the first to make us aware of the environmental crisis and our role in reversing it.
14. Thelander 1994 provides useful information on the role of reptiles and snakes within the California ecosystem.
15. Powell and Hogue 1979 offers an excellent guide to California insects.
16. Stokes 1983 provides useful information on observing and identifying insects.
17. Stokes 1983.
18. Flint 1990 includes a useful guide to wasps and their behavioral patterns.
19. Barnes 1993 summarizes some of the habitat found on riparian corridors in California.
20. For information on Partners in Flight, see Evans 1993.
21. See Terrill and Rigney 1993 for a fascinating report on bird migration.
22. Evans 1993 documents the decline in migratory flocks.
23. Stallcup 1993 documents the decline of migratory birds due to habitat loss.

EPILOGUE

1. There is a substantial amount of literature on the healing effects of plants and gardens. See, for example: Gerlach-Spriggs, Kaufman, and Warner Jr., 1998; Francis, Lindsey, and Rice 1994; Lewis 1997; and Ulrich 1993.
2. Berry 1988, 35.
3. Thelander 1994, 270.
4. E. O. Wilson 1992, 351.

REFERENCES

Ackerman, J. 1993. "When the Bough Breaks." *Nature Conservancy,* May/June: 8–9.

Adams, W. H., and S. Wrede. 1991. *Denatured Visions: Landscape and Culture in the Twentieth Century.* New York: Museum of Modern Art.

Appleton, J. 1975. *The Experience of Landscape.* New York: Wiley.

Arms, K. 1992. *Environmental Gardening.* Savannah, GA: Halfmoon Publishing.

Armstrong, J. 1993. "Standing by the Pine." *Orion,* summer.

Audubon Society. 1980. *The Audubon Society Field Guide to North American Insects and Spiders.* New York: Knopf.

Austin, R. L. 1984a. *Designing the Natural Landscape.* New York: Van Nostrand Reinhold.

———. 1984b. *Wild Gardening.* New York: Simon & Schuster.

Baines, C. 1984. *Wildlife Garden Notebook.* Oxford: Oxford Illustrated Press.

———. 1985. *How to Make a Wildlife Garden.* London: Elm Tree Books.

———. 1991. *A Guide to Habitat Creation.* London: Packard.

Bakker, E. 1984. *An Island Called California.* Berkeley: University of California Press.

Barbour, M., B. Pavlik, F. Drysdale, and S. Lindstrom. 1993. *California's Changing Landscapes.* Sacramento: California Native Plant Society.

Barnes, R. 1993. "Riparian Forests: Rivers of Life." *Observer* (Point Reyes Bird Observatory), no. 97 (fall): 8–9.

Beardsley, J. 1995. *Earthly Delights*. New York: Abbeville Press.

Beatty, R. 1977. "Browning the Greensward." *Pacific Horitculture* 38, no. 3 (fall): 37–46.

Benyus, J. 1989. *The Field Guide to Wildlife Habitats of the Western United States*. New York: Simon & Schuster.

Berry, T. 1988. *The Dream of the Earth*. San Francisco: Sierra Club Books.

———. 1995. "The Bush." In *Sculpting with the Environment: A Natural Dialogue,* ed. B. Oakes. New York: Van Nostrand Reinhold.

Blackburn, T.C., and K. Anderson. 1993. Before the wilderness: environmental management by native Californians. Menlo Park, CA: Ballena Press.

Blakey, L. 1985. *Our Hummingbirds*. Los Altos, CA: L. Blakey.

Bontrager, D. 1984. "Ecological Landscaping: Creating Bird Habitat in Suburban California Gardens and Public Landscapes." In *The Natural Sciences of Orange County,* ed. P. J. Bryant and J. Remington. Newport Beach: Natural History Foundation of Orange County.

Borman, F. H., D. Balmori, and G. T. Geballe. 1993. *Redesigning the American Lawn*. New Haven: Yale University Press.

Bradshaw, A. D., and M. J. Chawick. 1980. *The Restoration of the Land*. Berkeley: University of California Press.

Broadstreet, J. 1990. *Building with Junk*. Port Townsend, WA: Loompanics Unlimited.

Brown, V., and H. G. Weston. 1961. *Handbook of California Birds*. Healdsburg: Naturegraph.

California Department of Fish and Game. 1991. *Annual Report on the Status of California State Listed Threatened and Endangered Animals and Plants*. Sacramento: Resources Agency, State of California.

Calthorpe, P. 1993. *The Next American Metropolis*. New York: Princeton Architectural Press.

Carney, W. 1989. "Earth Ethic: Gaia Meets Landscape Architecture." In *CELA 89: Proceedings of the Council of Educators of Landscape Architecture Annual Conference, September 1989.*

Carr, A. 1983. *Rodale's Color Handbook of Garden Insects*. Emmaus, PA: Rodale Press.

Carson, R. 1962. *Silent Spring*. Cambridge, MA: Riverside Press.

Chatto, B. 1996. *The Dry Garden*. Sagaponack, NY: Sagapress.

Church, T. D., G. Hall, and M. Laurie. 1995. *Gardens Are for People*. 3d ed. Berkeley: University of California Press.

Connelly, K. 1991. *Gardener's Guide to California Wildflowers*. Sun Valley: Theodore Payne Foundation for Wild Flowers and Native Plants.

Conran, T., and D. Pearson. 1998. *The Essential Garden Book*. New York: Crown.

Cook, J. 1969. "Do the Gardens Fit the People?" *New Society* 13: 589–591.

Cooper, G., and G. Taylor. 1996. *Paradise Transformed: The Private Garden for the Twenty-first Century*. New York: Monacelli Press.

Corner, J., and A. S. MacLean. 1996. *Taking Measures across the American Landscape*. New Haven: Yale University Press.

Cosgrove, D., and S. Daniels, eds. 1988. *The Iconography of Landscape*. New York: Cambridge University Press.

Cox, J. 1991. *Landscaping with Nature*. Emmaus, PA: Rodale Press.

Crampton, B. 1974. *Grasses in California*. Berkeley: University of California Press.

Creasy, R. 1982. *The Complete Book of Edible Landscaping*. San Francisco: Sierra Club Books.

————. 1985. *Earthly Delights*. San Francisco: Sierra Club Books.

Crowe, S. 1981. *Garden Design*. London: Packard.

Cundiff, B. 1988. "Let Nature Do the Landscaping." *Canadian Geographic* 108, no. 4: 52–58.

Daniels, S. 1995. *The Wild Lawn Handbook*. New York: Macmillan.

Dannenmaier, M. 1998. *A Child's Garden: Enchanting Outdoor Spaces for Children and Parents*. New York: Simon & Schuster.

Dawson, K. 1990. "Nature in the Urban Garden." In *The Meaning of Gardens,* ed. M. Francis and R. Hester, 138–143. Cambridge, MA: MIT Press.

Dell, O. E. 1994. "Sources and Environmental Impacts of Some Common Landscaping Materials." Santa Barbara: unpublished monograph.

Deloria, V. 1994. *God Is Red: A Native View of Religion*. Golden, CO: Fulcrum Press.

Dennis, J. V. 1985. *The Wildlife Gardener*. New York: Knopf.

Deval, B., and G. Sessions. 1985. *Deep Ecology: Living as if Nature Mattered*. Layton, UT: Gibbs M. Smith.

Diekelmann, J. 1982. *Natural Landscaping: Designing with Native Plants*. New York: McGraw-Hill.

Dobyns, W. S. 1996. *California Gardens*. New York: Knoll.

Dramstad, W. E., J. D. Olson, and R. T. Forman. 1997. *Landscape Ecology Principles in Landscape Architecture and Land Use Planning*. Washington, DC: Island Press.

Druse, K. 1994. *Natural Habitat Gardens*. New York: Clarkson Potter.

Dubos, R. 1972. *A God Within*. New York: Scribner.

Eckbo, G. 1937. "Small Gardens in the City: A Study in Their Design Possibilities." *Pencil Points*, Sept.: 573–586.

————. 1950. *Landscapes for Living*. New York: F. W. Dodge.

Ehrlich, P. R., D. S. Dobkin, and D. Wheye. 1988. *The Birder's Handbook: A Field Guide to the Natural History of North American Birds*. New York: Simon & Schuster.

Elder, J. 1994. "The Big Picture: Sierra Club Critical Ecoregions Program." *Sierra,* Mar./Apr.: 52–57.

Emerson, R. W. 1983. *The Conduct of Life*. New York: Viking Press.

———. 1991. *Nature*. Boston: Beacon Press.

Emery, D. 1988. *Seed Propagation of Native California Plants*. Santa Barbara: Santa Barbara Botanical Garden.

Evans, D. 1993. "New Perspectives: For the Conservation of Migratory Songbirds." *Observer* (Point Reyes Bird Observatory), no. 97 (fall).

Everett, P. 1957. *A Summary of the Culture of California Plants at the Rancho Santa Ana Botanical Garden*. Claremont: Rancho Santa Ana Botanical Garden.

Faber, P. M., ed. 1997. *California's Wild Gardens: A Living Legacy*. Sacramento: California Native Plant Society.

Fiedler, P. L., and S. K. Jain, eds. 1992. *Conservation Biology: The Theory and Practice of Nature Conservation, Preservation, and Management*. New York: Chapman & Hall.

Flint, M. L. 1990. *Pests of the Garden and Small Farm: A Grower's Guide to Using Less Pesticide*. Statewide Integrated Pest Management Project, Publication no. 3332. Oakland: University of California Division of Agriculture and Natural Resources.

Francis, M. 1987a. "Gardens in the Mind and in the Heart." In *Proceedings of the 10th International Association for the Study of People and Their Physical Surroundings Conference*, 495–500. Delft, Neth.: Delft University Press.

———. 1987b. "Some Different Meanings Attached to a Public Park and Community Garden." *Landscape Journal* 6: 101–112.

———. 1995. "Childhood's Garden: Memory and Meaning of Gardens." *Children's Environments* 12, no. 2: 183–191.

Francis, M., and R. T. Hester, eds. 1990. *The Meaning of Gardens*. Cambridge, MA: MIT Press.

Francis, M., P. Lindsey, and J. S. Rice, eds. 1994. *The Healing Dimensions of People-Plant Relations*. Blacksburg, VA: People-Plant Council.

Franklin, C. 1997. "Fostering Living Landscapes." In *Ecological Design and Planning*, ed. G. F. Thompson and F. R. Steiner, 263–292. New York: Wiley.

French, J. 1993. *The California Garden—and the Landscape Architects Who Shaped It*. Washington, DC: Landscape Architecture Foundation.

Garth, J., and J. W. Tilden. 1986. *California Butterflies*. Berkeley: University of California Press.

Gebhard, D., and S. Lynds, eds. 1985. *An Arcadian Landscape: The California Gardens of A. E. Hanson, 1920–1932*. Los Angeles: Hennessey & Ingalls.

Gerlach-Spriggs, N., R.E. Kaufman, and S.B. Warner Jr. 1998. *Restorative Gardens: The Healing Landscape*. New Haven: Yale University Press.

Gilbert, O. L., and P. Anderson. 1998. *Habitat Creation and Repair*. New York: Oxford University Press.

Goldsworthy, A. 1990. *A Collaboration with Nature*. New York: Harry N. Abrams.

Grampp, C. 1985. "The California Living Garden." *Landscape* 28: 40–47.

Groth, P., and T. W. Bressi. 1997. *Understanding Ordinary Landscapes.* New Haven: Yale University Press.

Guinness, B. 1996. *Creating a Family Garden: Magical Outdoor Spaces for All Ages.* New York: Abbeville Press.

Harper, P. 1994. *The Natural Garden Book.* New York: Simon & Schuster.

Harrison, G. H. 1992. "Is There a Killer in Your House?" *National Wildlife,* Oct./Nov.: 10–13.

Hart, J. F. 1975. *The Look of the Land.* Englewood Cliffs, NJ: Prentice Hall.

Hay, J. 1992. "Swallows and Swallowtails." *Orion,* summer: 65.

Head, W. S. 1989. *The California Chaparral: An Elfin Forest.* Happy Camp, CA: Naturegraph.

Heisler, G. M. 1984. "Planting Design for Wind Control." In *Energy Conserving Site Design,* ed. G. McPherson, 165–183. Washington, DC: American Society of Landscape Architects.

Henderson, C. L. 1987. *Landscaping for Wildlife.* St. Paul: Minnesota Department of Natural Resources.

Hickman, J. C., ed. 1993. *The Jepson Manual: Higher Plants of California.* Berkeley: University of California Press.

Hogan, E. L. 1994. *Western Garden Book.* 11th printing. Menlo Park: Sunset Books.

Hough, M. 1990. *Out of Place: Restoring Identity to the Regional Landscape.* New Haven: Yale University Press.

Jackson, J. B. 1994. *A Sense of Place, a Sense of Time.* New Haven: Yale University Press.

Jameson, E. W., and H. J. Peeters. 1988. *California Mammals.* Berkeley: University of California Press.

Janssen, J. A. 1995. *Building with Bamboo: A Handbook.* London: Intermediate Technology Publications.

Jenkins, V. S. 1994. *The Lawn: A History of an American Obsession.* Washington, DC: Smithsonian Press.

Jensen, D. B., M. Torn, and J. Harte. 1990. *In Our Hands: A Strategy for Conserving Biological Diversity in California.* Berkeley: University of California Policy Seminar.

Johnson, S., G. Haslam, and R. Dawson. 1993. *The Great Central Valley: California's Heartland.* Berkeley: University of California Press.

Jones & Stokes. 1987. *Sliding Toward Extinction: The State of California's Natural Heritage.* San Francisco: California Nature Conservancy.

Kaplan, R. 1973. "Some Psychological Benefits of Gardening." *Environment and Behavior* 5: 145–161.

Kaplan, R., and S. Kaplan. 1989. *The Experience of Nature.* New York: Cambridge University Press.

Kastner, J. 1993. "My Empty Lot: The Natural History of an Urban Patch." *New York Times Magazine*, Oct. 10: 22–25, 41–44.

Keator, G. 1990. *Complete Garden Guide to the Native Perennials of California*. San Francisco: Chronicle Books.

———. 1994. *Complete Garden Guide to the Native Shrubs of California*. San Francisco: Chronicle Books.

Kourik, R. 1986. *Designing and Maintaining Your Edible Landscape Naturally*. Santa Rosa, CA: Metamorphic Press.

———. 1988. *Gray Water Use in the Landscape*. Santa Rosa, CA: Metamorphic Press.

Kreissman, B. 1991. *California: An Environmental Atlas and Guide*. Davis, CA: Bear Klaw Press.

Kress, S. W. 1985. *The Audubon Society Guide to Attracting Birds*. New York: Scribner.

Landau, D., and S. Stump. 1994. *Living with Wildlife*. San Francisco: Sierra Club Books.

Lee, D. 1987. *Freedom and Culture*. Prospect Heights, IL: Waveland Press.

Leigh, C. 1993. *California Gardens: A Nature Lover's Guide*. Santa Barbara: Capra Press.

Lenz, L. 1956. *Native Plants for California Gardens*. Pasadena: Abbey Garden Press.

———. 1981. *California Native Trees and Shrubs, for Garden and Environmental Use in Southern California and Adjacent Areas*. Claremont, CA: Rancho Santa Ana Botanical Garden.

Leopold, A. 1949. *Sand County Almanac*. New York: Oxford University Press.

Lewis, C. 1997. *Green Nature, Human Nature*. Urbana: University of Illinois Press.

Lowry, J. D. In press. *Gardening with a Wild Heart: Restoring California's Native Landscapes at Home*. Berkeley: University of California Press.

Luz, F. 1986. "Between Sidewalk and House: Suburban Frontyards." Master's thesis, University of California, Davis.

Lyle, J. 1994. *Regenerative Design for Sustainable Development*. New York: Wiley.

Lyle, J., and T. Quinn. 1991. "Ecological Corridors in Urban Southern California." In *Wildlife Conservation in Metropolitan Environments, Proceedings of a National Symposium on Urban Wildlife, Cedar Rapids, Iowa, Nov. 1990*, 105–116. Columbia, MO: National Institute for Urban Wildlife.

Lynch, K. 1984. *Site Planning*. Cambridge, MA: MIT Press.

MacDonald, S. O., and M. Myhrman. 1994. *Build It with Bales*. Tucson, AZ: BIWB.

MacFadyen, J. T. 1992. "A Celebration of Place: Landscape Architect Ron Lutsko Brings Out the Best in California." *Horticulture*, Jan.: 48–52.

Malitz, J., and S. Malitz. 1998. *Reflecting Nature: Garden Designs from Wild Landscapes*. Portland, Ore.: Timber Press.

Manning, R. 1988. "Nature in the City: The Creation of Nature-like Landscapes in European Parks and Residential Open Spaces." Master's thesis, Cornell University.

Marinelli, J. 1993. "Gardens for the Twenty-first Century." *Nature Conservancy,*
    May/June: 34.

McElroy, T. P. 1960. *The New Handbook of Attracting Birds.* New York: Knopf.

McHarg, I. L. 1994. *Design with Nature.* New York: Wiley.

———. 1996. *A Quest for Life: An Autobiography.* New York: Wiley.

McPhee, J. 1989. *Control of Nature.* New York: Noonday Press/Farrar Straus
    Giroux.

———. 1993. *Assembling California.* New York: Farrar Straus Giroux.

McPherson, G., ed. 1984. *Energy Conserving Site Design.* Washington, DC: American
    Society of Landscape Architects.

Meinig, D. W., ed. 1979. *The Interpretation of Ordinary Landscapes.* New York:
    Oxford University Press.

Milne, L. J., and M. Milne. 1990. *The Audubon Society Field Guide to North American
    Insects and Spiders.* New York: Knopf.

Moore, C., W. Mitchell, and W. Turnbull. 1988. *The Poetics of the Garden.*
    Cambridge, MA: MIT Press.

Morrison, D. 1987. "On Aesthetics and Restoration and Management." *Restoration
    and Management Notes,* summer: 3–4.

———. 1988. "Designing with Native Plants: Potential and Challenges." *Wildflower*
    1, no. 1: 13–18.

Morse, H. 1982. *Gardening in the Shade.* Portland, OR: Timber Press.

Muir, J. [1894] 1977. *The Mountains of California.* Berkeley: Ten Speed Press.

Munz, P. A., with D. D. Keck. 1970. *A California Flora.* Berkeley: University of
    California Press.

Nabhan, G. P., and S. Trimble. 1994. *The Geography of Childhood: Why Children Need
    Wild Places.* Boston: Beacon Press.

Nabhan, G. P. 1997. *Cultures of Habitat.* Washington, DC: Counterpoint.

Nash, J. M. 1993. "Gardening Nature's Way." *Time,* May 17: 53–57.

National Wildlife Federation. 1974. *Gardening with Wildlife.* Washington, DC:
    National Wildlife Federation.

Natural History Association. 1993. *The Outdoor World of the Sacramento Region: A
    Local Field Guide.* Sacramento: Natural History Association.

Neihaus, T., and C. L. Ripper. 1976. *A Field Guide to Pacific States Wildflowers.*
    Boston: Houghton Mifflin.

Noss, R. F., M. A. O'Connell, and D. D. Murphy. 1997. *The Science of Conservation
    Planning: Habitat Conservation under the Endangered Species Act.* Washington, DC:
    Island Press.

Oakes, B. 1995. *Sculpting with the Environment: A Natural Dialogue.* New York: Van
    Nostrand Reinhold.

O'Keefe, J. 1993. *Water-Conserving Gardens and Landscapes.* Pownal, VT: Garden Way.

Ornduff, R. 1974. *Introduction to California Plant Life.* Berkeley: University of California Press.

Osler, M. 1989. *A Gentle Plea for Chaos.* New York: Simon & Schuster.

Ottesen, C. 1987. *The New American Garden.* New York: Macmillan.

———. 1989. *Ornamental Grasses.* New York: McGraw-Hill.

Page, R. 1983. *The Education of a Gardener.* New York: Random House.

Palmer, T. 1993. *California's Threatened Environment.* Covelo, CA: Island Press.

Pavlik, B., P. C. Muick, S. Johnson, and M. Popper. 1991. *Oaks of California.* Los Olivos, CA: Cachuma Press.

Pearson, D. 1989. *The Natural House Book.* New York: Simon & Schuster.

Perry, R. 1992. *Landscape Plants for Western Regions.* Claremont, CA: Land Design Publishing.

Phillips, K. 1998. *Paradise by Design: Native Plants and the New American Landscape.* New York: North Point Press.

Pollan, M. 1991. *Second Nature: A Gardener's Education.* New York: Dell.

———. 1998. "Beyond Wilderness and Lawn." *Harvard Design,* winter/spring: 70–75.

Powell, J., and C. Hogue. 1979. *California Insects.* Berkeley: University of California Press.

Pyle, R. M. 1984. *The Audubon Society Handbook for Butterfly Watchers.* New York: Scribner.

———. 1990. *Butterfly Gardening.* San Francisco: Sierra Club Books.

———. 1993. *The Thunder Tree: Lessons from an Urban Wildland.* New York: Houghton Mifflin.

Reimann, A. 1993. "In Search of Ecological Alternatives for the California Home Landscape." Master's thesis, University of California, Davis.

Reingold, H., ed. 1994. *The Millennium Whole Earth Catalog.* New York: Harper Collins.

Relf, D., ed. 1992. *The Role of Horticulture in Human Well-Being.* Portland, OR: Timber Press.

Renaud, W. 1994. "High Style and Low Maintenance." *Fine Gardening,* Jan./Feb.: 45–48.

Rose, J. 1990. *Gardens Make Me Laugh.* Baltimore: Johns Hopkins University Press.

Saratoga Horticultural Foundation. 1983. *California Native Plants with Commercial Sources.* Davis, CA: AgAccess Books.

Sawyer, J., and T. Keeler-Wolf. 1995. *A Manual of California Vegetation.* Sacramento: California Native Plant Society.

Schama, S. 1995. *Landscape and Memory.* New York: Vintage Books.

Schmidt, M. J. 1980. *Growing California Native Plants.* Berkeley: University of California Press.

Schoenherr, A. A., ed. 1989. *Endangered Plant Communities in Southern California: Proceedings of the 15th Annual Symposium.* Southern California Botanists Special Publication, no. 3. Claremont, CA: SCB.

Schultz, W. 1989. *The Chemical-Free Lawn.* Emmaus, PA: Rodale Press.

Seager, E., ed. 1984. *Gardens and Gardeners.* New York: Oxford University Press.

Sharnoff, S. D. 1997. "Lichens." *National Geographic,* Feb.: 58–71.

Sime, J., and K. Michiharu. 1988. "Home Gardens: Attachment to the Natural Environment and the Experience of Time from a Western and Japanese Perspective." In *Paths to Co-existence: Proceedings of the 19th Environmental Design Research Association Conference,* ed. D. Lawrence and B. L. Wandersman, 105–111. Oklahoma City: EDRA.

Skinner, M. W., and B. M. Pavlik. 1994. *California Native Plant Society's Inventory of Rare and Endangered Vascular Plants of California.* Sacramento: California Native Plant Society.

Smyser, C. A. 1982. *Nature's Design: A Practical Guide to Natural Landscaping.* Emmaus, PA: Rodale Press.

Snyder, G. 1990. *Practice of the Wild.* Berkeley: North Point Press.

———. 1992. *No Nature.* New York: Pantheon Books.

Soulé, M. E., ed. 1986. *Conservation Biology: The Science of Scarcity and Diversity.* Sunderland, MA: Sinauer Associates.

Spirn, A. W. 1984. *The Granite Garden: Urban Nature and Human Design.* New York: Basic Books.

———. 1988a. "Nature, Form, and Meaning." *Landscape Journal* 7: 85–107.

———. 1988b. "The Poetics of City and Nature: Towards a New Aesthetic for Urban Design." *Landscape Journal* 7: 108–126.

———. 1998. *The Language of Landscape.* New Haven: Yale University Press.

Stallcup, R. 1993. "What We Can Do at Home: Welcoming Neotropical Migrants Home." *Observer* (Point Reyes Bird Observatory), no. 97 (fall).

Stebbins, R. 1978. "Why Are There So Many Rare Plants in California?" *Fremontia* 5, no. 4: 6–10.

———. 1985. *Western Reptiles and Amphibians.* Boston: Houghton Mifflin.

Stein, S. 1993. *Noah's Garden: Restoring the Ecology of Our Own Backyards.* New York: Houghton Mifflin.

———. 1997. *Planting Noah's Garden.* New York: Houghton Mifflin.

Stilgoe, J. 1988. *Borderland: The Origin of the American Suburb.* New Haven: Yale University Press.

Stokes, D. 1983. *A Guide to Observing Insect Lives.* Boston: Little, Brown.

Streatfield, D. 1985. "Where Pine and Palm Meet: The California Garden as Regional Expression." *Landscape Journal* 4, no. 2: 61–74.

———. 1994. *California Gardens: Creating a New Eden.* New York: Abbeville Press.

Sunset. 1990. *An Illustrated Guide to Attracting Birds.* Menlo Park: Lane Publishing.

———. 1997. *Sunset Western Garden Book.* Menlo Park: Lane Publishing.

———. 1998a. *The New Western Garden Book.* Menlo Park: Lane Publishing.

———. 1998b. *Sunset Western Garden Problem Solver.* Menlo Park: Lane Publishing.

Swain, R. B. 1992. "Editing Landscape: Nothing Is More Natural than a Self-Sow Garden." *Horticulture* 70, no. 3: 17–22.

Tekulsky, M. 1985. *The Butterfly Garden.* Boston: Harvard Common Press.

———. 1990. *The Hummingbird Garden.* New York: Crown.

Terres, J. K. 1980. *The Audubon Society Encyclopedia of North American Birds.* New York: Knopf.

———. 1994. *Songbirds in Your Garden.* Chapel Hill, NC: Algonquin Books.

Terrill, S. B., and M. Rigney. 1993. "The Marvel of Migration." *Observer* (Point Reyes Bird Observatory), no. 97 (fall): 2, 3, 15.

Thacker, C. 1984. *The History of Gardens.* Berkeley: University of California Press.

Thayer, R., Jr. 1984. *Water-Conserving Landscapes.* Sacramento: California Department of Water Resources.

———. 1989. "The Experience of Sustainable Landscapes." *Landscape Journal* 8, no. 2: 155–164.

———. 1994. *Gray World, Green Heart.* New York: Wiley.

Thayer, R., Jr., and T. Richman. 1984. "Hydrozones." In *Energy Conserving Site Design,* ed. E. G. McPherson, 185–213. Washington, DC: Landscape Architecture Foundation.

Thelander, C. G., ed. 1994. *Life on the Edge: A Guide to California's Endangered Natural Resources.* Vol. 1: *Wildlife.* Santa Cruz: Biosystems Books.

Thompson, G. F., and F. R. Steiner, eds. 1997. *Ecological Design and Planning.* New York: Wiley.

Tibbets, J. 1989. *The Earthbuilders' Encyclopedia: The Master Alphabetical Reference for Adobe and Rammed Earth.* Bosque, NM: Southwest Solaradobe School.

Treib, M., ed. 1993. *Modern Landscape Architecture: A Critical Review.* Cambridge, MA: MIT Press.

Treib, M., and D. Imbert. 1997. *Garrett Eckbo.* Berkeley: University of California Press.

Tuan, Y.-F. 1993. *Passing Strange and Wonderful: Aesthetics, Nature, and Culture.* Washington, DC: Island Press.

Tufts, C. 1988. *The Backyard Naturalist.* Washington, DC: National Wildlife Federation.

Tunnard, C. 1993. "Modern Gardens for Modern Houses: Reflections on Current Trends in Landscape Design." In *Modern Landscape Architecture: A Critical Review,* ed. M. Treib, 159–165. Cambridge, MA: MIT Press.

Turner, F. 1985. "Cultivating the American Garden." *Harper's,* Aug.: 45–52.

———. 1988. "A Field Guide to the Synthetic Landscape: Toward a New Environmental Ethic." *Harper's,* Apr.: 49–55.

Tuttle, M. D. 1988. *America's Neighborhood Bats.* Austin: University of Texas Press.

Ulrich, R. S. 1993. "Biophilia, Biophobia, and the Natural Landscape." In *The Biophilia Hypothesis,* ed. S. R. Kellert and E. O. Wilson, 73–137. Washington, DC: Island Press.

Urban Ecology, Inc. 1995. *Blueprint for a Sustainable Bay Area.* Oakland: Urban Ecology

U.S. Department of Commerce. 1992. " Industrial Production Indexes, by Industry: 1970 to 1991." *Statistical Abstract of the United States,* no. 1252.Washington, DC: GPO..

Vance, J. 1972. "California and the Search for the Ideal." *Annals of the Association of American Geographers* 62: 185–220.

Van der Ryn, S., and S. Cowan. 1996. *Ecological Design.* Covelo, CA: Island Press.

Van Sweden, J., and W. Oehme. 1997. *Gardening with Nature.* New York: Random House.

———. 1998. *Bold Romantic Gardens.* Washington, DC: Spacemaker Press.

Vessel, M., and H. Wong. 1987. *The Natural History of Vacant Lots.* Berkeley: University of California Press.

Walker, P., and M. Simo. 1994. *Invisible Gardens: The Search for Modernism in the American Landscape.* Cambridge, MA: MIT Press.

Walpole, H. 1995. *The History of Modern Taste in Gardening.* New York: Ursus Press.

Warowski, S. 1995. *Native Gardens for Dry Landscapes.* New York: Potter.

Waters, W. G. 1990. *The Pacific Horticulture Book of Western Gardening.* Boston: Godine.

———. 1993. "But Is It a Garden?" *Pacific Horticulture,* summer: 1.

Wilkinson, E., and M. Henderson. 1992. *Decorating Eden: A Comprehensive Sourcebook of Classic Garden Details.* San Francisco: Chronicle Books.

Wilson, E. O. 1992. *The Diversity of Life.* Cambridge, MA: Harvard University Press.

Wilson, J. 1992. *Landscaping with Wildflowers: An Environmental Approach to Gardening.* New York: Houghton Mifflin.

Worthen, H. 1975. "How Does Your Garden Grow?" *Landscape* 19: 14–27.

Yoch, J. J. 1992. "Arcadia in California." *Pacific Horticulture* 53, no. 2: 61–64.

Zagory, E. M. 1992. "Planting under and around California's Native Oaks." *UC Davis Arboretum Review,* winter.

———. 1997. "The Mary Wattis Brown Garden of California Native Plants." *UC Davis Arboretum Review,* fall: 1–3.

Zube, E. 1987. "The Advance of Ecology." *Landscape Architecture,* Mar./Apr.: 58–67.

GENERAL INDEX

Italic numbers indicate illustrations.

birdhouses, *55,* 76–77
birds
    attracting to the garden, 75–81
    bluebirds, 175
    California towhee, 83
    and cats, 60–61
    cedar waxwings, 78
    finches, 78
    garden habitats for, 73–75
    hermit thrush, 83
    hummingbirds, 79–80
    leaf-litter foragers, 83
    least Bell's vireo, 65
    mixed-species flocking, 81–82
    nest sites for, 76–77
    plants to attract, 122–24
    purple martin, 81
    and riparian habitat, 65
    rufous-sided towhee, 83
    swallows, 62–63, 80–81
    wrens, 75, 78
    yellow-billed cuckoo, 65
    See also songbirds
Black Hawk, 17
Blakey, Louise, 80
blocks, sculpting ground with, 103–4
borders, perennial, 129–30
brainstorming, 96–98
Brown, Mary Wattis, 117
bubble diagram, 98
Buchanan, David, *61, 112, 181*
building materials. *See* construction materials
bunchgrasses, 83
    for annual beds, 131
    for attracting wildlife, 124
The Burden Garden, *24*
butterflies
    habitats, 82, 83–84
    mission blue, 12
    and nonnative plants, 57
    plant hosts, 83–84, 122–24
    a Sonoma butterfly garden, 82, *83*
    and weeds, 139
buying nursery plants, 125

California Bluebird Recovery Program, 175
California Gardens: Creating a New Eden, 19
California Native Plant Society (CNPS), 56,
    121, 138, 192
California Native Plants with Commercial
    Sources, 137
California Partners in Flight, 176
California's Changing Landscapes, 58
California Wash Garden, 148
Carney, William, 36

Carson, Rachel, 169
catch basins, 151
cats and wildlife, 60–61
cattle grazing, 19
cedar waxwings, 78–79
Cenozoic era, 7
Center for Conservation Biology at
    Stanford University, 112
Central Park, Davis, *75*
Central Valley, 6, 7, 9, 10
Chainey, Steve, xviii, 87, *100*
Chainey/Schiller Garden, *100*
chamise, 128, 136
chaparral, 8, 67, 70, 128, 141
chemicals, 154–55
    avoiding, 40
    herbicides, 139
    overuse, xiv
    See also fertilizers, pesticides
Chief Seattle, 17
children, an adventure garden for, *62, 63*
Chiroptera, 173–75
Christoph, Ann, xviii, 87, *125, 131*
Church, Thomas, xviii, 23, *47,* 85
climate zones and plant selection, 120–21
coastal forest habitat, 7, 72–73
coastal sage scrub, *61,* 67, 70
coastal salt marsh biotic community, 58
Coast Range formation, 6
CoDesign, Inc., *60, 75*
Coleoptera, 172–73
community, sense of, 188–89
compromises, ideal gardens vs. real gardens,
    44–47
concrete, *158*
    as a construction material, 158
    pillars for rustic trellises, 90
conservation
    energy, 149
    and plant selection, 121
    water, 149–51
conservation organizations, 10, 197–99
construction materials
    adobe, 94, 163–66
    bamboo, 104–6, 162–63
    blocks, 103–4
    branches, *156, 157,* 162–63
    ceramic and pebble mosaics, 107–8
    concrete, 90, 158
    ecological, xv, 40
    environmental costs of, 156–57
    for garden ornaments, 166
    for live structures, 106
    local and accessible, 38, 157–67
    metal, 106–7

lawns, xiii–xiv, xvii, 22, 29–30, 44–45,
    45, 48
    and water conservation, 150
leaf litter as garden art, 73, *139*
least Bell's vireo, 65
Lee, Dorothy, 16
lichens, 13
lodgepole pine fir forest biotic community,
    58
lowland river forest biotic community, 58
Lutsko, Ron, Jr., xviii, 31, 53, 54, *86, 87, 102,*
    113, 114, 130
Lyle, John, xvi, 146, 147, *148*

magnolia ancestors, 7
maintenance, 155
Marysville Buttes, *10*
Mary Wattis Brown Garden, 117
meaning in the garden, 41–44
Medjeska, Helena, 21
memory and meaning in the garden,
    33–34
Mesozoic era, 6
metal, construction with, 106–7, *107*
microclimates, 102–3
Mihalko, Cheryl, 117
The Millennium Whole Earth Catalog, 194
Miller, Patrick, 99
Miller, Patrick and Jane, xviii, *87, 117*
mission blue butterfly, 12
mission gardens, 19
mosaics, *107,* 107–8
mosquito control, 69
mountain forest habitat, 72–73
mountain meadow biotic community, 58
mountain stream biotic community, 58
Muir, John, 10, 16, 21, 29
mulch, 103, 153–54
multicultural exchange, *43*
Murphy, Dennis, 112
myths and stereotypes of California,
    20–21

National Audubon Society, 56
National Gardening, 193
National Wildlife Federation, 54
Native Americans
    ideals and the environmental movement,
        18
    and sense of place, 28
native Californians, 5, 14–18, *15*
    and ecology, 14
    and fire, 15
    and interrelation with nature, 16

and land management, 14–15
native plants, xv, 9, 25, 45–46, 112, 113–15,
    125, 142
    and butterflies, 82
    chaparral and coastal sage scrub, 67
    container gardens, 136
    dry perennial border, 132–33
    Mary Wattis Brown Garden, 117
    nurseries, 199–201
    propagation, 137–38
    shrubs, *130*
    water requirements of, 136–37
    wetlands, 68, 69
Natural Habitat Gardens, xv
natural history and garden organizations,
    197–99
natural processes in the garden, 51–53
Nature Conservancy, 10
nest boxes for birds, 76–77
The New American Garden, xvi
nonnative plants
    assessing appropriateness, 45–46
    assessing impact of, 24
    and butterflies, 57
    grasses, 67
nursery plants, buying, 125

Oakes, Baile, *157*
oaks, *3, 11,* 116, 122
    natives, 11–12
    table of species, 127–28
    See also entries in Plant Index
oak woodland habitat, 58, 70–71
old-growth Douglas fir forest biotic
    community, 58
The Oliver Garden, *93*
Olmsted, Frederick Law, Jr., 21
open-channel drainage, 150
Organic Gardening, 193
ornaments, 166
Ottesen, Carole, xvi
outdoor living space, xviii
Out of Place: Restoring Identity to the Regional
    Landscape, 26
overgrazing, 67

Pacific Horticulture, 30, 193
parasitic wasps, 173
passive design principles, 38
passive energy features, 41
passive solar design, 149
path materials, 103
patterns, *49, 107, 165*
Pearson, David, 145

PLANT INDEX

Designer:	BookMatters
Compositor:	BookMatters
Text:	11/16 Monotype Columbus
Display:	Adobe Trajan
Printer and Binder:	C&C Offset Printing Co., Ltd.